IN LOVE WITH DEFEAT

ALSO BY H. BRANDT AYERS

You Can't Eat Magnolias (1972) CO-EDITOR

Bicentennial Portrait of the American People:
Southern Chapter (1972) CONTRIBUTOR

IN LOVE

≡ *with* ≡

DEFEAT

*The Making of a
Southern Liberal*

H. BRANDT AYERS

FOREWORD BY
GOVERNOR WILLIAM F. WINTER

NEWSOUTH BOOKS
Montgomery

NewSouth Books
105 S. Court Street
Montgomery, AL 36104

Library of Congress Cataloging-in-Publication Data

Ayers, H. Brandt, 1935-
In love with defeat : the making of a Southern liberal / H. Brandt Ayers.

p. cm.
Includes index.

ISBN 978-1-58838-277-1 (alk. paper)

1. Southern States—Politics and government—1951- 2. Southern States—
History—1951- 3. Southern States—Civilization—20th century.
4. Political culture—Southern States—History—20th century. I. Title.
F216.2.A94 2012
975—dc23

2012014900

Design by Randall Williams

Printed in the United States of America
by Thomson-Shore

All photographs courtesy of the author except
Willie and Lestine Brewster, P7, bottom right, © Bettmann/CORBIS
and author photograph, front cover, by Jeffrey Kinney, EA Photography

To my editor, my inspiration, my love, my wife Josephine,

and to all those other lonely souls who have wished for their beloved South to become fully a distinctive part of the nation.

Contents

A selection of photographs follows page 134

"A depressingly high rate of self destruction prevails among those who ponder about the South and put down their reflections in books. A fatal frustration seems to come from the struggle to find a way through the unfathomable maze formed by tradition, caste, race and poverty. In view of this record, for reasons of personal comfort, if for no other, the inclination to look for a ray of hope in the progress of the South is strong . . . Despair need not be the only outcome."

— V. O. KEY, IN Southern Politics in State and Nation

"I don't hate it," Quentin said quickly, at once, immediately. "I don't hate it, he said. 'I don't hate it,' he thought, panting in the cold air, the iron New England dark. I don't. I don't! I don't hate it! I don't hate it!"

— WILLIAM FAULKNER, IN Absalom, Absalom!

Foreword

There have been countless efforts by Southern and non-Southern writers—some highly regarded and many less so—attempting to interpret the uniquely complex region that is the American South. That remains an endlessly challenging task. It may be an impossible one. As an eighty-nine-year-old fifth-generation Mississippian, I have spent half of my life trying to figure it out.

In this insightful memoir, Brandt Ayers has come as close as anybody ever has to explaining who we Southerners are and why we act as we do. In addition, he has provided us a personally experienced commentary on many of the fascinating personalities and events that have shaped the region for better or worse over the last half-century.

As a newspaper reporter, editor, and publisher, he has been where the action was, but he has been much more than simply an astute observer and chronicler of the Southern scene. As a founder of the influential LQC Lamar Society to be a voice of reason in the 1960s, and as confidant and counselor to progressive Southern leaders including two presidents, he has helped make the South more prudent and responsible than it otherwise might have been.

I can testify out of my own bittersweet involvement in the often brutal electoral politics of my state of Mississippi how difficult it was to provide moderating influence in the closed society of which we were a part.

It was on a September evening in 1962 in my hometown of Jackson when I saw the frightening power of politically incited fear and prejudice overwhelm an entire state. I was there when then-Governor Ross Barnett walked on the field at halftime of a University of Mississippi football game and harangued thousands of well-meaning, Bible-reading, white Mississippians into believing that the sky would fall if one black man was admitted to Ole Miss. I finally understood how the calamitous Civil War had started a hundred years before.

How did this happen again a century later, we ask ourselves. It happened partly because not enough wise leaders and thoughtful people after the Civil War understood the immensity of the reconciliation that had to take place between the North and the South and between the races. With Lincoln gone, there were not enough like him to appeal to "the better angels of our nature." Mississippi's Lucius Quintus Cincinnatus Lamar was one. His nationally acclaimed eulogy at the funeral of the South's bitter enemy Charles Summer of Massachusetts implored his fellow Americans: "Know one another and you will love one another."

But bitterness ran too deep in the South and in the North. After all, three-quarters of a million human beings had died in that tragic struggle, and four million slaves, almost all illiterate and penniless, had been released from their bondage to fend for themselves. There was no safety net—no Marshall Plan. Cynical political deal-making took over.

With the country still torn apart and the old battle wounds, physical and psychological, slow to heal, it was left to the Supreme Court to kick the can down the road with its well-meaning but unfortunate "separate but equal" mandate in 1896. Most Southern whites heard the first word but ignored the second.

And so for another sixty years the South lived for the most part in a self-imposed political and pastoral isolation defending a past that it would not let die. That attitude was reflected in a story out of the old plantation town of Holly Springs, Mississippi, not far from where I grew up. It was there on a lovely June evening many years after the war that a visitor from New York City remarked to his hostess on the veranda of her antebellum home, "What a beautiful moon." "Ah, yes," she replied, "but you should have seen it before the war."

It took World War II to begin to break the South out of its fantasies. Millions of us Southern white segregationists and black GIs came home with a much-enlarged perspective of the world but nonetheless to the same totally segregated society that we had left four years before.

It was obvious to many that things were going to change. The unanswered questions were how and how long would it take. Again the Supreme Court stepped in, as it had sixty years before, to provide an answer. Only this time the unanimous decision in *Brown v. Board of Education* had the moral support of the country outside the South and the fervent interest of every black American.

Too many Southern whites did not understand the strength of that force, just as their forebears had underestimated northern resolve to save the Union in 1861. So in the 1950s we embarked on another lost cause, just as my Confederate grandfather's generation had done a hundred years before.

The latest effort was an even more hopeless crusade, but the arguments were the same. The issue of race cloaked in the garb of states' rights was the driving force. The South ensnared itself again in a myth of its own making. We wasted another twenty years fighting dead-end battles in the courts and often in the streets that were lost before they had begun.

Now thankfully at long last, we are seeing the repudiation of some of those myths—both by Southerners about themselves and also by those outside the South about the South. But old stereotypes die hard. What is most frustrating to us who live here is the lack of awareness on the part of so many who do not live here, or have never been here, as to how much the South has changed in so many positive ways since the 1960s.

For several decades the region has attracted an ever-increasing number of people from all races and from other states and countries. Many black Southern expatriates have discovered a more hospitable environment here than in the mean streets of Northern cities and now are moving back to their ancestral homes to add their talent and leadership to the communities they once rejected.

There are those who fear that all of these changes will make us less Southern. I submit that—without causing us to lose our Southernness —they will be making all of us more American by transferring to those outside the South an appreciation and acceptance of the distinctive cultural qualities about which Brandt Ayers writes so passionately in this book.

Impulsiveness may once have been one of those qualities, but hopelessness never was. We offer without apology a heritage of civility and courage and compassion. Even in the bad old days of segregation there were countless examples of kindness and generosity by blacks and whites toward each other. It is in the framework of our fascinating cultural diversity that we can embrace our common humanity. By sharing an understanding of its heritage and mystique, the South can contribute much to the richness of our national existence.

This is the process that, accompanied by a universal commitment to respect the dignity of all of our neighbors and to provide the opportunity for a competitive education for everyone, can lead us into an era when the South will be able to revel in its victories. Hopefully, it will not still be in love with defeat.

There will continue to be cynics and fear-mongers who would turn us back. My old friend, the late David Cohn, the great writer from the Mississippi Delta, warned us years ago of these charlatans: "With heaven in sight," he wrote, "they would lead us perversely into hell."

But how can a people so richly endowed with those human qualities that make for personal satisfaction and fulfillment, and with a natural bounty of almost all of the resources that contribute to good living, ever again be guiled into cutting our own throats as we did twice in our tragic history?

The South of the future must not be the South of romantic illusion nor of racial bigotry. I believe that it can be and still will be a distinctive South that we can enjoy and celebrate—yet a South that is committed to fairness and justice for all of its people and to the building of a more united country.

This is the kind of region that Brandt Ayers has devoted his extraordinary career to achieve. Thanks to his kind of vision and persistence, that newest New South is now within sight if succeeding generations of young Southerners do not let it slip away. I do not think they will.

Former Mississippi Governor [1980–84] William F. Winter was honored in 2008 with the Profiles in Courage Award *of the John F. Kennedy Presidential Library. He practices law in Jackson.*

Preface

I write of a place that was but is no more, the Deep South, which had a sudden violent rebirth as a New South but whose newness has long since worn off, and which contemplates in wonder and doubt the fact of a black man as President of the United States.

Born into a small-town publishing family in the Old South, I was a witness to the death throes of that civilization, which occurred between 1965 and 1970, and I was one of the leaders in what came to be called the "New South." Nothing can be "new" forever, and so the patina of newness began to disappear in the 1980s, soon after Jimmy Carter's presidency.

This is the story of that time.

To BEGIN AT THE beginning, my parents' house at 818 Glenwood Terrace was filled with books, Asian treasures, an expectation of achievement, and an air of adventure beyond the confining limits of Anniston. The publisher of the *Anniston Star* and his wife, Harry M. and Edel Y. Ayers, had a curiosity about world events and foreign travel that made them an unusual small-town couple and demanding models for my sister Elise and me, but their primary commitment was to one place, Anniston, Alabama, and to the people who lived there.

Next in order of lifelong influences was marriage in December 1961 to Josephine Peoples Ehringhaus, daughter of a distinguished North Carolina family. Josie, I called her as a bride, and now, Josephine, as I call her as editor of the high-style *Longleaf Style* magazine, which features fine writing by Pulitzer-winners and other authors. She is unique. She has an internal homing device that draws children, the wounded, seekers of companionship and at least one president of the United States to the warming beam of her personality. She has been a harbor in the tough times, a joyous companion in the good times, and a wonderful co-pilot of our captain's paradise, which keeps us rooted in a forest on the edge of our hometown but an airport away from the human and natural wonders of the world. I am also grateful to my daughter, Margaret Ayers, for her love and support.

A rough draft of an okay human being and an above-average career was crafted by a wonderful man and dear friend, the late John Verdery, headmaster of the Wooster School in Connecticut, where Masters Donald Schwartz and Joe Grover also put their stamp on and widened the world view of a Southern boy. At the University of Alabama, Dr. Donald Strong, a legman for V. O. Key's classic *Southern Politics*, began a lifelong quest to understand the South with his Socratic style and unconventional personality. At the University one night, Gene Patterson, then editor of the *Atlanta Constitution*, flattered me by joining me for a nightcap after his lecture. He gave me the key to the riddle of the South's apartness from the "other" Americans by suggesting that I read C. Vann Woodward's books. Southern journalists of my generation are eternally grateful to "Marse" Vann for teaching us why we are different. Gene also took a chance sponsoring me for a Nieman Fellowship at Harvard, a glorious year away from George Wallace's insurgency against the "integratin', scalawaggin', pool-mixin'" forces of the United States.

As a self-conscious Alabama boy, I would never have had the temerity to assault the high walls of intellect at Harvard were it not for former University of North Carolina President Bill Friday who encouraged me to apply. He also did me the favor of reading my chapter on North Carolina and offering a helpful suggestion. Ferrel Guillory, a Chapel Hill authority on the region whose advice is sought by journalists and political leaders alike, also gave the North Carolina chapter a thoughtful read, as did my brilliant sister-in-law, Susan Ehringhaus, a former long-term vice chancellor at UNC. My dear friend Hodding Carter, now an endowed lecturer at UNC, has been an enabler and influence of incalculable value in my career as well as a companion, drinking, talking and arguing late into the night at various venues, and gave an early version of the manuscript a careful read.

For the Washington chapter, three men provided essential details and insights: former Deputy Attorney General Nick Katzenbach; former Justice Department spokesman Ed Guthman, since departed; and Guthman's assistant Jack Rosenthal, later editorial page editor of the *New York Times*. Arthur Schlesinger, also now deceased, provided important insights about the Washington years; he was for more than twenty years a friend and colleague on the Twentieth Century Fund (now the Century Foundation).

I am greatly indebted to Kevin Stoker for invaluable research in his University of Alabama dissertation, "Harry Mel Ayers: New South Community Journalism in the Age of Reform." Stoker's 1998 work was both a compass and a gold mine of factual material.

If this were an academic book the bibliography from a lifetime of reading about the South would cover several pages. I have already mentioned V. O. Key's *Southern Politics* and the many significant works of C. Vann Woodward. A few other books and authors who have had a lasting and profound influence on my thinking include: W. J. Cash's *The Mind of the South* is essential bedrock for understanding the region. Diane McWhorter's *Carry Me Home* filled out for me in rich detail why Birmingham behaved as it did during the civil rights struggle and why it was so different from its post-civil war sibling, Anniston. Robert Schlesinger's *White House Ghosts*, about speechwriting in the Jimmy Carter presidency, filled in the blanks and provided answers to the strange reticence of that brilliant and moral man, a disability that helped doom his administration. Finally, if one is to understand the interior of the Southern soul, he or she must read James Agee, Clarence Cason, William Faulkner, John Egerton, and the Agrarians' *I'll Take My Stand*, as well as historians and journalists too numerous to mention.

My friend and colleague as the *Star's* vice president for sales and a consumer of history, Robert Jackson, carefully researched some of the chapters dealing with Anniston in the civil rights era. Local attorney Charles Doster gave flavor and substance to a crucial event, the violent integration of the Anniston library. The *Star* metro editor Ben Cunningham provided rich legal details about the Willie Brewster murder. Editorial Board colleague John Fleming added original reporting to the Brewster murder and its aftermath. He and *Star* editor Bob Davis read and gave reassuring validation to controversial portions of the "Afterword." Joel Sanders of Montgomery read the manuscript and made many useful comments during the final editing.

All the photos in the book were carefully scanned by the *Star*'s graphics chief, Patrick Stokesberry. Thanks also to the skill, patience, and encouragement of my editor at NewSouth Books, Randall Williams, and for the support of his partner, Publisher Suzanne La Rosa, along with the good work of staffers Margaret Day, Brian Seidman, Sam Robards, Lisa Harrison, Noelle Matteson, and Lisa Emerson.

Until hampered by the demands of her job, Kim Usey, an excellent former editor at the *Star*, did yeoman's work on the manuscript. To my surprise and delight, Kim's task was taken up by the managing editor of *Longleaf Style*, Theresa Shadrix, a sharp editor herself. My wife, *Longleaf Style* editor Josephine Ayers, also made the long march through a manuscript most of which she had seen or heard before. I am seriously indebted to both women.

Prologue

In Love with Defeat

The room clerk at Johannesburg's five-star Saxon Hotel surprised us as we checked in: "Mrs. Suzman called and said you are expected for dinner." That was unexpected, and in a way unwelcome; after the hassle of the flight from Cape Town, we looked forward to a shower and dinner at the famous new hotel's dining room. I called Helen immediately who said to come right over, several of our South African friends were already there. As we approached the house—gated as most in Sandton are—the hotel driver was excited. I had promised to introduce him to South Africa's most famous woman. Helen greeted us in the inner courtyard, shooing away the dogs as she let us through the gate. She focused the full power of her charm on the thrilled driver and then guided us to the living room, which was filled with smiling familiar faces from business, the professions, journalism and civil rights. They were into their second round of drinks so we were soon called to table.

Helen's slight figure presided, seating me at her right, a small tribute that pleased me. During a rare lull in the conversation I offered a Helen Suzman story from a decade earlier (Helen was not then in Parliament but served on the Electoral Commission that would soon oversee the election of her friend, Nelson Mandela): "This was in 1994. We were having an after-dinner brandy in her darkened dining room. At our end of the table were only the wife of the Swedish ambassador, Helen and me when, in a sudden, impetuous moment I asked a prying question, 'Helen, I have a theory about why people like you—and I too, in a comparatively minor way—have been so contrary to majority white opinion. My theory is that education and travel reveal the wider world, putting local loyalties and prejudices in clearer perspective. Is that why you did what you did?' You replied emphatically, 'No!' Then, what was it, I pleaded. You paused, drew a long breath and answered, 'INDIGNATION!'" Helen laughed along with the rest of the guests, enjoying being reminded of her feisty reputation.

At tea the following morning, a cool spring day in May 2005, she found a Southerner's preference for iced tea a wholly mysterious process but not in the slightest tempting. As conversation soon revealed, she was just as impatient with her nation's shortcomings as she had been in the thirteen years when she was the only opposition member of Parliament, calling for division which sent Afrikaner colleagues stomping on tree-limb legs across the aisle to vote "Aye" on some travesty against human rights. A slight woman, alone in a sea of green benches, she was a burning splinter in the body of South Africa's ruling National Party. But those days were long past. She was now nearing her eighty-eighth birthday, still energetic, capable of outrage but a caged tiger. She didn't hide her frustration. "I don't have the access that Parliament gave me," adding, as if it had just occurred to her, "I think access may be the most important word in the English language."

When we first met in Cape Town in 1977, she had already used her Parliamentary privileges to mount a hectoring campaign that so nettled the Justice Minister that he relented and allowed her to visit Robben Island. It is a barren spot of land in the bay about thirty rough minutes by jet boat from Cape Town where political prisoners were kept in cells that can only be described as cement boxes. It was she who introduced her country—and the world—to Nelson Mandela. And it was she who made it possible for books and writing paper to be brought to the tall man in Cell No. 5. Visitors to that desolate place today get an informed view of the rhythms of life on that barren rock because your guide will be a former inmate. They seem strangely detached, without resentment or visible emotion when describing, for instance, the stinking latrine dug out of a lime-pit wall as the only place prisoners could speak privately, because the guards would not enter. In the same passionless voice, guides speak of how Mandela would teach them about the moral power of nonviolence and advise his fellow prisoners to purge their hearts of hatred.

Only one other name is spoken of there: Helen Suzman.

On the day of our first meeting, freedom was years away for Mandela, and she was to speak in the morning as shadow Justice Minister for her minority party, the Progressive Party. I had just been introduced to her on the veranda of U.S. Ambassador William C. Bowdler's residence. She had been talking with the ruling National Party Justice Minister, a hulking tree of a man, who had been mocking her forthcoming speech, which the formality of introductions had interrupted. As I stood there, he resumed the disparaging remarks about his tiny opposite number. Helen had had enough; she did a smart left turn and kicked the Justice Minister in the shin. If there is such a thing as a tree in pain, the minister was one. I was a little shocked but curious about the tiny woman I'd just met.

At dinner, I asked Mrs. Bowdler, the ambassador's wife, about Helen and other mysteries of South African society that I had encountered in my few days there. I was midway in a month-long speaking tour, sponsored by the Institute of Race Relations, then South Africa's only legal civil rights organization. It had been a disconcerting journey, like flying into my own past, Alabama in the 1940s and '50s. Our societies had crossed in time; we had begun shedding legal segregation in the 1960s, while South Africa was tightening the divisions of apartheid. "Colored" and "White" signs were everywhere. I had a lot to learn, which must have been obvious to Mrs. Bowdler. She inquired about how I had come to know Vice President Mondale, who had briefed me before the trip, and I told her about becoming friends with Jimmy Carter and his family when I headed a New South organization with the preposterous, antique name of the Lucius Quintus Cincinnatus Lamar Society.

After dinner, the ambassador sent the conversation on a surprising turn. "How are things at the Calhoun County Courthouse?" he inquired. I confessed my surprise and asked how he happened to be in the county seat town of Anniston. He explained that he had been stationed at Anniston's adjacent Fort McClellan during World War II and had gone to the courthouse to have repatriation papers signed by the probate judge. Having grown up in Latin America where his family was in international business, they had given him the Spanish name for William, "Guillermo." He went on, "The judge looked at the paper with my full legal name, Guillermo C. Bowdler, looked up at me and said, 'Hay, buddy, you know you don't have to go through the rest of yo' liiif bein' called Gill-er-mo.'" Spontaneous laughter greeted the near-perfect Southern country pronunciation of his name.

Not only had the ambassador linked with my hometown, the whole Republic of South Africa was an echo of a former life. I found that I was comfortable with South African blacks, I knew them from birth, and with Afrikaners, whose loyalties, prejudices and good-ole-boy hospitality reminded me of friends, neighbors and family in the segregated South of my childhood. South Africans with a British background I equated with New Englanders whose high-minded morality blinded them to the subtle interplay of hating and loving, of the shades of light and dark in a Manichean society.

How did it all begin, the locked-down loneliness of a Southern liberal who cared about but was fated to live out his life at times far apart from most of the people in his hometown? There was no illuminating moment, no Saul of Tarsus lightning revelation. If I had to choose a place to start, it would be at the end of my parents' long journey from Anniston to Danbury, Connecticut, on the single-lane, pre-interstate roads. Eli Wilkins drove them in the family's black Chrysler in his smart, gray chauffeur's hat and uniform (which he hated and Mother insisted upon). The occasion was my graduation from the New England prep school to which they had sent me, and where Dad had been asked to do the principal address. It was a journey that would begin and end in the last year of normal sameness for the Old South. It was May of 1953, and I listened with mingled embarrassment and pride as Dad, the late Colonel Harry M. Ayers, gave his address at the Wooster School in Danbury. It was entitled, "Come South, Young Man," and seemed to have been well received by our popular headmaster, the Reverend John D. Verdery, and other adults. I guess it must have been pretty good, because *Time* magazine wrote about it, comparing it to the advice of another newspaper publisher, Horace Greeley's, "Go West, Young Man."

As we were packing the car for the trip home, the Head happened by and in the course of a brief conversation asked what I thought of a case then before the U.S. Supreme Court. The case was heavy with portent, but I didn't know anything about it—much less recognize its significance. Embarrassing. I liked the Head a lot and wanted to impress him, but I was clueless. He gave me an understanding smile, wished us a good trip and drove off. This failed legal quiz came after my roommates and I did something that turned out to be small-scale historic. We integrated Wooster. Adolescent hair-trigger justice inspired our breach of the social barrier, which came about this way: I had made reservations for Mother and Dad at the best local hotel, the Green, and tried to make one for Eli, too, but my Southern intuition moved me to explain, "He's colored." The reservations clerk explained that they did not allow coloreds to sleep there. It was understood Eli would have to make other arrangements, but before he took them to the hotel I wanted everybody to see our East Cottage senior suite, Eli wasn't impressed, "Lord," he said, "this looks like a prison," not knowing it would become his home for an evening. My two roommates and I were offended by his being refused lodging at the less than grand Green Hotel. So we provided a cot in the suite, where Eli spent an uncomfortable night "in prison" with three white teenagers. He was the first Negro to do so on campus.

The outside world seldom penetrated the monkish precincts of a New England preparatory school, which explains my ignorance about the case the Head asked me about, *Brown v. Topeka Board of Education*. The Court's unanimous decision was handed down the next year, my freshman year at the University of Alabama. The decision and what followed presented Southerners with a choice about which it was impossible to be ambivalent: Reason or Resistance. I ultimately chose the liberal course.

What is it like to be liberal-minded in the Deep South? It is to be pulled this way and that by complex, contradictory feelings about your own people—about yourself. It is to feel inescapably, even willfully one with a people who disappoint and hurt you, who make you laugh and bite your lip in frustration, whose charm and generosity live side by side with meanness and bigotry, who cling to the paraphernalia of the Lost Cause as self-defining symbols even as it holds them down. They so cherish the emblems and ensigns of the Lost Cause that they are literally — in love with defeat. They can move you to tears with their openhearted kindness and drive you mad with their narrow-mindedness. They will fight like crazed people to keep the Confederate flag, but won't vote an extra dollar in school taxes. Yet they will give that dollar, even if it is their last, to a friend or a stranger in trouble. Truth be known, their granddaddies were born into a third-world nation within a nation and worked for less than a dollar a day. They work so long and loyally; you'd think the Depression was just behind them, closing fast. They have been stifled by lousy schools, gulled by demagogic politicians, and scorned for their backward ways by elites, North and South. Life has dug a cultural canyon between them and those of us who escaped the once-and-future Confederacy through luck or education and travel. To be liberal in the Lower South is to know a deep, double loneliness: An object of condescension to the "other" America and yet never fully accepted by your own.

It has been puzzling and painful to see friends and neighbors reject men you know—flawed, surely, but extraordinarily talented—who speak for the best of the South and who were chosen to lead the nation for a while. Being casual friends with Jimmy Carter and Bill Clinton and watching the white South turn from them, crying, "Give us Barabbas!" has been wounding to Southerners who dreamed of a smart, confident South, a South with a wise heart. Certain Afrikaners and Russians know what it is like to be held by the invisible, unbreakable bonds of nativity to a society they love and despair of, to experience a brief epiphany of reform—the joyous lightness of release from scorn and separation—and then feel the old, familiar weight of depression return as bright promise dulled into the reality that the quest for a truly good society would go on beyond your own lifetime, would go on forever, maybe never be found. How could Americans born in California or Massachusetts, for instance, know what it was like?

To behold and fully comprehend the ironies and contradictions of the South, to understand how the resistant apartness of these people, my people, came to be, requires living a uniquely un-American story, a drama played out in a third-world region as it progressed through each level of development to a mature, post-industrial society—with the consequent values won and lost. The term "third world" is more literal than metaphorical. In the mid-1930s, when I was born, the per capita income of Alabama was less than $1 a day. Only one generation has lived at and beyond the intersection of the Old and New South, experienced the demise of an old civilization, and tried to define a better one—transforming and being transformed by a hard economic climb from poverty to post-industrial plenty.

This is a very personal story of that generation, my generation. I was born into a now-extinct civilization, but have lived the story as one of the leaders of that constellation of social and political forces that came to be known as the New South movement. I have taken the measure of my people—finding both confusion and common cause—in the White House, throughout the South and from foreign venues. Mainly, however, I have witnessed and lived the story from the perspective of a small-town Alabama newspaper publisher. A county-seat town is an intimate angle from which to witness a new nation emerging, decade-by-decade. It was also a place best to feel the impact of a simultaneous event—the moment when two cultures, one white, with well-worn rituals of civic and political life, the other black, new to positions of influence and power, came together as strangers. This was a moment when the old leaders experienced the shock of self-recognition and when the new leaders behaved distressingly like the old ones—like people.

Much of this journey was chronicled in the pages of my family-owned newspaper, which, with independent journalism itself, is an endangered species. At the end of World War II, almost all daily newspapers were owned by a family. As this is written, there were fewer than 300 of approximately 1,500 dailies that were still owned by families, which means an especially intense connection between a family and a community. The human dynamic of the relationship between one family and an entire community is unusual: close and caring, but sometimes jarring and painful. The emotional strings of such a relationship are tuned more like a Jacha Heifetz violin than, say, a Pete Sampras tennis racquet. The give and take, anger, celebrations, frustration, joys, sorrows and satisfactions that pass between publisher and community are acutely sensitive. And it is precisely that sensitivity that gives a family newspaper its unique personality. It may be less objective than a chain newspaper, but it is more caring. It scolds, supports, consoles and chides. It hurts and is hurt, and it loves — like any slightly dysfunctional family.

This is natural, because the publisher of a family-owned newspaper is more than likely a native son. The Ayers family has published newspapers in Calhoun County for more than a century, from the late 19th century to the early 21st century. The publisher's fate and feelings expand and contract with the rhythms of community life. It is this primary allegiance that a family-owned paper has to a place and its people that too often is missing in corporate journalism, and may explain its low esteem in the public's mind. Family newspapers have passionate critics, too, mine no exception. To save our friends and critics, too, from uncaring corporate journalism, our family years ago passed up a cash offer of $50 million for sale of our two daily and four weekly papers, and have since pledged our stock to a foundation. The foundation will keep our dailies and weeklies local; and, with the University of Alabama, supports an institute to further the arts of community journalism.

This newspaper has also provided a window to the larger universe: the state, the region, the nation and the world. The region is especially important to this publisher. There are many Souths but the main fault-line is between past and present, between visions of an Old South or New South. For most of my life, I have been puzzled, even contemptuous of those who cling to the dry bones of the long-dead Confederacy, who made a shrine of the Lost Cause, in effect, worshipped defeat, but in later years I had to acknowledge that the great schism in the nation's life ought to be memorialized and that there can be nobility in defeat. The innocent enjoyment of that heritage deserves respect. That being said, I have consistently spoken for those of my generation whose vision was future rather than past oriented. A consistent core philosophy connects us New South believers: Society benefits from bridges that the less fortunate can cross over to a good life. Dad put it this way in an article for a trade journal, words we quote daily on the editorial page flag, "A newspaper should be the attorney for the most defenseless among its subscribers." Those who would close the bridges breed turmoil, cap a social volcano that someday must erupt.

The civil rights movement was one such eruption. It grew in volume from the distant thunder of *Brown v. Board of Education* my freshman year at the University of Alabama. It grew louder with the lunch counter sit-ins I witnessed as a young political reporter in North Carolina, where two governors showed creative leadership, and then in Washington where I covered Bobby Kennedy's Justice Department and the March on Washington. Back home, it reached a personal crescendo—a nightrider murder following racist rallies on the courthouse steps. A major crisis was averted by rare and courageous statesmanship by Anniston's black and white leaders.

After the passage of the Voting Rights Act in 1965, the volcano began to cool. Looking back now, it seems as if the Old South disappeared "with deliberate speed" over the five years between 1965 and 1970, and where it had been, a wholly new place stood like a volcanic island, risen from the Gulf and the Atlantic. Even writers such as James Agee, Clarence Cason, William Faulkner and W. J. Cash could not have imagined this new civilization.

The first fruits of the new civilization astonished those of us born into the old one, but in time they became commonplace and the New South itself soon vanished. That is where the balance of my story ends, but the stunning cultural exclamation point of a black man as president requires an extended afterword.

In Love with Defeat

Ancient Civilization Revisited

The civil rights movement cut through the center of my generation of white Southerners like a turbulent canyon river separating an ancient civilization from a newly minted one. Long before we could imagine that there was another side of the canyon, there was only the Old South. It amazes me now to think that there actually was such a place—a distant planet, blurred by time and space, where graces for a few and a universal insistence on common courtesy masked the reality that we were born to a backward, unhealthy, undereducated, third-world nation, governed by laws that spawned violence and misfortune. Poverty, pellagra, and prejudice were the three horsemen of that society. We didn't have much but we had our pride. FORGET, HELL, read Confederate battle flag bumper stickers. As an unconscious antidote to the threadbare hardness of our lives, we did have a lubricant of human community—courtesy. We yes-sirred and yes-ma'amed everybody from barbers and store clerks to parents and teachers. It is a fact that in the South you can say anything, anything at all, if you have the right prefix or suffix: "That sure is an ugly baby, bless his heart."

When I was born in 1935 in Anniston, Alabama, on the second floor of the old Garner Hospital on South Leighton Avenue, Alabama was a third-world nation in a third-world region. The state's per capita income was $214—less than a $1 a day. But a boy growing up in the small county-seat town of Anniston, cupped by the blue foothills of the Appalachians, had no sense that he belonged to an isolated, impoverished culture that was mocked by the educated, self-confident people who lived in the "Other" America.

The wilderness from which the model "new town" of Anniston was carved had enough ore and limestone to lure an industrial odd couple, Sam Noble, a Confederate munitions manufacturer from Rome, Georgia, and Daniel Tyler, a Union general from Connecticut. The chance 1872 meeting between the two men in Charleston combined the main elements of the New South formula devised by Henry Grady, the peppery Atlanta editor. Grady reasoned that a region lying in the ashes of defeat, dehydrated by a capital drought, had to import capital in order to rise up as an industrial power. Yankee wealth matched with Southern sense of the geography, geology, and culture was Grady's formula for creating a New South. Noble and Tyler turned out to be corporate visionaries. From their Woodstock Iron Works my hometown was born as an elaborately planned model city. Grady was excited to see his concept taking shape in bricks and mortar, and confident enough to invest in the company.

The partnership added a new element to Grady's theory, a dimension that Birmingham lacked, the wedding of capital with an essential, extra ingredient—personal commitment. In fact, Anniston had come into being at the same time as Birmingham, the state's industrial capital. Both were post-Civil War towns that emerged in the 1870s and 1880s. But Anniston did not become the state's major business and manufacturing center—which is too bad, because its founders endowed Anniston with a civic ideal while Birmingham was a runaway frontier town. Anniston had tantalizing mineral deposits, but sixty miles further west lay the major deposits of coal, limestone, and ore needed to make iron and steel. These deposits in Birmingham's aptly named Red Mountain spawned a helter-skelter city—atop which a statue of Vulcan, god of fire and metalworking, stands today. One industrial titan whose personality dominated the erupting town was Colonel Henry DeBardeleben, described by the writer George Packer as a "coal-maddened Ahab." DeBardeleben's civic conscience was expressed in this pretty sentence: "I like to use money as I use a horse—to ride!" His defense against union organizers was a militia whose armaments included machine guns.

Birmingham's homegrown Tennessee Coal, Iron and Railroad Company fell under control of an entrepreneurial Texas stock gambler, John "Bet a Million" Gates. During the Panic of 1907, J. P. Morgan proposed to save the country from a stock market crash by buying TCI stock from the Wall Street brokerage that held a majority of the stock in Gates's syndicate. President Theodore Roosevelt endorsed the emergency scheme. Morgan bought TCI for roughly a dime on the dollar—thus eliminating U.S. Steel's major competitor and creating a steel monopoly that became the godfather of Birmingham. From the 1880s until about 1970, the city's soul was shaped by a succession of managers whose allegiance was to a corporation instead of the community, who helped guarantee that the world was safe for the Big Mules of industry and that the people and the press were orderly and respectful.

If Birmingham's corporate chieftains saw their community as existing for the company's benefit, Anniston's founders wanted their company to uplift the community. Noble moved his family to the nineteenth-century "new town" and General Tyler persuaded his son, Alfred, to take up residence and help run the company. They first chose the name Woodstock, after the ancestral English town of the Noble family near Oxford. When the founders discovered there was another Alabama town named "Woodstock," they named the new city for General Tyler's wife, Annie, thus Anniston. The two families were determined to make the place where they lived as attractive as possible. Sam Noble expressed the civic ideal: "Instead of dissipating our earnings in dividends, we have concentrated them here . . . These reinvestments were judiciously made, and every dollar was made to do its best." One of the earliest investments was a gilt-and-velvet jewel box of an opera house. Another gift was given in 1881, at Sam Noble's suggestion, when the town council authorized the purchase of 100,000 water oaks to line the orderly grid of broad, north-south avenues named for Episcopal bishops (both families were Episcopalians) and east-west streets. On the east side, Grace Episcopal, a little gem of a parish for the carriage trade, was perched prettily on two landscaped lots which, together with the rectory and a finishing school for young ladies, covered an entire city block. On the west side, St. Michael and All Angels, filled with Italian-crafted marble statuary and set grandly on its own city block, was a cathedral for the working class. The liberal ideal of the founders extended to the workers in other ways, too. General Tyler believed that good workers should be well paid—twice the prevailing wage of fifty cents a day. Instead of paying rent for company-built houses in perpetuity, Woodstock's workers accumulated equity in their houses, which encouraged upkeep and made the workers stake-holding, home-owning citizens.

In those days, Anniston had the best possible form of government—a visionary and benign dictatorship. As the Georgia-Pacific railroad pushed west toward Anniston, incorporation was required, which introduced democracy, that messy, necessary governing process which in time would clutter the founders' dream. Among the assets with which this self-governing town began was a newspaper, which the founders established to be an adhesive to community. The first issue hit the streets on Saturday, August 18, 1883, the year the city was incorporated. It is said that Henry Grady and Sam Noble were discussing what to name the paper over a "toddy" on the veranda of Noble's house when the Woodstock furnace lit the evening sky. "You've got to call it the Hot Blast," Grady is supposed to have said. Grady's "A Man and a Town," a reprint of an *Atlanta Constitution* column, covered four of the seven front-page columns of Volume 1, Number 1 of the *Anniston Hot Blast*. He detailed the city's founding and its guiding principles and described what he could see from Noble's hilltop house. Grady's excitement at seeing his capital-plus-commitment theory come so vibrantly to life was such that he hoisted the Noble-Tyler partnership to hyperbolic heights: "I thought, as I stood between their two houses, that . . . I had rather have been either of them . . . than to have been the president of these United States."

Even discounting Grady's exuberance, the founding vision was liberal to the point of utopian. Democracy's tendency to choose the means—often the lowest common denominator— couldn't maintain the brilliance of the dream that inspired the founders. By the time my generation was born, the slogan "Model City of the New South" was more than a little worn. But boys, having no past, are not interested in examining their own roots or that of their city. And having no way of comparing, I thought the place where I was born was pretty much all there was. It was very pleasant for those of us in my part of town, a white universe with black visitors who came on the bus or in old automobiles to cook, clean, garden, and drive for us. We called them "members of the family"; they came to our weddings and funerals, and we went to their funerals, but we all knew where the unspoken line lay between servant and employer. It was a line, not a wall, and thus easily breached by more powerful forces such as grief or affection. Despite that line, genuine bonds of affection and even love developed between individual "coloreds" (the polite term in the ancient regime) and their white employers. Alabama writer and former *New York Times* editor Howell Raines won the Pulitzer Prize for a magazine piece, "Grady's Gift," which poignantly probed such a relationship. It may seem saccharine to Yankees, but Southerners find authentic the line in *Driving Miss Daisy* when the old lady in the nursing home puts her hand on that of her former chauffeur/handyman and says, "Hoke, you're my best friend."

The late Willie Morris, an eloquent spokesman—drunk or sober— for our generation, recalled that his dying grandmother reached not for the hand of her daughter or any blood relative, but for the hand of the black woman who had lovingly looked after her every day for years. Willie and I, and anybody born to the small-town South, know that what passed between those two women was more important than race or station, and we are moved by the authenticity of the scene. Not to a well-known New York writer and his socially conscious wife, however. When Willie told that story at a sophisticated dinner party on the Upper East Side, the writer said, "That is the most racist description I've ever heard." His wife added, "It's a racist description of a corrupt and racist society." Poor woman; a head stuffed with stereotypes blinded her to the life-taught knowledge of human interaction. She did not have the key to unlock the attic-consciousness of Southerners: the knowledge of loving and hating, enduring without hope of prevailing through remorse and forgiveness, and caring, eternally caring. At a party once in Willie Morris's New York apartment, I asked Robert Penn "Red" Warren if he could explain why Southerners are more violent. He thought for a minute and said, "I think it has to do with caring more." His instincts about us are uncommonly true.

Lila Esau, my first nurse, cared about me, and I loved Lila. She is a fond presence in my memory—slender, small, the color of cured tobacco. After she escaped our narrow universe for the relative freedom of Brooklyn and became a nurse, there would be a birthday note from Lila for me every April 8. The notes stopped years ago, a closure I recall with a stab of regret. A very different personality was Mildred White, the cook, who lived in "the little house" behind our three-story residence. She was no Carson McCullers character, a mass of good will humming gospel hymns and providing a comforting bosom for a boy, sensitive to the sharp edges of childhood. Mildred was a big, strong, ebony woman, a touchy, hard-working loner. She had a talent for frying chicken; she tackled the task with assembly-line energy and efficiency. It was a wonder to watch her machine-like performance, rolling wet pieces in spiced flour, briskly dropping them in the sizzling grease and plucking each golden brown piece at precisely the right moment, as if she were an industrial engineer. I couldn't imagine Mildred crooning lullabies. Once she informed me sharply that she knew some French from school, her scowl surely born of resentment that she, an intelligent woman, had to cook fried chicken, cornbread, and greens for a white family instead of holding a real job. Mildred was management material, born in the wrong place at the wrong time.

Eli Wilkins was my laid-back buddy. Mother felt he performed his tasks as the family's butler, chauffeur, and yard man without enthusiasm. But he was my friend, somebody to play catch with, a passable Ping-Pong player who let me win sometimes. When I began to have aches in strange places and noticed girls, he explained the birds and bees to me in an arcane style that left me still clueless about female anatomy and the mechanics of "going all the way." He told me that the first time he had sex, he was embarrassed because he thought he had peed in the girl. This only deepened the alluring mystery. Once I embarrassed myself in Eli's presence by uttering a remark typical of the thoughtless racism of the time and place. He was driving a group of us boys to a party and the subject of mixed nuts came up. I said I liked everything but "nigger toes," our colloquialism for Brazil nuts. The word hung in the air, a frozen, ugly thing. I wanted to die, but Eli, either gracefully or with resignation, acted as if he had not heard me.

Though I never heard Mother and Dad utter the word "Nigger," I can only imagine the indignities overheard by Mildred and Eli from dining room guests in the 1940s and '50s. Mildred had room and board in a two-room apartment, with bath, attached to the garage. The pay back then was no more than seven to ten dollars a week; it hardly compensated for the social slights they suffered, though Eli's and Mildred's meager salaries put them in an economic bracket above the army of black and white sharecroppers.

Clarence Cason, a writer and University of Alabama journalism professor from neighboring Talladega County, explained the economics of sharecropping in his 1935 book, *90° in the Shade*. This is how it worked: In March, the typical tenant borrowed about $200 from his landlord or banker. Of this sum, $50 might be designated for the fertilizer dealer, $50 for stockfeed, and $10 for interest. With luck—which seldom visited tenants in the Depression years—the "cropper" would sell three bales of cotton for $200 in the fall. After paying off his loan, the tenant would have left about $15 for each of the next six months until March. Jimmy Carter described the same cycle of hard work and hard poverty in south Georgia in his book *An Hour Before Daylight*. These are the people about whom James Agee wrote in *Let Us Now Praise Famous Men*. Despite Agee's elegant and sympathetic account, the book shamed the families depicted in it because, among other details of their pinched lives, he revealed that the Whites and Gudgers had only two pairs of threadbare underwear. Agee pulled back the curtain so these formerly invisible people and their miserable lives could be seen by the educated, articulate, and well-heeled. He told the croppers' story in language that sophisticated readers could understand; it was their language, only better. It was important for that audience to know what life was like in the Black Belt but the book shamed the people about whom Agee wrote. They felt as if they had been exposed, in their threadbare underwear, inside a circle of wealthy, educated, fashionable, and powerful elites.

The Gudgers and Whites are also the people about whom the *Star* alumnus Rick Bragg wrote in his memoir of growing up dirt poor in Possum Trot, a cluster of rural Calhoun County houses whose post office closed decades ago. Bragg knew the people of the hardscrabble South, was one of them from his earliest memory: being dragged on the end of a cotton sack by his mother. His books *All Over But the Shoutin'* and *Ava's Man* gave Agee's people a voice, a story they could be proud of, written by one of their own. Bragg's work did not "sing the praises of famous men," as in the opening passage of the verse from Ecclesiastes. He wrote for those who "have perished as though they had never existed; they have become as though they had never been born, they and their children after them." They are the people you didn't know, if you were an east-sider like me. They lived in the weathered gray shacks on rural back roads, the people who fought and drank and populated the hospital and police reports in the paper. They were poor people with a code of honor we east-siders didn't know or understand, but which made them worthy of respect. About them, about his own black family, the late James Tinsley said, "They call it sharecropping, but the big man, he didn't do too much sharin'." Mr. Tinsley's parents escaped the farm to do "public work" in the textile mills for the lordly wages of $7.50 to $10 a week, which they stretched to send their son to Tuskegee Institute.

The Tinsleys' migration from farm to city came after the agricultural depression of the 1880s and 1890s. Families by the thousands fled from "Tobacco Road," the indentured servitude of sharecropping, to cities where the mill owners had jobs and housing for the workers—including the children. In fact, the small hands of children were more adept at working the machines than parents whose hands were gnarled by years of cotton picking. By 1900, 30 percent of Alabama's millhands were children, according to an essay in *Alabama Heritage* magazine.

Many of these children never saw the sun, trudging to work at dawn and dragging home in the dark for a few hours sleep. A brief survey at the time turned up 450 children under age twelve who worked twelve or more hours every day, Saturday included. They were an army of unschooled (many totally illiterate), indentured slaves—not unlike children in rural Turkey today who sit on stools weaving rugs for tourists all day—some, the family's only source of income.

Alabama children brought home wages of a dime to forty cents while the mill owners were cushioned by profits of 35 to 40 percent or more. In 1900, the state was no different than a small, third world nation today, ruled by an economic elite. The oppressed workers and yeoman farmers, especially blacks, were soon to be disenfranchised by the 1901 Constitution, written by a convention of our "best" citizens.

A generation of persistent effort, appeals to the conscience of many "best" citizens, and the shocking images of photography—as powerful then as TV was to the civil rights movement—eventually achieved some reform. Mill owners fought against the reformist onslaught in the legislature, arguing that the mills had saved white Southerners from the ravages of poverty, a generally accepted perception at the time; further, mill owners argued that mill parents would migrate to Georgia if the children's income stopped.

A partial victory for reform was won with the reluctant compliance of Governor B. B. Comer, himself a textile magnate. Even the minimal, sixty-hour week for children under fourteen proved unenforceable. Reform got another boost in 1911 when the National Child Labor Committee convention was held in Birmingham. Former President Teddy Roosevelt told a packed house that Alabamians, who had recently improved their livestock breed, should put equal effort to raising their children.

An exhibit of Lewis Hines's photographic essay on child labor dramatically galvanized public opinion. Photography was as new to the eyes of early twentieth-century citizens as television was in the 1950s and '60s. A shocked *Birmingham Age-Herald* reporter wrote, "There has been no more convincing proof of the absolute necessity of the child labor laws . . . than by these pictures. They . . . depict a state of affairs which is terrible in its reality—terrible to encounter, terrible to admit that such things exist in civilized communities." With the election of Thomas Kilby as governor, reform finally triumphed. In 1919, the Legislature passed an act reducing to forty-eight the maximum number of hours that children under fourteen could work. In addition, child workers were required to complete the fourth grade.

Working-class Southern blacks and whites, rescued from share-cropping, were in turn exploited by Southern mill owners, and also fell victims to national political and economic forces—the part Calvinist, part Darwinian belief that "to the victor belongs the spoils." No Marshall Plan cushioned the South's recovery from the error of attacking the great industrial nation to the north. When the war ended in 1865, capital in the South vanished. Confederate currency and bonds were worthless. A hundred million dollars in insurance investments and twice as much bank capital evaporated. Merton Coulter, who authored the *Reconstruction* volume for the LSU *History of the South* series, estimates the lost capital from the emancipation of slaves to have been between $1 and $4 billion. The desolation couldn't have been more drastic if mid-nineteenth century Europe had been transformed into the Indian subcontinent.

A society without any currency, and few opportunities to earn any, must invent its own peculiar economic and social system. Of course, a nation without capital will not grow industries and cities where the arts, finance and health care are connected to vibrant, life-giving golden arteries. The shrunken economy of the South, a region as large as Europe, invented the crop-lien system—essentially, a barter economy that perpetuated poverty and such pastoral flowers as Erskine Caldwell's famous Jeeter Lester in *Tobacco Road*.

Of course, there were exceptions such as the entrepreneurial McGowin clan of Chapman, Alabama. Their unique story is a metaphor for how the South could have grown if national policy had been development instead of regional advantage. James Greeley McGowin was one of those rare people who, set down on the surface of the moon, would invent some way to develop an interplanetary market for dead rocks and a personal life of high culture. From a class of farmers, small-town merchants, and sawmill operators in the pine wilderness of south Alabama, James Greeley McGowin—in a single generation—created a land barony, jobs for impoverished backwoods people of both races, and an aristocracy.

The handsome Greeley and his talented, desirable wife Essie Stallworth McGowin crafted a family heritage of refinement from the materials of culture, education, hard work and travel, set upon a bedrock of indomitable will. The boys' education included graduate study at Pembroke College, Oxford, and the daughter at Vassar. Essie's insistence that they all master a musical instrument filled the thick, moist night air of their mill town and the surrounding pine forest with sounds to compete with the symphony of cicadas and bull frogs—a family string quartet. If Chapman's baronial seat, Edgefield, was a center of civility, grace and learning, life in the "benign dictatorship" of the company town was a far sight better than the rutted, hopeless, treadmill existence of sharecropping. The company provided a steady job, a place to live with a garden, schools, and churches for blacks and whites, as well as a clinic staffed by a doctor and a nurse.

The McGowins could make money from their lumber mills and live baronial lives because they were in a free zone untouched by the punitive economic policies laid down by the Radical Republicans after the Civil War, and perpetuated into the middle of the twentieth century by the interests they protected. Essentially, the South was to be a producer of raw materials in a revival of the mercantile system abandoned by the British in the 18th century. The Louisville and Nashville Railroad provided the company access for its lumber to markets in the northeast and abroad through the port of Mobile, and later to markets in the middle west. When Greeley died in 1934, his sons Floyd, Earl, and Julian, continued to operate the company and used imagination, salesmanship and inventive reforestation to govern Chapman as a highly profitable enterprise, owning some 222,000 acres. As in most enterprises owned by large families, the pull of distant family members who own stock worth millions but wonder if they can afford a new car eventually dismantled the family business, and the company was sold to Union Camp in 1966. By then, a New South was in economic ascendancy and the Old South was about to become a fictionalized memory. The "boys" are long since dead, the mill town has vanished, Edgefield was put up for sale and family cellos and violins no longer competed with crickets and frogs. The entrepreneurial spirit, however, still courses in the veins of the third generation. A grandson, Earl's son, Mason, has installed a $30-million computer-driven machine to process smaller pine trees (overlooked by previous generations) into lumber. Mason, a big, friendly, emphatic man, likens himself more to his all-business grandfather, Greeley, than his charming father, Earl, but good-naturedly takes his pretty wife Suzie's ribbing, "The bigger the boy, the bigger the toy." Sawmills can do what Mason's magical machine can do, he says, "but not as fast, as much, as cheaply." Edgefield still stands, as a museum that recalls the charms of a life that was but will be no more.

Railroads provided the McGowins a way to create a good life, because they fit the colonial mercantile system erected by Eastern politicians and interests: Ship us the raw materials and we'll send them back as finished goods. Henry Grady lamented the South's peonage in the story of a Georgia funeral in which the casket came from Cincinnati, marble and nails came from New England, and all Georgia supplied "was the body and the hole in the ground." As if to ensure that the South would not rise from its humid cage, the dominant East imposed a system of discriminatory freight rates that inhibited the growth of industry, cities and capital in the region. Complicated rule making by the Interstate Commerce Commission had this effect: a refrigerator manufactured in Birmingham would cost more to ship to Pittsburgh than the same appliance shipped from Pittsburgh to Birmingham. Why build manufacturing plants in the South if you had to pay an extra tariff to ship the product?

Southern governors, frustrated by the added barrier to development posed by these discriminatory freight rates, formed what became the Southern Governors Conference. In 1937, Alabama Governor Bibb Graves filed a complaint with the ICC on behalf of the Conference. The issue won the sympathy of President and Mrs. Roosevelt. FDR and his chief of staff, Harry Hopkins, cited unfair freight rates as central to the South being "the Nation's number one economic problem." The cause of reform was pushed along to the U.S. Supreme Court by Georgia Governor Ellis Arnall, but was not finally resolved until the spring of 1952. I was a seventeen-year-old fifth-former at the Wooster School in Danbury, Connecticut. That year in Mr. Grover's class I wrote an enthusiastic essay about the South's growth rates exceeding that of the nation, and got an "F" on the paper. Exuberant Dixie chauvinism met precise Yankee superiority, and Yankee superiority won.

Still, that year, the economic shackles had been struck from the limbs of the South. The economic stimulus of World War II, elimination of the freight rate differential, and the delightful invention of New Yorker Willis Carrier—air conditioning, which became widely affordable in the 1950s—combined to give the South its economic takeoff speed. Irony of ironies, the South's final recovery from its war came at the same time as the recovery of the Germans, Italians, and Japanese. Because of that bitter irony, perhaps we can be forgiven sullen reflections about how rapidly the South would have recovered socially and economically—thus coaxing the national economy to a faster gallop—if the nineteenth century Radical Republicans had been men of vision such as twentieth-century Republican statesmen Henry Stimson, John J. McCloy, Robert Lovett, Arthur Vandenberg, and Dwight Eisenhower. The bipartisanship that remade the world by the enlightened self-interest of helping our fallen foes to their feet could have made America a much better place, much sooner. Perhaps it might even have accelerated civil rights reforms.

However, we're not in a mood to dwell on that old mistake, because—

irony of ironies, again—the economy of Anniston and a large slice of Alabama across the I-20 corridor is being occupied by the former Axis Powers. Germany's Mercedes-Benz is on the western side of I-20 and Japan's Honda has built a plant thirteen minutes from our major shopping mall on the eastern end of I-20. To make the ironic triangle complete, Italy's Fiat has a plant just forty miles to the south. Of course, the boys and girls with whom I grew up so happily in our third-world cocoon had never heard such exotic names as Honda or Toyota, and if they had, they would have belonged to the enemy. It was beyond our powers of imagination to think that one day the Axis Powers would be our welcomed neighbors.

2

Growing Up—
Cracks in the Cocoon

Ve were innocents, focused on the pleasures of the present. It was pleasant on Glenwood Terrace, a street divided by a grassy median, which supported a line of antique streetlights marching six blocks up to Tenth Street Mountain. Our house was the fourth on the south side of the median, number 818, the only one sitting on two corner lots. Glenwood Terrace was and is a premiere address in Anniston, but I didn't know it at the time. Even if I had, we were taught that it is pretentious (a cardinal sin) to say so. My family was part of what passed for aristocracy in a small town, though we didn't put on any airs. That "wasn't done." Besides, you couldn't get away with such affectations in a small town.

Had there been a social register in Anniston, though, Mother and Dad would have been listed. Mother was an athletic, beautiful, and talented woman, star of the Little Theater and a state doubles tennis champion. From childhood, she had pulled a whole caravan of Norwegian maiden names—Edel Olga Leonora Ytterboe—that embarrassed her when she had to recite them before a first-grade class in the Minnesota college town of Northfield. Her father, Halvor Tykerssen Ytterboe, whom I knew only as a lithe, athletic-looking man in the portrait hanging in our dining room, played football for the University of Iowa and was a founder of St. Olaf College, as well as a popular professor and playing coach of the baseball team. His unsmiling face in the portrait and photographs concealed a playful nature. In letters he was sure chickens were calling Mother's name "Edel, Edel Edel." In another, he teased his wife, "Just got up and feel that I love you still. I don't see how I can with all your faults—but it seems I can't help it." St. Olaf's original mission was to acclimate Norwegian immigrants to

16

the new American society without discarding all of their original culture. The young athletic professor, whose fund-raising had helped save the college, undertook even menial duties. One was fumigating the boy's dorm with formaldehyde after an epidemic of scarlet fever. The fumes poisoned him and, cheerful and playful to the end, he died at forty-six. Mother, who worshipped him, was six years old.

Years later in New York at graduate school, she accepted a fateful invitation to venture South from a classmate in the Columbia University School of Education. Young Edel Ytterboe's Southern friend was another pretty athlete, Palmer Daugette, whose father, Dr. Clarence W. Daugette, was president of the State Normal School in Jacksonville, ten miles north of Anniston. The two girls taught physical education that summer of 1921, when Edel met the Colonel . . . by accident of a coin flip.

Colonel Harry Mel Ayers, my father, was already a substantial man in Calhoun County and the state of Alabama, whose military title was awarded for service on the staff of his best friend, Governor Thomas E. Kilby, former president and CEO of Anniston's Kilby Steel. Dad owned a daily newspaper, the *Anniston Star*, and had managed Kilby's winning gubernatorial campaign. For his time and place, he was also a worldly man. He had lived and traveled in Asia with his father, Dr. Thomas Wilburn Ayers, one of the first Southern Baptist medical missionaries to China (1901–26). By Dad's own estimate, he was far short of handsome: a slight man of medium height with sloping shoulders, receding hairline, and a substantial nose rudely sculpted on the football field of then Jacksonville Normal School, but bright and intellectually inquiring. His manly charm made him a popular and natural leader who would dazzle young Edel Ytterboe in their first lengthy and close encounter, which was by chance. Dad had lost a coin flip and had to drive the ten-mile, washboard dirt road to Jacksonville to pick up Edel and Palmer for a Rotary Club picnic. A dance number performed by Edel and the Daugette girls, Kathleen and Palmer, entertained the Rotarians and guests. The thirty-six-year-old publisher followed the moves of the blonde Nordic beauty and he fell, hard.

Their whirlwind romance was climaxed by an anti-climatic automobile journey to Minnesota by Dad and several of his friends, all expecting to bring home his bride. When the Alabamians entered a Minneapolis hotel in their seersucker suits and straw hats, it was as if there had been an aboriginal invasion of Scandinavia. The room clerk, curiosity mingling with alarm, asked, "What are you . . . Baptists?" No, the ecumenical delegation answered, worse . . . "We're Democrats." When the squad of exotic strangers reached thoroughly Lutheran and Republican Northfield, they and Dad were met with deep skepticism. The president of St. Olaf, Lars Boe, grilled Dad for hours and sent forth a blizzard of telegrams inquiring about the character of this alien being from the deepest, snake-infested jungles of Alabama. A crestfallen Colonel returned home sans bride. Shortly after, when President Boe's telegrams yielded nothing but affirmative reviews of Dad's character and history, the odd couple—or so it seemed to Minnesota Lutheran eyes—was wed on September 28, 1921 at Northfield's St. John's Lutheran Church.

The *Star's* legendary society editor, Miss Iva Cook, whose story reached for, and almost went, over the top, reported the affair. She described the wedding as "a very notable event, which has been the occasion of much interest throughout Alabama, where the groom is well-known and prominent." The bride was "very charming and accomplished, possessing many social graces, which will make her a lovely addition to Anniston society." If Miss Iva said it, then it must be so, for she was the social tyrant of northeast Alabama. She chose and dictated the size and display of the bridal pictures each Sunday. If your daughter was not one of the three large pictures at the top of the page, then your family dined below the salt or at the second table. If your daughter's picture was in the center, elevated slightly above the other two, then you were the pinnacle of Anniston society. Typical of Miss Iva's imperious touch was her account of a garden party hosted by Mrs. Kilby, wife of the former governor. In almost sensual detail, Miss Iva described the day, the garden, the texture and make of the tablecloth, the silver, the food, and the medley of colorful frocks, and then listed some of the guests by name, concluding . . . "and several others." Mother made the list, but imagine the distress of local matrons awakening to discover that Miss Iva had assigned them to an anonymous social purgatory of "several others."

THOSE GROWN-UP SOCIAL NUANCES meant nothing to us local boys. We were no more aware of such distinctions than we were of the huge and omnipresent structure of segregation which, to us, was normality, the way things were, always had been, and always would be. The adult obsession with race was invisible to my buddies and me. I heard few telltale signs at the dinner table of the torturous grip the issue had on Dad or about his courageous and conflicted struggle to balance his belief in educational, economic, and political equality for blacks—within a segregated system.

We knew about the custom that reserved the back of city buses for Negroes, but we violated that taboo frequently, happily commandeering the prized long seat in the very back of the usually empty bus on Saturday afternoons. Saturday's ritual was as permanent and predictable as the order of service at any of the town's six jillion churches. The bus stopped at the main downtown intersection of 10th and Noble streets, where the elegant old Opera House had become the Noble Theater, venue for Roy Rogers cowboy movies and Batman serials. Riveted by the good-guy, shoot-em-up action of Roy and his horse Trigger, and by Batman's weekly escapes from near death, we did not notice that the once-elegant Opera House, where Shakespeare had been performed, was now a derelict old lady, her velvet dirty, her ceiling murals caked with dust, her gilt cracked—genteel poverty at its most abject, vulnerable to the cocky, tasteless New South real estate economy soon to destroy her. She would be dismantled to make room for a furniture store—later closed. But in boyhood days, the Noble was the first of four downtown theaters with the Cameo, the Calhoun and the Ritz, one-to-a-block that lined the west side of Noble Street.

All are now erased, but then the Noble was the branch-head of the stream of ceremonial Saturdays in the happy, opaque, all-white world where we grew up. Every Saturday, as we exited the cooler darkness of the un-air-conditioned Noble Theater into the bright humidity of Noble Street, we speculated excitedly about Batman's fate. Then we might get a cherry Coke at Wikles or Scarborough drug stores, but a necessary part of the ritual was to walk the two blocks up tenth Street to view the treasures of Carnegie Library. The library then housed the Regar Collection, beautifully mounted native birds in their natural habitat. A favorite was the steely-eyed eagle, its noble head capped in white, perched high on a limestone outcropping.

In its claw was a lamb, a realistic drop of blood on the little animal's white fur. Next, we mounted the stairs to the balcony to stare at the case with the Ptolemaic Period mummy, its colored wrapping faded by the centuries. But underneath, we knew, was the deadness—a dark, scary concept, beyond our imagination or experience. We regarded the dead Egyptian woman with silent respect.

There was one delicious year during construction of Memorial Hospital that the walk home took us by irresistible cliffs and valleys of red dirt. On dry days, conditions were just right for painless dirt-ball combat. Painless because the red clods crumbled when they struck. The year of the great mud-ball civil war, however, was real combat, with real casualties. The eastside was divided into two rival armies of boys, one defending in the woods above Governor Kilby's house. When the invaders approached our roofless log fort, commanded by the governor's grandson, George Kilby, I at first threw mud balls fearlessly—until one struck me in the chest. From that moment on, I was a cautious soldier. The battle was a formless affair, boys running through the woods tossing and ducking mud balls with high anxiety, as if there were real danger. Our side caught and briefly imprisoned a few invaders in the pool house but there were no real victors or losers; just boys excited by imagining we were real soldiers.

Casualties of similar skirmishes today might still face the unpleasantness of the Saturday bath, but their battle-soiled clothes would be dropped in the washing machine. Back then, dirty clothes were collected and taken to Jensie's house in the Southside colored neighborhood. In her backyard was a giant black iron pot where the clothes were boiled (perhaps, I imagined, while Jensie uttered black-magic incantations as she stirred). Within the week, they would reappear, starched and folded in a wicker basket and giving off a neutral scent, the smell of clean. Jensie's house was one of the stops on the Christmas delivery route, too. Mother insisted I deliver her present personally, which I did awkwardly, not knowing what to say to an older person who was owed respect but who also had to endure the humiliation of washing other people's clothes. She always greeted me warmly, with self-confidence rooted in the belief that the service she performed was not demeaning but a way to make a few extra dollars.

A REAL WAR CAME to us mud-war veterans on the radio with the shocking news that the Japanese had attacked Pearl Harbor. The most immediate and visible sign of threat to me was Dad on Civil Patrol with a World War I helmet a size too small and a flashlight as long as my six-year-old torso. The blackout—shades lowered and no outside lights—lasted only a few days. Adults concluded that the Japanese weren't going to bomb Anniston. Ritual summer Saturdays and the winter walks to Woodstock School, hated corduroy knickers marking time—swish, swish, swish, swish, swish—rolled on with little sense that people were actually killing each other way over there in Europe and Asia, wherever those distant galaxies were. One summer during the war, when I had been sent off to Camp Yananoka in North Carolina, Mother committed a famous malapropism. Chatting cheerily on the phone with a friend, she said, "Oh, yes, Brandy's having a wonderful time—canoeing, riding horseback. Where? Okinawa." The friend was puzzled and horrified.

Those great and terrible years when the world was on fire, when American heroes were white knights in khaki pushing back the evil hordes, Nazis and Japs, are compressed in child-time. The war years are a cadenza of memories: my victory garden that yielded only radishes, war bonds in Christmas stockings, "America the Beautiful" sung joyously off-key in the Woodstock School cafetorium; Mother playing "There'll Always Be an England" with anthem solemnity on the baby grand in our living room; the "essential occupation" gas rationing stamps on Dad's Chevrolet; playing French Resistance fighters with George in the fields behind the governor's house; pictures I drew of P-50 Mustangs with grinning shark's teeth on their noses and of GIs mowing down Nazis. All these and the Movietone newsreels narrated by a doomsday bass are the ways a boy remembered a war that didn't touch his family directly—minutia interrupted by two dramatic jolts and the first smack of cynicism to adolescent idealism.

The first shock came when Marian Huey and I were doing something that might have earned us a spanking if we'd been caught. We'd sneaked into Mr. Acker's car to listen to music on the radio—not to deliberately run down his battery, but that could well have been the result, which would have brought with it the consequence favored in that time. Those were the days when spanking was as American and Southern as fried chicken on Sundays. Marian usually had it a little worse than I did judging from the sounds of her yells and her mother's smacks ringing from the pre-air conditioning open windows at the corner of Glenwood and Highland. Mother gave me a few light lickings and Dad's one performance was a bit comical as he searched for a hairbrush that had not been used for its original purpose in decades. On this occasion, however, it wasn't corporal but God's punishment we got. We had scarcely taxed Mr. Acker's battery when the music was interrupted to announce . . . PRESIDENT ROOSEVELT IS DEAD! It was as devastating as if a parent had died. He had literally been father to the country, the only national father we children had known, who drew even Dad and Mother to the sound of his voice coming from Dad's old shortwave radio by his red leather chair in the library.

Less than four months later, I was at my good friend Lloyd Brinkley's house across the alley, a second home, when the second surprise shook our world. Lloyd's father, Bill Brinkley, was managing editor of the *Star* and, because of our dads' occupations, Lloyd and I had passes to all the Anniston Rams home baseball games. We were allowed to climb the wooden ladder, straight up on top of the bleachers, and lie on our stomachs right under the radio booth and behind the screen, where we would involuntarily reach for an occasional foul ball inches away. Heedless of our station as children of privilege in that all-white cocoon long ago, from our perch under the WHMA announcers, we were fascinated by "Cotton" Hill's curve balls and hump-backed sinkers.

Evidently, Lloyd's dad made just enough at the *Star*—about $100 a week—to support his wife, Ida Lee, two sons and a daughter. The Brinkley kitchen did not have a refrigerator. It had an icebox, whose top compartment held a block of ice, delivered weekly by a muscular man wielding a large pair of iron tongs. There was a wide income and power gap between the two families that the adults understood but that had no meaning to their pre-teenaged children. I looked up to Lloyd, a year older and adolescent handsome, with slicked-back dark hair, whom the girls called "Id'n" (for idn't he cute. I would have done anything short of treason to be called "Id'n.") Mrs. Brinkley seemed to have an inexhaustible supply of sandwiches for

Lloyd and me, the boss's son. It was on her screened back porch one morning in early August when the voice on the ubiquitous radio announced in sepulchral tones that a "device" of indescribable destructive force had been dropped on the city of Hiroshima, Japan. (Many years later pictures in the Hiroshima Peace Memorial Museum portrayed for me the instant of horror and the piteous aftereffects, but outside, when I found that a sports bar occupied ground zero, the museum's gloom was lifted.)

Three days later, August 9, a second "device" was dropped on Nagasaki, and within a week of the introduction of atomic warfare by the United States, World War II was over. When V-J Day was announced, my older sister, Elise, was home. She was to me, eleven years her junior, a wondrous being who lived away from us in Tuscaloosa, a romantic place of such Wagnerian heroes as Harry Gilmer, the All-American halfback for the Alabama "Crimson Tide." She would be a senior at the University that fall. She and a contemporary, Anne Gambrell McCarty, decided to drive downtown to observe the spontaneous celebrations of V-J Day. In the front seat, I was happily wedged between actual college girls. Downtown we saw a good deal less than a Times Square celebration: happy people greeting each other on the sidewalk, and some honking of horns. Anne Gambrell viewed the scene unsmiling, and deflated my sense of celebration when she said the strangest thing: "The war's over; the breadlines start tomorrow." Her cynicism, uttered with quiet but impressive certainty, was strange to my ears, like nothing I had heard at home. Her worldview was foreign to her place and time. Anne was a liberal, a real left-winger for whom the flaws and evils of our "way of life" were more obvious and detestable than the gracious speech and manners with which they were camouflaged. She would later get in trouble in Louisville for the mortal sin of helping an African American couple buy a house in a white neighborhood—prima-facie evidence of communism in those days. Neither she nor I suspected at the time that one day I, too, would be branded a liberal and our family newspaper derisively called, principally by racists, "The RED Star."

In 1945, downtown was just as it had always been. Hidden economic forces—wheels within wheels within wheels—had not yet engaged to signal the economic takeoff point of the Southern economy, marking its long-delayed recovery from the Civil War. Not yet risen were the winds of social change that would turn "our way of life" upside down. On Noble Street, stood the magical kingdoms, Kress's and Woolworth's five-and-dime stores. The warm parfait of scents from the candy counter tantalized children as they entered Kress's to shop for Halloween masks and hats or inexpensive Christmas presents for friends and teachers. Of course, there were also the twin, hospital-white drinking fountains, one marked "White" and the other "Colored." The wife of an Air Force officer, Rosalie Reynolds, was home on leave in the early 1950s from Germany where her seven-year-old son, "Studie," had been born. She took the boy shopping at Sears and Roebuck, the fabulous, large store at 17th and Noble. Studie confronted one of the drinking fountains for the first time, and he was charmed. "Look, Momma," he said excitedly. "They've got colored water!"

It was just such innocent discoveries that made my generation aware of the parallel universe where "colored" lived behind a barrier that read, "Do Not Enter." I was about twelve when I first noticed the barrier as an inconvenience. I was buying a ticket at the Calhoun Theater simultaneously with a boy who'd played touch football in our unselfconscious, interracial games. He was on the other side of the glass ticket box. Inside, I waited for him to come in, but there was no door. It was then I understood why there was a red velvet rope blocking the stairs to the balcony.

Thoughts of social justice did not disturb the pleasant sameness of growing up at 818 Glenwood Terrace in the 1940s. We had rituals as perfect and predictable as Saturday afternoons at the movies. Dinner, cooked by Mildred and served by Eli, was at 6:30 sharp, when conversation was suspended to hear the radio commentary of Quincy Howe from Boston. Then Mother and Dad would discuss the events of the day. Countless times Dad punctuated the discussion with favorite quotes. "Noblesse Oblige, to whom much is given, much is expected." "Duty is the sublimest word in the English language, quoth Robert E. Lee." "He who fails to take heed of events far away will soon find trouble near at hand." Whether or not those aphorisms were meant to instruct his children, they stuck with me and helped shape my view of the world.

Sunday dinner, served after church, was always fried chicken—a Mildred specialty: juicy meat covered with a golden brown crust. Often during the war, soldiers would be at the table, knights in khaki. In those days, before air-conditioning, the house was always dark in summer and the basement fan perpetually stirred the moist air. On rare occasions, Stephen Foster melodies would float from outside through the closed blinds into the dining room. The family would leave the table and assemble on the front porch to enjoy the serenade by a trio of black musicians who did not ask for but received a gratuity from our parents. The sound carried on the humid Alabama air was sweet; the memory is sad. They were the last troubadours of a dying civilization—a society with a rotten legal core but which had its charms.

Dad's words may have been more memorable, but Mother was at the center of family life, planning meals, birthday parties, grown-up parties, and family vacations. Perversely, every August just as the hurricane season started our family headed for the Ponte Vedra Beach Resort and Club in Florida (welcomed "home" by the familiar staff). Mother was the producer and stage-manager of a series of birthday parties at which I, as guest of honor, got the prime slice of chocolate cake, "the chicken coup," so-called because it was a corner piece with icing on two sides as well as the top. The calorie and cholesterol content could have measured in megatons. One birthday, she organized a midget baseball game at which she pitched and our then-butler-chauffeur-gardener, George Hillman, was the catcher. Bushes obscured the whole scene from neighbors across the street—except for the pitcher and catcher—and next day our across-the-street neighbor, Mrs. Miller, called to ask Mother if she enjoyed her game of catch with Hillman.

Christmas was Mother's *pièce de résistance*, the beating heart of family ceremony. Christmas was also a celebration of community life. Before the boom times down South, before suburban sprawl brought us developments with names nearly as pompous as "Grande Dame Estates," before malls and multiplex theaters, Noble was the main street. Crowded with Christmas shoppers, the vital pulse of commerce beat from Gus "Nick" Nichopolous's community-central Sanitary Cafe to the Commercial National Bank presided over by big, friendly Marcus Howze and quiet, sweet-natured Guice Potter Sr. We even had our own Lilliputian Macy's Day Parade. Children wedged and squeezed through the forest of adult legs to get close to the grand progression of high school bands, including the high-stepping Cobb High (black) entourage, capped by the appearance of a magnificent Santa—sowing the fields of spectators with wrapped candies, children grabbing at them in the air and scurrying to rescue fallen pieces.

At home, Mother's much-anticipated production began with the ritual gathering of the smilax, which meant a perilous ascent of an extension ladder to clip the vines from trellises on the side of the house. Smilax was a main feature of Mother's decorations. Lush garlands snaked up the banisters of the hall stairway and were draped over all the pictures, including the flat likeness of Grandfather, his white VanDyke beard above white tie and tails that set off three colorful medals awarded by Chinese presidents for his public health contributions to that poor nation—objects of awe, envy, and mystery to me. His picture was faced by a lovely portrait of Mother, painted by cousin Ted Mohn, hanging above the fireplace mantel on the opposite wall of the living room. The two paintings were silent witness to the ritual Christmas Eve. The perfect, undeviating sameness of those evenings, with their constant moral core, took on an almost sacramental quality. The evening began with a scratchy 78-rpm recording of Dickens's "A Christmas Carol," starring British actor Basil Rathbone as Scrooge. Its undisguised message—the evils of greed and the joys of charity—were taken seriously by our family and we never failed to be moved when Tiny Tim piped, "God bless us, every one!"

Next in the order of service came family carols, an uncertain chorus of Dad, Elise, and me, accompanied on the piano by Mother, who, as the family musician, played with firm confidence. The only flaw in the ceremonial re-enactment was the perfectly awful Christmas Eve dinner of backbone—a fat, greasy, barely edible black mass whose roots in tradition are lost, a tradition to be honored in the breach. Because there was no strong pull of anticipation associated with that meal, the family listened with patient appreciation as Dad found the Second Chapter of Luke, beginning with: "And it came to pass in those days, that there went out a decree from Caesar Augustus . . .

"And she brought forth her firstborn son, and wrapped him in swaddling clothes, and laid him in a manger; because there was no room in the inn . . . And there were, in the same country, shepherds abiding in the field, . . .

And, lo, the angel of the Lord came upon them, and the glory of the Lord shone around them, and they were sore afraid."

The majestic language of the original King James translation awakens a cluster of powerful feelings of home, family, happy times during the delightful irresponsibility of childhood. Modern versions, which substitute "strips of cloth" for the magical "swaddling clothes" and the shepherds were "frightened" for "sore afraid," trigger no emotion but regret. Mystery has been robbed to achieve a too-familiar accessibility. Important traditions are not improved by modern-day tinkering. It's the faith of my father, King James, for me, and I never found any version of Dickens's classic quite as satisfying as those old, scratchy recordings. I can't explain why those Christmas Eves rank in my memory above the exquisite torture of the following morning's anticipation—Dad's interminable breakfast—which kept us from the treasures under the tree in the library.

Nostalgia plays funny tricks but it must know what it is doing. Its authority cannot be disputed

TURNING TWELVE AND ENTERING sixth grade was a milestone. It meant leaving the familiar habitat of Woodstock School. My all-white grammar school was a place of happy memories, minor disappointments, and one great crime. Heroism and celebrity were near-misses in those years. I had a chance to score a touchdown during recess tackle football games—a signal achievement for a slow, chubby boy who was not a favorite receiver—but Jimmy Hannon's bullet hit me in the mouth and I dropped the ball. Neither did I get the coveted appointment as captain of the Safety Patrol—the white cap and belt with the silver and blue badge—opening car doors as they delivered children at school and, grandly stopping tenth Street traffic for students crossing. I was merely fire chief, with a red cap and belt and red-rimmed badge.

Woodstock was also the setting for my brief and inept criminal career. The summer after graduation from Woodstock, Tommy Butler, Ronnie Hicks, and I were camping out in an army tent in the side yard. We relieved the boredom by egging neighbors' houses—not very cleverly leaving my house untouched. Next, we targeted the school. We crouched behind a row of hedges separating the west side of the building from a rocky, unpaved alley where ammunition was plentiful, smooth throwing stones. Among the most delicious moments of childhood is that instant after launch when you wait to hear if your missile hit brick—or, ahhhhh, GLASS! Bold and invisible in the dark, we moved closer, concentrating fire on the office of the feared principal, Miss Meigs. She used switches on malefactors and always held a handkerchief in her hand—to cover a missing finger, clear evidence of sinister doings. Suddenly, a light flashed around the north side of the school. Like two dumb, frightened deer—one skinny, the other chubby—Tommy and I fled due south, up a rise where, at the front of the school, we were stabbed by a constellation of lights. We froze, while Ronnie smartly veered off to the west and escaped. The cops took Tommy and me to the station and put us in a cell while they made the fateful calls to our parents. Elise was at home and described the scene. Mother took the call, heard the news, and dramatically held the phone out to Dad, "Harry, your son is in prison!" Dad's recommendation was to leave me there, which meant the police had to take me home. Among the physical and financial punishments that resulted was an audience with the Mayor Himself, the Honorable Ed Banks. Worse, Dad ordered our misdeeds exposed in the paper, which meant everybody in town, peeking through their blinds, spied Public Enemy Number One as he trudged remorsefully around town, bent under the weight of Cain's crimes.

Sweeter memories of Woodstock begin at the beginning, when I fell in love with my first-grade teacher, Margaret Griffis. Miss Griffis was also our "Miss Manners," teaching children the distinction between "excuse me" and "I beg your pardon." "Excuse me," is appropriate for a trivial offense such as brushing against someone. But for serious breaches of etiquette (her example, knocking a lady's sable coat to the floor) "I beg your pardon," is required—as in begging clemency from a king. She was not out of touch with the seamier side of life, but viewed it with droll worldliness. When a prostitute claimed a candidate for lieutenant governor had tied her up and done unspeakable things with her, Miss Griffis observed, "If that gul did all of the things she is supposed to have done, Ah think she sold herself too cheaply."

My feelings for her didn't achieve closure until the fall of 1998, when the still-slim and still-beautiful Margaret, in a white silk dress and spiked heels, had a birthday party. For herself. To celebrate her ninetieth birthday. In my toast, I invited the guests to go back with me fifty years and look in on Miss Griffis's first grade class. The children were bent to their task—copying the alphabet, making vowels with great oval swoops—all but one boy. So smitten was he by the beauty of his teacher, he could do little but stare. That Christmas, his mother suggested cologne for the teacher. The boy protested, "Mother, that's not good enough for Miss Griffis. We should give her an evening dress." The mother prevailed, of course. I was that little boy, and the oversight so many Christmases ago had been a burden on my conscience—until her party—where, to her delighted astonishment, I whipped out a fire-engine-red sequined number. With tassels. Would she wear it? A friend asked her that and she gave a revealing reply, "Oh, it's much too tight."

She died in 2006, an original and, in our informal, unceremonial contemporary society, an unrepeatable heirloom—with just a dash of flirtatious devilment.

Inevitably, the day came when all twelve-year-old boys and girls were launched from their grammar schools and met in a war of the planets: eastside vs. westside, Venus vs. Mars. We were all white, but we had been formed by life into two separate and incompatible worlds. We eastsiders had been coddled and sheltered by the more spacious incomes of our parents. The westside kids had been toughened, made streetwise by growing up in blue-collar neighborhoods. One of the friendlier westside girls shocked me with an admission that seemed commonplace to her. The family would take Sunday sightseeing drives to Glenwood Terrace and other neighborhoods on my side of town: to see how the "rich" people lived.

Not all the westside boys were friendly. One of the tough ones roared back to life for me in the summer of 2000 when the Atlanta Braves' ace reliever, John Rocker, launched some wild verbal pitches, sounding off about New York's "foreigners," "queers," and welfare mothers. Rocker was for me a junior-high terror come to life. I recognized in him the feral breed. He drove a battered pickup on reckless Saturday nights up to and over the edge of danger. In his blood, a six-pack mingled with the genes of wild Celtic ancestors. He was a descendant of fearless Highland warriors, Irish rebels, Viking plunderers and lonely Southern pioneers pushing back the wilderness in solitary sorties—a familiar Southern type, a redneck. Anybody who grew up in the small-town South knows a John Rocker. I first met him in junior high school where boys from the "right" side of the tracks merged with their scary classmates from the "other" side. He was the tallest, most muscular, and scariest of them all. He knew the unprintable names of certain parts of the female anatomy and spoke them in a way that suggested he might actually have explored those secret, unattainable kingdoms. He was an object of fear and admiration.

In the universe of junior high and high school, he was Braveheart, with a mean streak, whom no paddling principal could tame and bring to heel. His independence was crafted by earlier generations that, in contrast with the westward exploration of Easterners in communal wagon trains, wrested the land from the wilderness as lonely, single pioneers. W. J. Cash in his classic *Mind of the South* wrote, "He had much in common with the half-wild Scotch and Irish clansmen of the seventeenth and eighteenth centuries whose blood he so often shared . . ." A history he didn't know or understand formed the John Rocker of my junior high: athlete, lover, king of his adolescent universe.

From an unlikely source, former United Nations Ambassador Andrew Young, came a tolerant understanding of how a small-town Southern tough felt on being stranded in an alien land—the sophisticated, urban, multiethnic planet upon which he had landed. When the two met, Young knew what it was like for Rocker to have exploded from a Macon neighborhood onto the national stage. In so many words, Young said that Rocker was an innocent country boy who had never been anywhere or met anybody who was different. A baffling world came at him, and he balked. "Besides," Ambassador Young added, "Yankees are different." True enough, as he illustrated with an ironic anecdote: years ago, a rude New York merchant had sent his wife from a store in tears when, in the segregated South, Young said, a shop owner would have treated her with courtesy.

The year, 1949, was a kind of educational "phony war" for me. It was to be my freshman year at Anniston High School, but the day for registration, buying schoolbooks, and the first day of classes all passed without any command from Mother and Dad about school. What I didn't know, and only vaguely suspected from taking a battery of tests none of my friends did, was that a decision had been taken from on high—long before family conferences came into vogue. I was being sent away, to a small Episcopal boarding school near the then-grimy manufacturing town of Danbury, Connecticut. Mother and Dad decided on the Wooster School, because the "name" schools such as Andover and Lawrenceville would have to put me back a year or two. Anniston schools evidently weren't up to speed. Wooster would take a chance, because I had a detectable IQ pulse and because my family liked the values Wooster put up front in its catalogue: "Religion, Simplicity, Intellectual Excellence and Hard Work."

The announcement of my fate was duly made and I awaited banishment with trepidation. Elise tried to calm my fears, without success. Finally, the day came for Dad and me to board the train for New York. In Manhattan, dressed in my favorite powder blue suit and whitebuck loafers, we went to Brooks Brothers to buy weird, pinched, dull, gray and blue suits and a gray jacket made of little Vs. I was outfitted as a proper preppie, and I hated the look. Dad took me to school, where we met the friendly headmaster, the Reverend John D. Verdery, and finally the dreaded moment came when Dad left me alone on the stone walk leading up to the New Building. It was a gray, cold September day in the foothills of the Berkshires—just right for a sense of desolate abandonment.

Before the mood could overtake me, however, a couple of older boys greeted me, one wearing a white sweater with a maroon "W"—a figure of awe to a third former. The older boys were kind, and I soon discovered that Wooster was a friendly, special place, a formative experience in my life. The student pool was not as old-money, first-family New England as Groton under its fabled Rector, Endicott Peabody, but it bore a resemblance to the model he cast. "If some Groton boys do not enter public life and do something for our land," intoned the Rector, "it will not be because they have not been urged." The handsome young headmaster of Wooster, John Verdery, was not so formidable as Peabody and his masters did not preach public service so didactically. Wooster did not hide its values, but it wasn't grim about them. Without trivializing either school, Wooster was Groton Lite. The style of the place and what I took from it are summarized in the citation that was given to me as the Alumnus of the Year for 1998 [see Appendix].

The citation's style fit the place: just short of jaunty, no strained praise or funereal solemnity, an honest, not terribly impressed salute to a life that, on balance, had been above-average okay. It was read in the school's spare, old chapel where, in my speech I acknowledged the presence of so many friendly ghosts . . .

One was John Verdery, who preached there every Sunday, but whose manly, understated grace was a more lasting model than any of his sermons. His wife, Sue, whose slightly scatter-brained charm, good looks, and mastery of French cooking made their house a warm haven as a student and for years afterward. Babysitting their children gave me a feeling of family far from my real home. In my senior year it also got me close to their nurse, the full-lipped, shapely Mitzi Henz, the only girl our age on campus, which made me the envy of the class.

Another was Joe Grover, who tried to bring order to my chaotic essays. Still another was the rumpled "Mr. Chips" of my years there, Donald Schwartz, whose all-day final exam in the combined American history and literature class asked us to use our readings to respond to William Faulkner's Nobel Acceptance Speech that year, "man will not only endure, he will prevail."

I don't recall if after the award and speech in 1998 I looked deliberately at the spot outside West Cottage remembering how the Head had queried me about a pending Supreme Court decision that I knew nothing about, but surely I must have. If I had I would have shaken my head in wonder that I left Wooster completely innocent of the thunderclap that would shake the South in the second semester of my freshman year at the University of Alabama.

3

A Civilization Dies—Unnoticed

A whole civilization lay dying around me in the six years after prep school, but I was too self-absorbed to notice. For four of those years, I was concentrated on the pleasures of sorority girls, bad sex, and cheap bourbon as an undistinguished undergraduate at the University of Alabama, and for two more as a U.S. Navy enlisted man. A classmate who truly was distinguished, David Mathews, later became president of the University, Secretary of Health Education and Welfare in the Ford administration, and president of the Kettering Foundation. We didn't know each other in school but became friends when he was a dean of students at UA. Once during his presidency I asked, "David, why didn't I ever see you drinking beer in any of the fraternity basements?" He answered, "Why didn't I ever see you in the library?" That pretty well summed up my first wave of university life—a sensual explosion on escaping the monastic restraints of prep school and entering the relative license of college.

At the white-columned brick Phi Gamma Delta house, we paid scant attention to news of the outside world, which came to us on a black and white TV set in what was laughingly called the library. TV told, for instance, about a governor of Virginia invoking a shadowy power called "interposition" to prohibit blacks from going to white schools. Mildly interesting, but of more immediate interest were the weekend parties. The nuances of federal v. state authority gave way to defining the corporate personality of the top sororities: Kappa Deltas, bitchy but interesting; Tri Delts, too sweet for our taste; Kappa Kappa Gamma, natural and fun, good ol' girls.

While most of us grieved at the mighty Crimson Tide football team's losing seasons, beneath us the socio-political geology rumbled on its axis. But we could not feel or hear it. A warning tremor had been felt by Dad's generation earlier, in Birmingham at the July 1948 "Dixiecrat" convention led by former Alabama Governor Frank Dixon. Among the delegates, five Southern governors mingled with a who's-who of such violent racists as Gerald L. K. Smith and J. B. Stoner. They nominated South Carolina Governor Strom Thurmond as their presidential candidate to oppose the reelection of President Harry Truman, and to preserve "States' Rights," meaning a state's right to deny Negroes the vote, and the minimal conveniences of dining, sleeping, or using bathrooms when and where they were needed. The 1948 Dixiecrat convention was the first in a series of "Pickett's Charges" in the war to preserve white supremacy.

But we happy-little-idiot fraternity boys didn't know we were playing on a social fault line that was in motion. We knew we had a genial giant as governor, six-foot eight-inch James E. Folsom, because we sang a song about his paternity problems. Well-to-do parents were embarrassed by what they considered his crudities, and didn't care for his populist appeal. "Y'all Come" was the slogan of his second successful gubernatorial campaign, an appeal to all the bypassed working folks, urban and rural, to come visit him in the Governor's Mansion. We chuckled at the disarming honesty of his sexual exploits: "If they bait a trap with a pretty woman, they're gonna catch Big Jim every time." There is a story repeated so often that, if it isn't true, it ought to be. It stands as a metaphor for dealing with a sexual scandal that might have instructed President Clinton. In the story, Governor Folsom is confronted by reporters who ask if it is true that he slept with a "colored" girl in a Phenix City motel the night before. Folsom answered, "It's a damn lie; not a word of truth to it—didn't sleep a wink! " Over beer and cheap bourbon in fraternity basements, we sang a song about our colorful governor:

> She was poor, but she was honest.
> Victim of a rich man's whim;
> 'Til she met that Christian gentleman Big Jim Folsom,
> And she had a child by him.
> Now he sits in the governor's chair,
> Makin' laws for all mankind
> While she walks the streets of Cullman, Alabama
> Sellin' bits of her behind.

We also listened to the popular idol of the fifties, Elvis Presley—and we hated him. Only when his death in 1977 set off a shock wave of grief did I begin to understand the tragedy and the enduring power of the man. Elvis's fans don't see the fat man who died alone in his bathroom a generation ago. They only see the slim, hip-pumping boy with the glistening pompadour, heavy sideburns, and outrageous clothes who was both vaguely threatening and vulnerable. They crowned him King: sovereign in the kingdom of rock and roll, rhythm and blues, country and pop. They've made him into a memorial, a statue, totem, icon that has rendered the real man-boy unknowable. But the image fills a need in those who have to remember him a certain way. As always, those to whom we give symbolic power tell more about us than they do the object of our love or scorn.

Elvis Presley is a symbol for millions: of being born poor and making it? of fantasized fame and celebrity? Perhaps more of innocence lost. Thomas Wolfe was half right—you can't go home again. If Elvis had survived his fame, he might have gone to the fiftieth reunion of Humes High School, his high school in Memphis, Tennessee, but at seventy, he couldn't be that teenaged boy, raging with energy and mischief. Nor can the women who surround themselves with Elvis memorabilia go home again and revive the aching tenderness and insecurities of teenaged love, so they play the old records and blow on the dying embers, trying to recall how it was, enjoying the delicious sorrow of lost youth and innocence.

Elvis and I were the same age, and I thoroughly disliked him. I loathed what I took to be a sneering mouth—resented the attraction his rebellion had for girls our age, just as I was vexed by the appeal that the local "baaad boys" had for some girls I knew. Elvis was a shock, a threat to me and the well-protected cocoon in which I had been nurtured. We were from the right side of town—a family his people would call "rich." He was from the wrong side of town, violated every convention I knew, and he was getting the girls. I hated that.

Now, having ventured far and wide on the discovery craft of journalism, learning the values of other worlds, plain and fancy, Elvis's honeyed voice crooning "Love Me Tender" and the film clips of the girls squealing and swooning strike home with the combined power of innocent charm and nostalgia.

Elvis was an emotional force that attracted two small-town Southern presidents. When Elvis performed at the Omni in Atlanta in 1973, Jimmy and Rosalynn Carter went backstage to meet him. In the White House, Carter took a call from the singer just weeks before he died. Presidential hopeful Bill Clinton appeared on the "Arsenio Hall Show" in 1992 and paid a musical tribute to Elvis with a saxophone performance of "Heartbreak Hotel." The American presidency is a unique office, respected everywhere, but presidents' popularity doesn't match that of a dead singer. We have always needed to create heroes and kings, but we exact a terrible price from them. We demeaned Carter and Clinton, and bestowed such high-voltage charisma on Elvis that it killed him.

Our adolescent resentment of Elvis was a more potent emotional presence than the great events unfolding in Montgomery. Like a war on another continent, the first skirmish of full-scale civil combat, the Montgomery bus boycott, occurred beyond our notice on December 1, 1955, when Rosa Parks refused to surrender her seat on a city bus to a white man. The story of the determined passenger in the Montgomery bus has been told and retold so many times, it need not be repeated here, but one picture from that historic episode still surprises. It is a picture of the leader of the boycott, Dr. Martin Luther King, so slender, and so very young. Could it have actually happened? That slight, serious, twenty-six-year-old in the picture, young Martin King, could he actually have caused the sinking of an antique civilization and the rise of a wholly new society! It seems shockingly out of proportion until you remember that the Founding Fathers were mainly young men. Thomas Jefferson was thirty-three when he wrote the Declaration of Independence. Another young man in his early thirties remade much of the world, a young Jewish man with revolutionary ideas—Jesus of Nazareth.

What even fraternity boys could not avoid noticing for a few days in February 1956 at the University of Alabama was Autherine Lucy, the first Negro admitted to an all-white Southern university, and Leonard Wilson, an intense young man who led student protests against her enrollment. As student protesters' ranks swelled with the addition of some of the state's most diabolical racists, striking rubber workers, Ku Klux Klansmen and their allies from out of state, the crowds became more and more vehement and violent. On the morning of February 6 in New Orleans, where a fraternity brother and I had taken dates for the weekend, we awoke to radio news about the commotion on campus. We decided Tuscaloosa was more interesting than New Orleans and drove back. That night, the trustees met and decided to "exclude Autherine Lucy until further notice," for the safety of the students. She had been a student for five days. The mob had won. Lucy later married and moved to Texas. Leonard Wilson was expelled from the university for his role in the riots, but became a celebrity racist as executive director of the Alabama White Citizens Council until it expired, along with the civilization that spawned it, in 1969.

At the time, I wasn't stabbed by sympathy for Lucy or burning with moral indignation against the mob. I just wondered what all the fuss was about. She was just another student, a momentary celebrity whom I never saw but would have liked to have met. An amusing irony from that time, told to me by a girl from Anniston, was the real story behind the two-page photo spread in *Life* magazine of what appeared to be a racist thug stomping the roof of a Cadillac. As it turned out, the boy trampolining atop the car had been partying all weekend and was so drunk he didn't know—or care—who was in the car: frightened black tourists, unaware of what had been unfolding on campus. Historian Culpepper Clark in his indispensable account of the times, *The Schoolhouse Door*, confirmed the true story. Historical accounts of those few days now, when African American students are so ubiquitous as to be invisible, have the texture of a distant reality like Dickens's London or Hugo's Paris—events from a past century, a past civilization, which in fact they were.

The White Citizens' Council is a blur in my memory—the Klan in a business suit, with a college degree. If it had many members in Anniston, Dad was certainly not one of them. I recall his criticism of the white resistance movement, and by the time I returned to Alabama, such middle-class bigotry had been marginalized by real-man racists such as our famous fellow townsman, Asa "Ace" Carter, one of the authors of George Wallace's 1963 "Segregation Forever!" speech. But I'm getting ahead of my story. It is 1956, and the place is Montgomery.

These were serious times, but my awareness of them remained dim as

I engaged in fraternity house frivolity. Novels and trendy nonfiction such as Phillip Wylie's sardonic *Generation of Vipers* fed my intellectual appetite rather than textbooks. My grades were passable, but class attendance wasn't, and those were the days of in loco parentis—university administrators who treated us as their children. The university "family" reached an instant consensus about my value to the academy, and the next thing I knew, I was at the U.S. Naval Training Center in Bainbridge, Maryland, in a boot-camp company under the tender care of a man named Tarango, said to be the all-service heavyweight boxing champion.

After two years in the peacetime Navy, I returned to the University, a more serious student. The seeds of social conscience sown by family and the Wooster School were nourished and began to take root in discussions with Dr. Donald Strong. He was a political science professor who had been one of the two main researchers for Harvard professor V. O. Key's classic, *Southern Politics*. Dr. Strong's graduate course of the same title began to shape my intellectual and ideological foundation. A foundation stone was set when I asked a dumb question after class one day, "Wouldn't society be more stable if the vote were restricted to the educated and propertied classes?" Dr. Strong answered with a question, put something like this: "Do you think a person without a high school degree should be able to make a political statement about his life?" I could not think of a good reason why he shouldn't have that right. Which, of course, meant that my west-side classmates in junior high—even the black sailors I avoided in boot-camp—had the same political rights I had. It was so basic that it should not have been such a memorable insight. Donald Strong's graduate seminar in a tower of the library was a high place where I could look down on my life and inbred assumptions, putting them in perspective.

Key's text and the supplemental readings began to reinforce in my consciousness something else—the knowledge that to be Southern was to be somehow different. Of course, that distinction had been noticeable when I was the only Southerner in my prep school class, where I had organized a Confederate underground and actually raised the Stars and Bars on Wooster's flagpole. Clues to a more complete architecture of Southern uniqueness came my way one evening in the spring of 1959. The celebrated journalist Eugene Patterson, then editor of the *Atlanta Constitution*, spoke to our journalism fraternity and flattered me by accepting an invitation for a nightcap in the bar of the Stafford Hotel. He advised me to read everything C. Vann Woodward had written. Eventually, I made my way through most of Woodward's seminal series of books and got to know slightly the man we called "Marse Vann." In particular, his slim volume, *The Burden of Southern History*, shaped my generation's sense of the singularity of being Southern.

Gene Patterson's reading list would be completed in time, but immediately on graduation from the University, I first had to announce the happy news of my availability to the *New York Times*, the *Washington Post*, and the *Miami Herald*. A humbling wave of apathy greeted my applications to those great journals. Forced to live at home, under the roof of the publisher of the *Anniston Star* as the greenest of cub reporters at the paper inspired in me a powerful desire to . . . get the hell out of there.

Before I could escape, two reportorial diversions developed into lifelong anecdotes: the story of the ax murderess and the African prince. Every reporter remembers his first murder story, and mine was a doozie. The mystery began in the summer of 1959 with the grisly discovery in nearby Gadsden of a legless, armless, faceless torso. A day later, a couple picking berries pulled back a branch and uncovered a horrifying sight—a second legless, armless, faceless torso. Associated Press labeled the mysterious slayings the "X" and "Y" murders. We speculated that they were "gangland" murders, possibly the result of an underworld civil war between the Alabama hill-based white-whiskey ring and the Tennessee red-whiskey ring. The speculation ended when employees at the Anniston Army Depot noticed that the Harper brothers, Emmet and Lee, had not been at work for several days.

They had been living in a trailer on a farm in Rabbittown where Viola Virginia Hyatt lived with her father. All Viola said about motive was: "They done me wrong." In fact, she was alleged to have been in the midst of a dual sexual encounter with the brothers. Her business with one concluded, something was said, and the other brother covered himself with a handkerchief in a manner she found insulting. The punishment she exacted was hardly commensurate with the offense. She stole into their trailer at night with her daddy's shotgun, emptied a chamber into each brother's face, and dragged the bodies outside. There, in order to fit the disposal task to the dimensions of a wooden wheelbarrow, she cut off their arms and legs with her daddy's double-bit ax. Making several trips, she deposited the parts on a tarpaulin in the back seat of the family car. She drove through the night on a journey that touched several northeast Alabama counties, throwing an arm out here, a leg out there, rolling out the two torsos. After her arrest she took sheriff's deputies on a ghastly treasure hunt to relocate the pieces, and deputies stated as fact that she kept more private "treasure" in the freezer. Lorena Bobbitt never attained such rank as a folk villain.

I met Viola in the basement of the old county jail when she returned from her sanity hearing at Bryce Hospital, the state mental health facility in Tuscaloosa, where she was declared sane and competent. A big woman wearing a simple, camellia-red dress and red shoes appeared in the door, dwarfing little Sheriff Roy Snead Sr. She walked past me with a dignified strut toward a tiny elevator, guided by the sheriff who turned aside my interview request with, "She's going to jail." Intrepid reporter that I was, I entered the elevator with them, and found myself belly-to-belly with an ax murderess. My congealed brain could produce only the question, "Are you afraid?" Matter of factly, she replied, "No. Why should I be?" She had me there. We chatted through the bars for a few minutes, but I didn't have the experience and composure to get her to talk much about her life. Viola—ever mysterious and taciturn—pleaded guilty, was a model prisoner in Julia Tutwiler Prison, and returned home after 10 years to lead a quiet life until she died in 2000.

The saga of the prince began with a cryptic note in my typewriter from the city editor, Cody Hall: "Talk to African prince in hospital with kidney stones." "A prince," I thought, "How do you talk to an actual prince, especially African royalty in the segregated South?" Dr. Phil Noble, minister of the First Presbyterian Church, was already there in the administrator's office when I arrived. Soon a dignified young West African, Majuba Lapola Setewayo, eldest son of the Emir of Upper Volta, joined us. Regal in bearing, he tapped a cigarette on a gold lighter and lit it, sending thick tusk-like streams of white smoke curling from his nostrils. He explained that he was an exchange student at Stanford and had been taking the train to Atlanta for research at Morehouse University when he had a kidney-stone attack as the train approached Anniston. He was feeling better when we met, and told intimate tales of other African rulers such as the anti-imperialist first president of an independent Ghana, Kwame Nkrumah. Writing the story, I was acutely conscious that Prince Setewayo would one day rule another nation and I wanted to make a good impression—for Alabama and for the United States. Then, a few days later, Phil Noble called with shocking news. The prince was an impostor. Majuba Lapola Setewayo was in fact Eddie Lee Woods of Waycross, Georgia. He was a drug addict who to get a fix faked kidney stones by pricking a finger to show traces of blood in his urine samples. He was a talented actor. One of his many successful performances earned him a police escort from O'Hare Airport to a Chicago hospital. Under my shamefaced byline, the *Star*'s second story about him began: "The African prince, who was paid court briefly in Anniston last week, actually is only the Prince of Phonies."

4

Model Southern Governors

As far as I could see, the Old South was under no immediate threat in 1959, when my search for a "real" job—away from the sheltering family—led me to Raleigh, North Carolina. But it was not without a sense of adventure and its sibling, anxiety, that I headed down Quintard Avenue pulling a U-Haul-It filled with furniture from Mother's attic. I had landed a job as a political reporter for the now-defunct *Raleigh Times*, an afternoon paper owned by the Daniels family that was a training ground for at least one other publisher of a family paper, Arthur Sulzberger of the *New York Times*. A gubernatorial election was going on up there, and the issue was the same as it had been—which one of the segregationist candidates was the better man? Present, however, was a North Carolina difference that wasn't immediately apparent to me at the time: a patina of moderation covered the race issue there that would have melted in the blazing racial rhetoric of Alabama and Mississippi.

Once in Raleigh and situated in a one-bedroom apartment in Cameron Village, a real estate development surrounding one of the South's earliest suburban shopping centers, I began to sniff around, looking for girls and absorbing the different character of the place. There were three things afoot about which I knew little or nothing. A now-celebrated research park was forming in a wasteland bordered by Raleigh, Durham, and Chapel Hill, a crucible where government, business and education came together in a chemistry that produced a fabulous sprouting of wealth and social enrichment. A non-hysterical, undefiant roadbed of laws, lubricated by moderate rhetoric, was allowing social revolution to overturn the established order without Alabama's blood and fury. And finally, the state was making sense of its scattered colleges and universities by assigning accountability for the planning and coordination of the system to a single entity, the Board of Higher Education.

The Daniels family, which owned the *Raleigh Times* and the famous *News and Observer*—Frank Sr., Frank Jr., and most assuredly, Jonathan, a former press secretary to President Truman—were Carolina natives, steeped in its culture and politics. They knew what was going on. They had been cussed and discussed by Tarheels since the time of Josephus Daniels, the founder of the old "News and Disturber," a lifelong progressive Democrat who had been Wilson's Secretary of the Navy and later ambassador to Mexico for Franklin Delano Roosevelt (who had been Daniels's assistant secretary at the Navy Department). Mr. Josephus and my grandfather were contemporaries as Bryan Democrats in the late nineteenth century and the Danielses have been friends of our family for three generations, prominent in the network of a dozen or so moderate-to-liberal Southern papers.

As a pea-green reporter for the *Times*, I could see clearly about six feet in front of me. Unaware of the labors of gubernatorial and legislative commissions, and what in time their labor would bring forth, I had only a vague sense that North Carolina and Alabama were not the same. They were, in fact, remarkably different. Geology and history combined in North Carolina to create a culture defined by a business-political oligarchy so unashamed of its more humble past as to be, in Jonathan Daniels's phrase, a militant mediocrity, yet one that was a model of progressivism in the South. Alabama's more numerous land barons continually fought to control affairs of the state, subduing the white yeomanry and working class by scaring them with the threat of taxes and black domination. The result was an almost anti-progress electorate, a plurality which was willing to accept things as they are, whose buried resentments flare only when breached by meddlesome government, do-gooders, and liberals. Alabama's culture is one of fighting-mad resignation.

North Carolina did not regard itself as a kind of agricultural Versailles, the self-image held by the haughty "plantaristocracy" of South Carolina and Virginia. Neither did it have the nouveaux land-riche pretensions of Alabama's Black Belt plantation society and the Delta planter culture of Mississippi. It had no reason for such pomposity, because its "black belt"—soil suitable for large-scale cultivation by slave labor—was a comparatively little patch in the northeast corner of the state. In 1860, North Carolina had 744 plantations (fifty slaves or more) while Alabama had 1,687 and Mississippi had 1,516. If you think of slave labor as the human equivalent of thousands of six-figure modern combines, imagine the capital investment that vanished with the end of the Civil War. North Carolina didn't lose so much in the Lost Cause and so the state was not quite as enthralled by the dry bones of past graces and glories. It might have taken some pleasure from its snobbish neighbors being brought low. The lofty disdain of its two adjoining states, however, wasn't lost on my wife's family, which came from the plantation patch.

THE EHRINGHAUS CLAN TOOK pride in having an ancestor who served on George Washington's staff during the Revolution. In 1932, it gave the state another in a line of "education governors," J. C. B. Ehringhaus, my wife's grandfather. If not unique, Ehringhaus was an unusual candidate who promised during the campaign that if it took raising taxes to keep North Carolina schools open during the Depression, he would raise taxes. From a tax-toxic Alabama perspective that was a damn fool thing to promise and Alabama would have set him down. Tarheels elected him anyway. The new governor found keeping that promise hard going. Discovering that increases in corporate franchise and income taxes wouldn't cover school expenses, he turned to a sales tax. In a 1934 address to the Medical Society, he fixed on the results of the battle: "After trying to find any form of tax that would eliminate the danger . . . we went to the much 'cussed' and discussed sales tax, and whatever may be said in criticism . . . , we have saved the schools of North Carolina for the little children." Another address piped into schoolrooms statewide would be remembered for its surprise ending, a notorious example of the misplaced pause. Emphasizing the use of every resource in a time of scarcity, he concluded, "Now children, remember, every night when your momma puts that supper plate in front of you, I want you to eat every bean (pause) and pea on your plate." Necessity being the mother of invention, a more lasting and significant claim to the title "education governor" rests on his consolidation of the state's universities as a Depression inspired, cost-cutting measure. Later governors would thank him.

One of the state's historical treasures is the family's plantation, Greenfield, near Edenton. I visited that fine old house when Josephine toured me through what seemed the entire eastern third of the state to stand inspection by her relatives—the equivalent of sniffing a strange dog. Of course, I was shown the famous Edenton Tea Table, an unpretentious piece of furniture that still resides at Greenfield. It was upon that table in St. Paul's Episcopal Church, the first church built in the state, that fifty-one Edenton ladies on October 25, 1774, held the famous Edenton Tea Party—following the more-publicized December 1773 Boston Tea Party. The spunky group resolved: "We, the Ladys of Edenton, do hereby solemnly engage not to conform to the Pernicious Custom of Drinking Tea," or that "We, the aforesaid Ladys will not promote ye wear of any manufacturer from England until such time that all acts which tend to enslave our Native country shall be repealed." Despite the family's distinguished past, I kept hearing from them during our "inspection tour" a self-conscious phrase: "North Carolina is a vale of humility between two mounds of conceit." It finally dawned on me that Tarheels are mighty cocky about their humility. North Carolina, as Jonathan Daniels and others have suggested, is Mediocrity, Militant.

Having lost relatively little in the war, North Carolina went briskly about the business of building a better state for all its people. Alabama—Ashley Wilkes with an attitude—moped about, plotting revenge. Leaders in both states recognized that newly enfranchised, illiterate former slaves were being manipulated at the polls. Both set about constitutional reforms—reforming black citizens out of the political life of the South in 1900. North Carolina sent its black citizens to wander in the political wilderness with kind words. Alabama banished them with a vengeance, and tried to get rid of poor whites, too. Alabama's aristocracy reserved noblesse for itself and gave the burden of oblige to lesser sorts.

Unlike Alabama, illiterate whites were exempted from Carolina's 1900 literacy law, but it wasn't deaf to the siren call of racial prejudice. Even one of North Carolina's icons, its first "education governor," Charles Brantley Aycock, was swept into office as leader of a White Supremacy movement.

White Democrats with ferocious determination set out to recapture state government from "Fusionists" (Republicans and Populists), which included a number of black office-holders. The Fusion ticket won a majority in the legislature in 1894 and elected a governor in 1896 with a significant black vote in both elections. During the legislative races of 1898, Aycock winked at the activities of the hundreds of mounted and armed Red Shirts who intimidated black voters in the heavily black counties along the South Carolina border. Democrats won two-thirds of the General Assembly and promptly passed a constitutional amendment disenfranchising blacks. In the governor's race of 1900, the Red Shirts were out again. A Colonel Waddell in black-dominated Wilmington illustrated the temper of the times in an election-eve speech. The Colonel advised white men to go to the polls armed "and if you find the Negro out voting, tell him to leave the polls and if he refuses, kill him, shoot him down in his tracks. We shall win tomorrow if we have to do it with guns."

Once in office, Aycock governed with exceptional vision and liberality for the time. In and out of office, he was a passionate advocate of public education. As governor, he persuaded the voters to pay the taxes to create universal education and prevailed in getting increased appropriations for the state university over the opposition of denominational colleges. He planted the seed from which grew a first-class state university system. And, though elected in a great racial upheaval, Governor Aycock proved to be a defender of the black man. He was a vigorous opponent and prosecutor of lynch mobs. In a speech opposing a plan to limit support for Negro schools to taxes collected from black property owners, the governor said: "The proposal is unjust, unwise and unconstitutional. It would wrong both races, would bring our state into condemnation of a just opinion elsewhere and would mark us as a people who turned backward. Let us not seek to be the first state in the Union to make the weak man helpless." No such benign words accompanied the 1901 Alabama Constitution, which banished blacks and eliminated as many poor whites as possible through a cumulative poll tax.

Once set in motion, historical inertia holds fast and steady, rolling through the decades. Alabama fought integration with bombs, blood and frenzy, while its "better" class preserved its favored tax status in the Constitution and cowed the white majority with fear of property taxes and hints of black domination. History bred into too many Alabamians a bitter resignation that says: "Our lousy schools were good enough for me and my kids. I don't want none of your progress, race-mixin', taxes and home rule. I'm all right, just don't mess with me." In North Carolina, by contrast, forward historical forces prepared Carolina to build the wealth-fountain that is Research Triangle Park, for peaceful integration, and a consolidated university system with top-ranked research programs.

All that would become clear to me in time. But the gubernatorial campaign going on when I arrived had all the elements of a traditional no-party election of that time, the only question being which one of the segregationist candidates was the better man—whether conservatives or progressives would govern. Those were the two wings of the Democratic Party, the arena and the contrasting ideologies, which would have divided the two parties, if there had been a competitive Republican Party. The first primary was a culling process, which discarded the lesser candidates and chose the two prime contenders for governor.

It would become apparent to me in later years that a far bigger story was going on than the traditional cleavages within the all-segregationist, all-Democratic South. That was the story of progressive Southern governors channeling the churning white waters of racial turmoil into pools of relative peace. The state was also finding ways to accelerate the waves of economic growth that had been unleashed in the South by, among other causes, the end of discriminatory freight rates in 1952. That was the story of Luther Hodges and Terry Sanford who stood at the head of an invisible line of progressive Tarheel governors stretching back to 1900 and before, and who became my models for judging political leaders in Alabama and the rest of the South.

This 1960 runoff election was taking place just six years after *Brown v. Board of Education*—that first rumbling edge of the approaching civil rights storms. North Carolina had developed a political culture that provided some sanctuary from the storm fronts. The march of progressive education governors included Charles Brantley Aycock in 1900; the more conservative, J. C. B. Ehringhaus in 1932; and the populist-progressive, W. Kerr Scott, in 1948. It would certainly have to include Luther Hodges, who saved the public school system in the immediate aftermath of the *Brown* decision and Terry Sanford, who blunted race as a political issue and rationalized the state's higher education system.

Sanford was to be part of the North Carolina continuum of education governors. Ironically, his runoff opponent was himself an educator, a racist with a Phi Beta Kappa key, Dr. I. Beverly Lake. Dr. Lake was no shirttail demagogue. He was Harvard-trained, had studied utility law at Columbia, won a reputation as a consumer advocate as a state assistant attorney general, and had taught law at Wake Forest College. In short, he was a bigot with refinement. Dr. Lake would have been an ideal candidate for Alabama, reminiscent of former Alabama Governor Frank Dixon, east coast-educated, with the dignified good looks of a Methodist bishop. Governor Dixon gave a fighting keynote address at the Democratic breakaway "Dixiecrat" Convention in 1948, damning the Democratic Party and asserting that the States' Rights movement would defend "against those who would destroy our civilization and mongrelize our people." Later, Governor Dixon muted the racial themes, putting a high-minded gloss on the Dixiecrat movement in order to attract allies from outside the South. In private correspondence, he was more candid, lamenting that "the Huns have wrecked the theories of the master race with which we were so contented so long" and referring to blacks as "apes" and "gorillas."

The flame of demagoguery, which would roar to life in the flammable Alabama atmosphere, was banked by the determined common sense of North Carolina leaders. Within weeks of the May 1954 *Brown* decision, a mortally ill Governor William B. Umstead had appointed a commission to study the state's response, headed by a distinguished former North Carolina Speaker of the House, Thomas J. Pearsall. Before the year was out, Governor Umstead had died and was succeeded by the lieutenant governor, Luther Hodges, a former textile executive and Marshall Plan administrator in Germany. Hodges retained the Pearsall commission, which by December reported a plan to transfer pupil assignment from the State Board of Education to city and county boards. It was a local-choice solution, which did not defy the Supreme Court, made it possible for enlightened systems to gradually integrate—or to mount legal resistance—without locking the entire state in one immobilizing court order.

While North Carolina was adopting the Pearsall Plan and reelecting Governor Hodges in 1956, Alabama was adding Amendment 111 to its constitution, which exempted the state from the responsibility for educating its children. The amendment was described clearly as segregationist in newspaper articles at the time. "This is the intent and purpose of this amendment. (It) will prevent any child in Alabama being compelled by Alabama law to attend a mixed school," said F. E. Lund, then the president of Alabama College at Montevallo, in an August 25, 1956, story in the *Montgomery Advertiser*. In the same story, former State Superintendent of Education W. J. Terry said passage of the amendment was needed so "we can make sure that Alabama's public school system will continue to function in every county of our state on the segregated basis which has always been maintained." The amendment was recommended by a legislative committee established in 1953 to study ways to maintain school segregation. In an August 26, 1956, article in the *Advertiser*, state Senator Albert Boutwell of Jefferson County said the amendment would allow the legislature to abolish a public school system to avoid a court order to integrate a school. Another article quoted then-Lieutenant Governor Guy Hardwick as saying the amendment gave the people of Alabama an opportunity to answer the U.S. Supreme Court and "the radicals of the north."

North Carolina's Pearsall plan finally approved by voters in 1956 was chameleon-hued. It provided comfort for segregationists and realists alike, but its very centrist sensibility put Hodges in no-man's-land between hostile extremes—outspoken racists such as Beverly Lake and liberals such as Jonathan Daniels at the *News and Observer*. The most ungovernable rhetoric came from Lake, who fumed all the way through an integrated meeting on the Pearsall plan called by the governor, and seemed to regard the NAACP as a personal affront. A few days after the meeting, Lake told the Asheboro Lions Club: "We shall fight the NAACP county by county, city by city, and if need be school by school and classroom by classroom to preserve our public schools as long as possible, while organizing and establishing other methods of educating our children."

It was the language of "Massive Resistance" preached by the courtly scion of the Virginia political machine, the gentleman farmer, newspaper publisher, and U. S. Senator Harry F. Byrd Jr. It was the bitter-end resistance that would be waged by the handsome young Alabama governor John Patterson, a year after North Carolina adopted its moderate Pearsall Plan. In his 1958 campaign, Patterson courted the Ku Klux Klan and won its formal endorsement in his victory over a then-statesmanlike George Wallace. On election night Wallace pledged to intimates that he would "never be out-nigguhed again," and he wasn't. Patterson, soon after his election, assembled constitutional lawyers who advised a campaign of delaying tactics—a chief element of which was to drive the NAACP underground.

Alabama and North Carolina presented a duel between reason and emotion: a thoughtfully articulated vision opposed to a clutch of inarticulate feelings—resentment, insecurity, and anger. Alabama's constant harangues against the government of the United States and hysterical posturing in opposition to its laws would infect the state with a kind of psychosis. This verbal Niagara of fear seemed consciously designed to create mass dementia: A belief that our nation's government was malevolent, infected by alien ideology bent on crushing long-held values, forcing obedience to unnatural associations and patterns of daily life. Molded by such behavior and speech, the minds of too many Alabamians were conditioned to believe they were doomed to a perpetual Pickett's charge against a hated enemy, and forever fated to be crushed by it—a predestined defeat to be borne with sullen resignation.

North Carolina governors Luther Hodges and Terry Sanford were bookends of statesmanship on either side of George Wallace's energetic manipulation of popular anxiety and indignation. The chronology was: 1954—*Brown v. Board*; 1956—Pearsall Plan, Alabama's Segregation Amendment 111, and Hodges reelected; 1958—Patterson wins with Klan support and tries to banish the NAACP; 1960—Sanford beats educated racist Lake; 1962—Wallace wages defiant segregationist campaign and wins. We are left to wonder whether Patterson and Wallace could have led against the pull of popular agitation and followed the path of prudence and progress exemplified by Carolina leaders. At any rate, a self-confident Governor Hodges, two years after *Brown*, presented the Pearsall Plan to North Carolina voters. It was approved by 80 percent and carried all one hundred counties. Hodges that year won the Democratic nomination (tantamount to election in those days) with more than 400,000 votes to his closest rival's 29,000. In the fall of 1957, schools in Charlotte, Greensboro, and Winston-Salem were quietly, voluntarily integrated.

In February of 1957, Governor Hodges gave a budget speech to the General Assembly unlike any heard by the Alabama Legislature in my lifetime. His vision was:

> I see a land of thriving industry in well-planned small towns and medium-sized cities, without the slum conditions, the polluted air, and the unmanageable congestion of the typical American industrial center. This is a land where all workers are landowners and homeowners, rather than modern-day cliff dwellers, cramped in gloomy rented flats and furnished rooms; a land with prospering farms no longer dependent on a one-or-two-crop market. I see in every community well constructed, modernly equipped and modernly run schools, supported by enthusiastic people who demand nothing less than the best for all children. This is a land where all citizens have sufficient economic opportunity and education to enjoy the best in life. And in this land, looking out over all, there are towers of colleges and universities—for it is an enlightened land—and the spires of many churches—for it is a moral land.
>
> This is the vision, the North Carolina dream. It is not an unattainable thing. We have a great heritage of courage and faith and hard work. We have the people and the resources to turn this dream into reality. You and I, in the years remaining to us, can only lead our state a little way, but if we do that, and hand over to those who come after us the courage and faith which were given us, then, God willing, this vision of North Carolina will become her destiny.

Alabama saw no similarly inspiring vision. It saw a young governor conditioned by the culture in which he was raised, Patterson, wrestling with the NAACP, and the needy, crafty little wizard, George Wallace, booming defiance while behind the screen he was on his knees before a federal judge. When ordered to turn over voting records to the U.S. Civil Rights Commission in 1959, the public saw and heard stage-managed defiance, but as Dan Carter recounts in his biography of Wallace, under the cover of darkness late at night Wallace slunk into Judge Frank Johnson's home. Mrs. Johnson, awakened by the doorbell, heard Wallace plead, "Judge, my ass is in a crack. I need some help."

The wizard's machine worked wonders. The fighting little judge secretly arranged to surrender the voting records while dominating the headlines with a blazing anti-government grand jury statement that Wallace crafted and personally typed. The wizard won the 1962 governor's race and turned the state into his own Land of Oz. It started with an inaugural address in which he said the federal government encourages the "false doctrine of communistic amalgamation" and "encourages everything degenerate and base." The most memorable rhetorical flourish, of course, was: "I draw the line in the dust and toss the gauntlet before the feet of tyranny, and I say: Segregation today, Segregation tomorrow . . . Segregation forever!"

The gauntlet thrown by Wallace got a lot of wear—most famously when he threw it at the feet of U.S. Deputy Attorney General Nicholas deBelleville Katzenbach at the University of Alabama to prevent enrollment of a young black woman and man, Vivian Malone and James Hood. That was another Wallace-produced classic: Defiant special effects, which masked the planned and scripted end—surrender. And the medieval glove he flung "at the feet of tyranny" was pretty beat up by thousands of school buses running over it en route to integrated schools. There was no magic in it, only an invitation to a preordained defeat—as tragic as Pickett's Charge at Gettysburg and stupid as the charge of the Light Brigade into the Russian artillery in the Crimea. Nothing was left after Wallace's rhetorical fireworks but the ash of pointless defiance.

Meanwhile dull, old, commonsensical North Carolina was methodically building the fabulous fountain in the Research Triangle that in time would spew high-salaried jobs by the thousands, and raise towers of nationally ranked research universities. The benefits would prove larger than economic development. It became an importer of intellectual capital. The companies attracted to its agreeably landscaped campus brought the state an infusion of ideas and vision that raised North Carolina business, education and government leadership to a new, more global plateau.

On the surface, the Lake-Sanford campaign did not seem to threaten the ancient regime of segregation into which every Southerner living at the time had been born. Both men spoke in favor of segregation, but Lake opposed the Pearsall Plan and was race-obsessed, threatening "to drive the NAACP from North Carolina." Sanford assured voters he, too, was against integration but defined Lake as reckless, someone who would let the barbarians through the gates. In a crucial television interview during the runoff, Sanford faced the WRAL cameras and said of Lake: "He is injecting a false issue on integration and it is false because I am, and he knows I am, opposed to integration. The difference is that I know how to handle it, and he doesn't . . . Professor Lake yells about mixing of the races, about NAACP domination, and is appealing to blind prejudice for the pure and simple purpose of getting himself a few votes." Then Sanford drew the bright line between recklessness and reason. "Professor Lake has put us in a perilous, dangerous position. His talk is not going to stop anything but his reckless words could start something we can't stop . . . And though we don't like it, the Supreme Court has the last word. He is inviting the Supreme Court to step into North Carolina."

In the anxious climate of the time, Sanford could not allow himself to say what was on his mind—and in his heart. He knew that segregation was finished and believed it was right that it should be. That would become clear in yet another juxtaposition of crazy Alabama and calm Carolina. Four days after Wallace's inaugural, Governor Sanford announced his statewide Good Neighbor Councils to create equal opportunity for black citizens. He told the audience at Chapel Hill's Carolina Inn: "We cannot rely on law alone because much depends upon each individual's sense of fair play . . . We can do this. We should do this. We will do it because it is honest and fair for us to give all men and women their best chance in life." Alabamians aren't any different from North Carolinians—our blood is coded with the same wild Highland Scotch, rebellious Irish and tribal African genes. We might have responded to a sensible, local-choice integration plan. Our legislators surely would have thrilled to visions such as those of Hodges and Sanford. We didn't, because shortsighted, hotheaded leaders manipulated us. Must it be said that we got the leaders we deserve? Surely not.

The significance of those events was not clear to the young, expatriate Alabama reporter, but everything about Sanford just sounded and felt right. In later years, I thought of him as a model. In fact, the night before he died I spoke to the Alabama Political Science Association on a "Tale of Two States" in which Terry shone as a statesman. On learning of his death, I was struck with an eerie connection my family had with North Carolina statesmen. Dad had been in the audience in Birmingham when Governor Aycock began his speech, "I have always spoken of education . . ." A shocked audience then saw him slump to the floor, having just uttered his own epitaph.

Though North Carolina's democratic oligarchy has produced a line of solid and sensible governors, not all of its public men belonged in a statuary hall of statesmanship. Neither has its story been one of perpetual placidity, undisturbed by the winds of controversy. The state had suffered strikes, labor upheavals of violence by unions and the National Guard. A wave of passive resistance—deeply disturbing to its white citizens—rippled through the state in February of 1960, the lunch counter sit-ins by black students that began in Greensboro and moved to Winston-Salem, Charlotte, Durham, and Fayetteville, reaching Raleigh on Wednesday, February 10. The neatly dressed, quiet black students first sat in at the downtown Woolworth's lunch counter, which promptly closed as did counters at the other stores visited by the student demonstrators. They were heckled by white teenagers, but there was no real violence. The most violent act was by a red-faced man who raked his lighted cigar across a young woman's sweater. He then stared at her, arms folded, unaware that embers had landed in the crook of his arm. A thin stream of smoke curled from his burning sleeve. The sit-ins worried moderates in the Sanford camp, fearing that the campaign would inflame racial feelings and help Lake.

North Carolinians were not immune to racial appeals. The revered former president of UNC, Frank Porter Graham, had been defeated in a U.S. Senate campaign by A. Willis Smith, whose campaign exploited racial prejudice, including doctored photographs of Mrs. Graham dancing with a black man. Young Jesse Helms got his start in Tarheel politics by writing advertisements for the Smith campaign and has gone on to earn a place in the pantheon of bigotry. In a phrase credited to Helms, the initials UNC, which Dr. Graham had raised to the first rank of state universities, stood for the "University of Negroes and Communists." A candidate for mayor of Durham, later chancellor of UNC and acting president of the University of Alabama at Birmingham, Paul Hardin, claimed Helms referred to him on the air as "a nigger-loving Communist sympathizer." (No tapes exist to validate the claim.) Young Jesse, who had the brassy bigotry of a John Birch believer, ripened into a courtly caricature of old-fashioned manners and prejudices.

What made Helms so hard to read or predict is that he was an anachronism: cussedly, proudly out of sync with his times—a man stranded by the turbulent river of history on the other side of the canyon—left behind in an Old South tradition with many charms and a great evil. He could be a character out of the 1970s TV series, *The Waltons*, about a large, likable white rural Virginia family during the Depression. He is Grandpa Walton with courtly concern for the sensitivities of the little old ladies of the UDC.

He appealed to Tar Heels who yearn for the simple values of Walton's Mountain—life as it is remembered rather than the cruelties of life as it was lived in the Depression South. His appeal to the prejudices of his home state was mellow, Old South condescension: One must be polite to the "coloreds," but they should know their place and station in life. Helms kept winning because he was only a faded, brown, daguerreotype demagogue—not dangerous as Wallace was. He connected with voters because he honestly believed that the vanished civilization he represented was superior to anything and everything that has happened from the 1950s forward. His likeness will not be found in the pantheon of statesmen, but he deserves a place in the museum of national antiquities.

Now, reviewing those years from the distance of forty-plus years, I am of course amused at my own innocent astigmatism, I shake my head in wonder that a state which could produce Luther Hodges and Terry Sanford also regularly elected Jesse Helms (though Tarheels had the good sense to ship him off to the attic of Washington like a goofy uncle). But more importantly, I am struck by the significance of Sanford's and Hodges's leadership. Terry was a model of effective and moral governance, and later an admired friend. He elevated what Hodges saw as industrial trade schools into a system of comprehensive community colleges, wedding academics and skills for the modern workforce. It was his Commission on Education Beyond the High School that laid out a sixteen-college higher education system finally implemented by his friend, Governor Bob Scott. "It was a monumental piece of work," former UNC President Bill Friday said in a letter to me, " . . . Terry was really the architect and visionary when it came to reorganizing public higher education." Hodges had the advantage of being in office for most of two terms in a then one-term state. On balance, it is fair to say that he would have to rank a nose ahead of Sanford in the state's history. Add up his accomplishments: the Pearsall Plan that saved public schools and broke the back of the race issue in the state, the beginnings of a community college system—and the Midas touch of the Research Triangle Park. A half-century of Alabama governors could claim only one accomplishment of similar significance, an overbuilt, unplanned and disoriented trade school and junior college system.

In terms of personal and professional moment, my one noteworthy journalistic achievement was revealing the plight of migrant labor in North Carolina in the wake of Edward R. Murrow's "Harvest of Shame" broadcast on CBS. However, there were moments in the 1960 campaign with multi-tiered significance. The first televised presidential debates affected the work of local reporters, and gave me a chance for a memorable encounter with the plainspoken former President Harry Truman. During the third debate Vice President Nixon took advantage of a question to criticize Truman's language during the campaign. Senator Kennedy's response was: "I really don't think anything I could say to President Truman that is going to cause him at the age of seventy-six to change his particular speaking manner. Perhaps Mrs. Truman can, but I don't think I can." The next morning President Truman arrived at the Raleigh-Durham airport, where I began a question about Nixon's criticism. Truman interrupted, "Don't talk to me about that man, boy. It's liable to start me to cussin'."

The next day, I puffed along beside the former president on his early morning walk and asked him to respond to Republican charges that his own Secretary of State, James Burns, was for Nixon. Truman's response was: "Jimmy and I split when I sent him to Russia and didn't hear a god-damned word from him until an assistant told me he was arriving at Patuxent River Naval Station and that he was setting up the networks to report to the American people. I sent him a handwritten note that said, 'Jimmy, you better get your ass up here and report to the boss, first.' He resigned a few weeks later for reasons of health—and the old scudder ain't dead yet!"

Television was decisive in carrying North Carolina for Senator Kennedy, but it was not the TV debates that turned the tide. Voters in the thirty counties west of Raleigh, where Democrats traditionally got their majority, did not warm to the notion of having a Catholic in the White House. They were going fishing until late October when the handsome young senator campaigned "Down East," and more significantly, the regional TV stations ran non-stop commercials of the candidate's meeting with the Greater Houston Ministerial Association. Among Kennedy's remarks that made a personal connection with the predominantly Protestant ministers was when he wondered aloud whether anybody asked defenders of the Alamo what church they belonged to.

OF MUCH GREATER AND more lasting personal significance was a blind date with an attractive Raleigh girl, 18-year-old Josephine, who was then known as Josie, Ehringhaus, the governor's granddaughter. The date went badly. I wore a straw hat, which she thought "fruity." When we arrived at my apartment and encountered a couple campaigning for Terry Sanford, she treated them rudely, because her father, J. C. B. (Blucher) Ehringhaus Jr., was supporting Lake. Inside the apartment, I angrily made a comment not calculated to endear me, "If I knew you better, I'd spank you." Still, some kind of connection had been made. Josie was beautiful, though I resolutely declined to admit it when she asked if I thought she was, instead substituting another adjective: "arresting." In spite of the rough launching, I pursued her because she was smart and good looking, inviting her to an invitation-only premiere rerun of *Gone with the Wind*. We began to click and fell in love when Terry brought dancing back to the Governor's Mansion—a black tie affair with the North Carolina symphony playing waltzes. My standing as a likely son-in-law was cemented with Josie's witty and charming mother, Margaret, when Josie begged off a date to stay with her. Blucher was out of town and there had been a serious crime in the neighborhood. The "girls" would keep each other company and watch Margaret's favorite show, *The Untouchables*. That night, I sent a telegram to Margaret: "Don't worry, my agents have your house under surveillance. Signed, Elliot Ness." When Margaret discovered the author, I was *in*.

Josie and I were married in the chapel of her old school, St. Mary's, on December 9, 1961, and had an extended honeymoon as I had been assigned as the *News and Observer* Washington correspondent, reporting after the first of January. There would never be another time quite like the next two years. We were young, just married and living in Camelot—far from troubles at home.

5

Camelot Interrupted

The only South I had ever known was about to sink to the bottom of history, but Josie's and my immediate concerns were finding a place to live and learning a new job. We moved temporarily into the friendly, funky Congressional Hotel on Capitol Hill, and my office was in suite 1253 of the National Press Building, one floor beneath the seedy old National Press Club. The Bascom Timmons Bureau was named for and presided over by a lanky, ancient Texan who originally came to Washington as an aide to former Vice President John Nance Garner (he who famously described the vice presidency as "not being worth a bucket of warm spit," except he used another word for "spit"). Timmons's news bureau provided Washington coverage for some thirty Southern and Southwestern newspapers too small or too cheap to have their own bureaus.

Among Timmons's cheap publisher friends were the owners of major Texas papers in Dallas, Houston, Amarillo, and Wichita Falls—which gave our reporters access to Vice President Lyndon B. Johnson—and North Carolina papers in Raleigh and Winston-Salem. The latter two, the *News and Observer* and the *Journal and Sentinel*, were the major papers on my beat, but as the last man on board I also got the "dirty detail"—representing the *Clarion-Ledger* of Jackson, Mississippi.

I learned quickly that the *Clarion-Ledger*'s worldview extended only as far as April 12, 1861, the day Fort Sumter was fired upon. My first day on the job was an object lesson in roughing-the-politician penalties levied for noncompliance with the preferences of the paper's owners, the Hederman family. The breaking news was that Mississippi legislature had just "taken care of" the only congressman who frequently voted with the Kennedy administration, U.S. Representative Frank Smith, by redistricting his home county entirely into the district of conservative Representative Jamie Whitten, whose office sent over a press release accusing Smith of voting in favor of the fiendish United Nations. When I routinely called Smith for comment, he said: "Who'd you say you work for . . . the *Clarion-Ledger*? You know they're not gonna put anything I say in that paper." When I assured the congressman otherwise, he asked how long I'd worked for the Jackson paper. Learning it was my first day, Smith said: "Meet me in the Speaker's Lobby, boy, there's some things you need to know."

The Speaker's Lobby then was a comfortable arcade of open ended booths where congressmen and constituents could sit and talk in relative privacy just off the House floor. A feature of the lobby was rows of newspapers hung in the fashion of men's clubs. I was surprised and delighted to find the *Anniston Star* there. I sent a note through a congressional aide to alert the congressman that I was in the lobby. Smith soon appeared—an intelligent mass of good cheer wrapped in an off-the-rack blue suit. What the congressman told me that afternoon was a revelation, and my reaction was further evidence that I had evolved into a committed Southern liberal—a lonely species, too hot for home, but not hot enough for high-church liberals in Manhattan and Los Angeles.

WHAT SMITH EXPLAINED AND I subsequently observed was that Mississippi's political culture was a continuation of the civil war by another name; the federal government being the enemy. One of the *Clarion-Ledger*'s regular columnists was an example of the archaic attitudes. One column almost sensually recounted the penalty for a slave committing perjury—cutting off an ear. The columnist went on, "it should have been another appendage . . . They should have had their tongues cut out, then we wouldn't have to hear the wild talk coming from so-called civil rights leaders."

The medieval nature of Mississippi politics and the *Clarion-Ledger*'s ethics, shocking even by the Deep South standards of that day, said to me that if those qualities define Southern conservatives, then I am the opposite. My conversion wasn't dramatic. I didn't get up from my desk and shout: "Glory be, I have seen the light." Rather, my accumulating experiences triggered beliefs planted by Dad, Wooster, Donald Strong, and the statesmen governors that I had covered in Raleigh. If North Carolina governors

Hodges and Sanford could simultaneously build the economic and social cornucopia of the Research Triangle and calm the racial passions stirred by school integration, then it seemed obvious to me that Southern liberals were the best models.

Of course, parents fundamentally shape attitudes. It wasn't until reading his work later in my life that I realized how closely I hewed to the views of my father, the late Colonel H. M. Ayers.

In 1943, Dad had a vigorous but good-natured editorial battle with his friend, the columnist John Temple Graves. The conservative Birmingham editor, weary of President Franklin Roosevelt's reforms, declared, "the New Deal is dealt." Not so, wrote Dad:

> It will never have been dealt here in the South until we shall have supplied better schools, better homes, better roads, better medical care, larger economic opportunity in the city and on the farm and more general use of the ballot on the day of election. Inherent in the New Deal is the concept that every man is his brother's keeper, that democracy imposes responsibility to "combat the autocracy of both the classes and the masses," and that a social consciousness is best derived from the Sermon on the Mount, which is the derogation of greed, selfishness and an excessive inequality in the distribution of goods of the world.

Convictions seeded by family, church, school, and work were sealed by a Mississippi newspaper and political culture. Taken together, they were the origins of a Southern liberal. That personal revelation was a tiny current in the tidal forces that were remaking the political landscape. The liberal consensus that had kept Washington in Democratic hands for more than thirty years—when civility reigned—was still intact when we lived there, but it wouldn't last. Even before the 1980s' Reagan Revolution, the political-cultural compact that had cemented the nation was being swept away on a riptide of history by two turbulent, converging currents—race and Vietnam.

The convergence shattered the American agreement, leaving a bitterly divided, sulfurously partisan country. Two unrelated events in 1954 mark the origins of the tsunami that exploded the liberal consensus. No one in the freshman class at the University of Alabama thought to link the *Brown v. Board of Education* integration decision with the French defeat by Ho Chi Minh at Dienbienphu in the same year. The Vietnam/civil rights parallels are uncanny: 1954—*Brown* and Dienbienphu; 1955—the Montgomery bus boycott and South Vietnamese President Diem's rejection of national elections, certain he would lose to Ho Chi Minh; 1957—Little Rock boils over and the Viet Cong begin filtering south. From 1960 on, the U.S. commitment to Vietnam grew, while at home the American conscience and black impatience ignited revolutionary change.

Before race and Vietnam began to tear apart the national compact, Americans agreed on a lot. We had the same enemies in the Depression and World War II, and most of us thought of President Roosevelt as a kind of national father (though, as Arthur M. Schlesinger Jr., among others, has pointed out, the anti-New Deal forces were more virulent than even "the vast right-wing conspiracy" of the Clinton years and beyond). From Truman through Eisenhower up to Kennedy and Johnson, there was a national consensus of fairly liberal social values. We all thought veterans should go to college and get houses—and we all floated happily on the swells of prosperity those Democratic measures produced. We also believed old folks should be looked after, and that if you were laid off, you should have something to tide you over.

We were the kind of people who helped fallen foes and wounded friends to their feet with the Marshall Plan. And we'd send allies good NATO cops to protect them from Soviet burglars who were carrying off whole countries. When Josephine and I went to Washington in 1962, this was a happy land, an optimistic one. John F. Kennedy's eloquent inaugural address summed up our resolve, and our destiny was manifest.

MOST AMERICANS OUTSIDE THE South agreed with the Kennedys that images of civil turmoil on our TV screens in the 1960s were troubling. Why shouldn't polite, well-dressed young black students like those at Woolworth's in Greensboro be able to order a Coke and a sandwich at dime store counters? As distant witnesses in North Carolina in May 1961, Josephine and I were puzzled and worried reading news accounts of a burning "Freedom

Rider" bus on the outskirts of Anniston and of brazen and brutal beatings of Freedom Riders in downtown Birmingham. An undertone of anxiety grew from knowing we would soon return to a civil equivalent of a war zone, which now had touched Anniston. We read in the New York and Washington papers, as if they were reports from a third-world nation, news that in Birmingham and Montgomery the police had deliberately abandoned Freedom Riders to the waiting white mobs.

I learned later that the FBI knew in advance that the Klan planned to attack when the buses reached Alabama but did nothing to prevent it. At the bus station in Montgomery, female students were beaten almost as badly as the men. Our friend, John Seigenthaler, now the retired publisher of the *Nashville Tennessean* and editorial director of *USA Today*, was in 1961 an administrative assistant to U.S. Attorney General Robert Kennedy. After the violence in Anniston and Birmingham, Seigenthaler had been sent to Montgomery to keep an eye on things. A blow to the head by an iron pipe as he was attempting to rescue one of the girls from the mob sent him to the hospital in serious condition. From his hospital bed, he gave Bobby Kennedy sound advice: Don't run for governor of Alabama.

The next night at Montgomery's black First Baptist Church there was a gathering which included principals of the movement, Dr. King, and the young organizer of the Rides, John Lewis. An angry white mob of roughly 3,000 laid siege to the church, held off for a while by federal marshals. As it became apparent that the outnumbered marshals could not contain the mob, there was a round of frantic phone calls from Dr. King, in the basement of the church, to Bobby Kennedy and his brother John at the White House, and from Bobby to Governor John Patterson in Montgomery. Finally, Patterson acceded to Bobby's pleas and activated the Alabama National Guard to disperse the surging crowd.

On May 4, 2011, exactly fifty years later, former governor Patterson and now-U.S. Representative John Lewis met for the first time at a commemoration of the Freedom Rides in Montgomery. As two veteran politicians do, they took the measure of each other, hit it off and got along famously.

At that meeting, Patterson got word that the executive committee of the Alabama Academy of Honor, also meeting in the capital, had counted ballots for election to the body, defined as the one hundred living Alabamians deemed to have brought honor to the state. John Lewis had been one of six elected and would be asked to speak for his class.

How a civil rights icon and native Alabamian was welcomed into the embrace of the state's elite is a run-silent, run-deep example of how some things in the state (good on this occasion) get done. I had unsuccessfully nominated Lewis three times previously, the last two with former U.S. Secretary of State Condolezza Rice as co-nominator. I called and wrote members of the executive committee early in 2011 to see if another nomination would succeed. Some time later I got a friend-of-a-friend call suggesting that I back off the nomination. After that, I got a call from a former chairman who said the leadership really wanted to elect John and suggested that John Patterson make the nomination this time: "As you know, John is a former chairman of the Academy and is well thought of by the membership [pause], as are you, of course." I bowed out.

A few weeks later, members, new inductees and their families crowded into the historic old House chamber in the State Capitol and John Lewis spoke with emotion of his roots and referred to Dr. King's concept of "the beloved community." It was a moving occasion for Josephine and me who have known John and Lillian Lewis fondly for decades. And it was a closing of a circle that had begun in fury but closed in gentle companionship.

THE FEROCITY OF THE events in Montgomery heralded the next phase of black protest—which by 1962 was clearly visible from my vantage point at the U.S. Department of Justice. What could be seen ahead held the department's attention and mine—the rapidly approaching and expanding civil rights movement.

At the center of the massive gray building at 10th Street and Constitution Avenue is the spacious fifth-floor suite of the Attorney General of the United States. An attractive young woman guarded the entrance to the working spaces occupied by Bobby Kennedy and his staff. She liked to tell the story of her embarrassing faux pas on the day First Lady Jacqueline Kennedy unexpectedly appeared. Wheeling and rising simultaneously, her leg touched a security button under her desk, setting off alarms and summoning a squad of U.S. Marshals to surround the startled wife of the president.

Inside, a visitor in 1962 would meet a slight, wiry, thirty-seven-year-old with the sleeves of his blue button-down shirt rolled above his elbows. His office would inspire envy in most Russians who could only dream of a whole family living in such spacious quarters. Its oak-paneled walls were covered with an incongruous riot of children's crayon drawings. After brief pleasantries, U.S. Attorney General Robert Francis Kennedy would sit down, throw a leg in a lower desk drawer and, *click*, fix the visitor with penetrating blue eyes. My reportage from the Justice Department appeared in the *Star*, including interviews with Kennedy, which inspired a letter from my mother who wrote: "So many of my friends have mentioned how 'interesting' it is that you have become such a close personal friend of the younger Kennedy." When I quoted her letter to the attorney general, Bobby said in his distinctive Bostonese, "Waaaal, Braaandt, that must work a considerable haaaadship on you."

It was in this expansive office that a partner in the prestigious Covington, Burling law firm, Burke Marshall, was one of several lawyers interviewed for the crucial position of Assistant Attorney General for Civil Rights. The two equally taciturn men apparently spent a good bit of time staring at each other. Burke thought the interview had not gone well. Ed Guthman, spokesman for the department, said Bobby wondered if he and Burke would ever have anything in common. "Okay," Guthman asked. "Why did you pick him?" Bobby replied, "Because everyone in Washington said Burke was the smartest young lawyer in Washington."

There was another reason, about which Bobby and the president agreed. As Ed Guthman put it, "In the gathering struggle over civil rights, they decided that someone who had been prominent in the civil rights struggle would be handicapped by ideology or past association in heading the Civil Rights Division." When Bobby eventually offered Marshall the post, he wanted to think about it. That evening he asked his wife, Violet, to mix drinks so they could discuss Kennedy's offer. Excited by the unusual promise of consultation, she produced the drinks and sat down, anticipating a good discussion. Burke spoke first: "I'm going to take it."

Little did he and Bobby know what lay ahead. Much misfortune might have been avoided if the president, the attorney general, and his assistants had been willing to impose the power of the federal government on more local situations—as some civil rights leaders gripped by the perpetual danger of battle wanted them to do. Instead, they waited for the crisis.

The reactive Kennedy style, a step or two behind the rush of events, wasn't enough for unbending liberals, and it was frustrating for civil rights generals and troops on the front lines in Mississippi and Alabama. In 1964 Bobby himself put it this way: "You would have accomplished much more if you had had a dictatorship during the period of time that President Kennedy was President . . . We could have sent perhaps large numbers of people down to Mississippi and be able then to protect that group down there. But I think that it comes back to haunt you . . ."

Arthur Schlesinger said, "A generation rendered sensitive by Watergate to the case for constitutional processes finds this view more persuasive than did the men and women who went South in defense of elemental rights in the early 1960s." Later revelations of an illegal, secret war being run out of the basement of the Reagan White House underscores Kennedy's wisdom about restraint. And still later, a misshapen war in the deserts and back alleys of Iraq, conceived in deceit and mangled at birth, underlines in blood and fire the commandment: Our power is great; it should be exercised with discretion.

Jack Rosenthal was twenty-five at the time. Today, from his home in Portland, Oregon, he recalls that "horrors like the lynching of Emmett Till fired the passions of people like me." He was a young man attracted by causes, on strike from his reporting job at the prestigious *Oregonian* when offered the job of assistant press secretary at Justice. Like many of his generation and mine outside the South, he said, "We burned to impose racial justice on murderous bigots." Horrified by the Montgomery mob that nearly killed the Freedom Riders and John Seigenthaler, fearing for the lives of friends and colleagues pinned down by the mob at Ole Miss the next year, "we were certain that change had to be forced down the throats of the South. Civil Righteous, you could have called us." He admitted to being perplexed by Burke Marshall's disciplined restraint, and learning from it. As Marshall wrote in 1964, at the boiling peak of the struggle, "Only political power, not court orders or other federal law, will insure the election of fair men as sheriffs, school board members, police chiefs, mayors, county commissioners, and state officials." Years later, Rosenthal shook his head remembering his youthful, hair-trigger passion—*just send the troops and crush the bigots.* And he marveled at "Burke's faith in democracy, and how it transcended anger or vengeance."

As it turned out, the Kennedys did have to send large numbers of people to Mississippi. In September 1962, the only things Washington and Mississippi shared were suffocating humidity and mutual dread. A genial, pathologically dumb, soul-deep segregationist, Governor Ross Barnett, was determined that James Meredith would not enroll at the state university in Oxford. Twice before Mississippi had dealt with Negroes who tried to enroll. One was committed to the "colored" insane asylum at Whitfield. The other was later arrested and put on the chain gang for seven years. Clearly, seeking a higher education at Ole Miss was a cardinal affront to white civilization and womanhood. The governor wouldn't stand for it. Only this time "that boy," as Barnett called him, was backed by the United States Supreme Court—in an order signed by an Alabama country Baptist, Justice Hugo L. Black—and by the United States Department of Justice.

As Bobby sensed in a series of some twenty conversations with Barnett, the governor wanted to be a nice fellow, didn't really want to take on the federal government. But the shame he believed white Mississippi would shower upon him if he allowed a "colored boy" to defile their beloved Ole Miss was too abhorrent. In a telephone conversation on September 25, he told Bobby: "Must it be over one little boy—backed by a communist front—backed by the NAACP which is a communist front . . .? I'm going to treat you with every courtesy but I won't agree to let that boy to get to Ole Miss. I will never agree to that. I would rather spend the rest of my life in a penitentiary than do that."

Tragedy, as inevitable as if the gods had been moving the players in Jackson and Washington, was enacted five days later. Deputy Attorney General Nick Katzenbach, John Doar and Chief Marshall James McShane escorted Meredith to Baxter Hall dormitory, where he spent the night guarded by two dozen U.S. Marshals. A force of five hundred marshals formed a cordon around the Lyceum Building, where Meredith would register the next morning. An increasingly angry and violent mob attacked the marshals there. Most of the Mississippi state troopers chose that moment to leave the campus. Marshals held the mob off with tear gas, while at Justice and in the Oval Office orders for intervention were given to a National Guard which executed them with glacial dispatch. As the marshals ran out of tear gas, a by-the-book Guard commander took an hour to move the last half-mile from the airport. The casualty count in the morning was 160 marshals wounded or injured—twenty-eight by gunfire—and two people dead. In some reports the dead were said to be students but historian E. Culpepper Clark reports they were an Oxford jukebox repairman hit in the head by a stray bullet and a French correspondent for the *London Daily Sketch*, shot in the back.

Senator James O. Eastland was aghast, but not that a third of the marshals had been hit with gunfire, steel pipes, and rocks on a Mississippi college campus. He claimed to be horrified that the marshals had "brutalized Ole Miss coeds." The *Clarion-Ledger* bannered my story carrying the news that their senator would get to the bottom of the atrocities against the flowers of Southern womanhood, Ole Miss's gardenia-skinned coeds. He was going to empanel a special investigating committee of the Senate Judiciary Committee to expose federal brutality. Southerners on the committee, such as Olin Johnson of South Carolina and Sam Ervin of North Carolina, were honorable men who wouldn't think of falsifying a U.S. Senate report, so I pursued the story with a vengeance. I thought the natural evolution of the story would expose Eastland's demagoguery in the *Clarion-Ledger*, one of his favorite propaganda organs.

In the end, of course, truth was defeated by the conspiracy of silence. If the *Clarion-Ledger* wouldn't print the story—and it wouldn't—it might as well never have happened. The episode ended with the last of many requests for an update on the investigation. I was put through to the senator himself. "Senator, as you know, my paper is very interested in your investigation of the Ole Miss incident . . . ," I started, at which point Eastland broke in, "Son, I spoke to your publisher this mornin' and I can assure you that he's not interested in any such story." It was another lesson in the education of a Southern liberal, a glimpse of the face behind the shield that "preserves our precious Southern heritage," revealing how the soft patina of courteous speech covers the hard character beneath.

THUS SPAKE THE MISSISSIPPI Establishment in 1962, a view of the world echoed by its immediate neighbor to the east, Alabama. Together, the two states were a nation apart. Their mores, their loyalties, their prejudices, their understanding of right versus wrong rose up like a force field to repel disturbing views from the outside and to reinforce—by repeated exhortations from such living icons as Eastland and such institutions as the *Clarion-Ledger*—the view that "our way of life" must be protected at all costs. There were, of course, enlightened voices such as the Hodding Carter family, owners of the brave and feisty *Delta Democrat-Times* of Greenville. They were "the enemy within," regarded by the Establishment as aliens in a Looking Glass world, a world where evil was good, right was wrong and Christianity had been constituted by God to keep white people separate and superior to black people, "hewers of wood and drawers of water." Mississippi was no more a part of America than Yemen was a part of Scandinavia.

The Alabama megaphone for those inverted values was Circuit Judge George Wallace, who in 1962 was running for governor trumpeting defiance publicly while surrendering privately. My father's endorsement of Wallace in the Democratic primary—which he later regretted—was a shock that exposed the generational gap between Southern liberals of his generation and mine. Men like the Richmond editor Virginius Dabney and Dad were honorable and progressive, but they could not bridge the logical inconsistency of liberality within segregation. Dad, for instance, as de facto chairman of the State School Board, insisted that black professors at State colleges be paid the same as white professors—a bold stance for the time. He believed that the "Separate but Equal" doctrine meant exactly what it said: the equal part, too. Black people should be accorded the same dignity as whites, he believed. To enforce that view, he physically confronted printers at his paper who balked at using courtesy titles—Mr. and Mrs.—for blacks. The Colonel told the men, "You're going to do it, if I have to whip every one of you.

Now who's first?" At most, fair-minded Southern liberals of his day could conceive of gradual integration beginning cautiously in an undetermined future so misty as to be fantasy. But neither revolution nor white resistance could wait for the evolution of that imagined and immaculate future, a sweet bye-and-bye where blacks and whites would live happily in parallel societies, separate but equal.

Dad had championed equal educational opportunity, opposed race bait-ing in all its forms, and beginning in the 1940s advocated voting rights for blacks, all in opposition to the governor and state Democratic leadership of the time. He skewered the Dixiecrat rebellion against President Truman's integrating the armed forces and wrote editorials condemning the 1948 Birmingham convention that nominated South Carolina Governor Strom Thurmond to oppose Truman. His was a lonely stance: too liberal for most Southerners and too wedded to the past for Northern opinion. The trap of intellectual contradiction—change in a static system of forced segrega-tion—closed on him cruelly at a vulnerable time. He had suffered a coronary and was in the early stages of Alzheimer's in 1956, when at seventy-one he shocked a meeting of the American Society of Newspapers.

Fairly chastising Northern hypocrisy on race, he went on in rambling confusion, attributing to Negro educator Mary McLeod Bethune remarks made at a black church in Anniston that out of context seemed to represent his own belief that Negroes were "by and large . . . dirty, shiftless, liars and cheats and undependable in almost every way . . ." He actually voiced the myth that Negro men had a consuming desire to have white women.

His vision that one fine day blacks and whites would look at each other as brothers across an invisible color line was an optimistic fable, a sweet, old-time liberal's dream, true to the nature of the man I knew. His ASNE remarks are too painful to believe, contrary to a lifetime of beliefs for which he had paid by enduring threatening night-callers. The speech was alien to everything I knew about my father. I can only think it was the dementia speaking. His humiliating performance was painful, igniting a sense of outrage among younger Southern editors. A *New York Post* editorial ended gently: "Possibly we are being too wistful, but we had the sense that Mr. Ayers of Anniston belonged to the past." The editor was right.

The Southern fantasy built by such honorable men as Dabney and Dad was interrupted by the voices of revolution shouting, "What do we want?" The chorus answered: "FREEDOM!" "When do we want it?" "NOW!" The answer to the black chorus from armed defenders of "our way of life" came in the person of Sheriff Jim Clark on the Edmund Pettus Bridge in Selma in 1965: "Get those god-damned niggers! Get those god-damned white niggers!" History couldn't wait for that orderly, slow transition to a God's green acres on earth envisioned by Dabney and Dad.

ALEXIS DE TOCQUEVILLE OBSERVED in the 1830s that the principal cause of revolution is social inequality. But social convulsions are triggered only when there is hope in the hearts of people that there is a realistic possibility of throwing off the yoke of oppression. Young Martin King must have sensed that real possibility in the Montgomery bus boycott and pursued it to Birmingham, Selma, and eternity.

Dad, who was disappearing sweetly into a mist of his own, did not live to see the debacle of Selma, but one of his last coherent thoughts was an expression of disappointment in Wallace. Dad explained that Wallace persuaded him to support his candidacy in a one-on-one meeting between the two men. The judge came to our house and, in the library, asked, "Colonel, what will it take for you to endorse me?" Dad asked what Wallace's education platform would be. "You write it," the candidate replied. That was the first and last time the *Anniston Star* endorsed Wallace. To his credit, in his first term he raised teacher salaries and created a statewide system of junior colleges and trade schools, one within thirty minutes drive of every citizen. But these achievements were overshadowed by the lightning and thunder of his demagoguery on the race issue.

From my viewpoint in Washington, the 1962 Wallace campaign was muted, reports from the front to the civil society far from the scene of battle. Though distant, the sound was discordant compared to the reasoned rhetoric I'd heard in North Carolina, and the elegant, content-laden Kennedy speeches. But campaigning on Alabama ground, Wallace must have been something to behold. The same Wallace who pleaded privately at night with U.S. District Judge Frank M. Johnson Jr., "I need some help, my ass is in a crack," turned his own surrender into a public victory. If the federal courts say they didn't back down, he shouted, words landing like punches: "They're integratin', skallawaggin', carpetbaggin', pool-mixin', bald-faced LIARS!" He vowed to oppose federal tyranny "ruinin' our schools, our unions, our whole way of life." He'd face despotism "standin' in the schoolhouse door."

What drove him—other than the bantamweight boxer's driving need to win? What was the source of the fire in his brain that erupted in language that was the verbal equivalent of physical violence? The Old South had always had a surplus of bigots, such as that more recent Tarheel anomaly, Senator Jesse Helms. But Helms was a benign bigot; not tinged with danger as George Wallace was. Wallace's 1968 speech at Madison Square Garden could have been in Munich in the Thirties where crowds engorged by hatred shouted, "Juden! Juden!" What set Wallace off that night was black hecklers who had to be rescued from the pro-Wallace crowd screaming: "Kill 'em, kill 'em, kill 'em!" Wallace's anger touched deep chords of resentment in the crowd, setting off reverberating roars when he shouted, "We don't have riots in Alabama. They start a riot down there, first one of 'em to pick up a brick gets a bullet in the brain, that's all. And then you walk over to the next one and say, 'All right, pick up a brick. We just want to see you pick up one of them bricks: Now!'"

Wallace's inner volcano had to be triggered by something deeper; dual insecurities that erupted in combustible language so real, so authentic to the by-passed and scorned rural and working-class whites—and so frightening to non-Southern middle-class America, especially to intellectuals. At one level, he felt personally the real and implied damage to self-respect that affects most Southerners: The sense that Boston, New York, and Washington look down on us for our backward, country ways—scorn descending from the moral mountain top. At another level, he chafed at the wounding glances and superior attitudes of more refined, educated Southerners. Wallace grew up in Clio, a tiny Black Belt town whose location might be described as just this side of "Resume Speed." His father owned land but drank up the income. Though his grandfather was a respected country doctor, the Wallace family was several social rungs beneath the barons and dukes of the Black Belt plantaristocracy, the multi-generational landed gentry, lovely people, a few of whom attended Oxford and played in family string quartets. He would never have been comfortable at Edgefield, the mansion home of Oxonian cello-and-tennis-playing timber baron, Earl McGowin. He would have been hurt by that Black Belt aristocrat's dismissal of him as a populist demagogue. Wallace wanted everybody to like him; he wanted ME to like him. His need was so great that only amphitheaters filled with cheering crowds were enough to feed his hunger. He was a black hole of insecurities. Condescension real or imagined set off his volcanic insecurities. They erupted in a violent bout of whisky drinking and cussing at Judge Frank Johnson's dryly amused exposure of Wallace's surrender to the U.S. Civil Rights Commission. Wallace later told historian Dan T. Carter that Johnson "made fun of me." That, he could not stand. Though his volatile class-consciousness often touched the danger zone, he also could amuse the crowd by pricking the pompous—always with a sting. I would be stung personally by his barbs after returning home as Terry Sanford was campaigning in the 1972 North Carolina presidential primary. Asked what he thought of his opponent, Wallace said, "Terry Sanford is a fine man, an intelligent man. He might be the most intelligent man in the United States, but you know, he'll bore your ass off."

FOR JOSIE AND ME in 1962–63, newlyweds in a Washington infatuated with the Kennedy clan, the bombardment of headlines from Alabama and TV pictures of fire hoses and police dogs set upon students in Birmingham were disturbing. However, distance robbed them of immediate impact. Washington then was a good and innocent town: Drugs had not yet seeded menace into every shadow, terrorism was yet to lock down every national institution in tight bands of security. It was fun, free, and open. Josie and I were tucked into a roomy basement apartment on South Glebe Road in Arlington, with a view of an all-night bowling alley. A couple of times a week, she'd make the ten- or fifteen-minute drive down Shirley Highway to meet me for dinner at Costin's steak house in the basement of the National Press Building. One typical Saturday afternoon we had lunch at the Press Club and then walked around the corner of F and Pennsylvania to see a James Bond movie (JFK's favorite mystery series). After the movie, we strolled over to the White House. I flashed my White House press card at the guard who nodded us through open gates and into the untidy West Wing lobby—then a lounging area whose worn red leather chairs and sofa seats bore the depressions made by generations of reportorial rears. Henry Hall Wilson, a former North Carolina party chairman and White House congressional liaison, was in his office. He took us through the cabinet room and to the Oval Office, appointed with JFK's famous rocking chair.

On another occasion in that famous house, May 14, 1963, to be exact, in the State Dining Room, Dad and I disgraced ourselves—at least from the perspective of Mother's meticulous view of proper etiquette. Our social transgressions were minor comic relief in a spring that had been taut with tension and stress in Alabama and Washington. On Good Friday, sixty-three "Negro Leaders of Metropolitan Birmingham" had begun demonstrations, explaining why they could wait no longer. Bull Connor's men arrested Martin Luther King Jr., grabbing him by the seat of his overalls—a creative flourish designed to humiliate. Four days later, King finished "Letter from a Birmingham Jail," in which he set forth the Gandhian distinction between just and unjust laws: laws which "degrade the human personality" are unjust and thus in conflict with a Higher Law. Meanwhile, children had poured from 16th Street Baptist Church into the streets and into Kelly Ingram Park, where they were met on May 3 by Bull Connor's fire hoses and police dogs.

On Saturday night, May 11, dynamite ripped through the house of Dr. King's brother, the Reverend A. D. King. A mob of angry rock-throwing blacks was set upon by 250 of Public Safety Director Al Lingo's state troopers swinging clubs. Another date loomed before Bobby Kennedy, Burke Marshall, and other Justice Department aides. On June 11, two young blacks, Vivian Malone and James Hood, were to register at the University of Alabama, backed by federal court orders. What would Wallace do? Would the innocents be set upon by grotesques again—as in the Ole Miss tragedy? Buford Boone, publisher of the *Tuscaloosa News*, who had won a Pulitzer Prize for his principled stance during the Autherine Lucy incident in 1956, summed up Wallace's choices in a Solomonic private letter to the governor:

I have feared and I still fear, that inciting statements will encourage people to violence because they think it is expected of them. You are going to lose, as John Brown did, as Lee did and as Barnett did. But are you going to lose with dignity, with intelligent courage, and with proper regard for the long-range welfare of our people in Alabama? Or, are you going to take the low road and work the situation for all it is worth in current popular support and with too little thought of the tomorrows that will come?

More enlightened business leaders such as Buford Boone were needed to counsel calm civic peace and to encourage Wallace to do the right thing. Various Kennedy cabinet and subcabinet officials contacted Alabamians they knew in an attempt to ignite a backfire of reason. It was as part of that effort—outlined by the dynamite's red glare, the children's crusade, and the looming confrontation of June 11—that President Kennedy invited twenty Alabama newspaper publishers to lunch at the White House. Because Dad's dementia was beginning to take possession of him, White House Press Secretary Pierre Salinger allowed me to accompany him. I anticipated my first White House meal with excitement and anxiety. How does one behave in the presence of American royalty? What is the protocol? The wife of a Timmons Bureau colleague, Daisy Cleland, was the daughter of a former cabinet officer. She explained that the only ironclad rule was: You do not leave a room before the president of the United States makes his exit.

We picked up Dad at Union Station, had coffee at the Willard, and then hurried to the White House in a cab that drove right under the north portico—what would have been an astonishing breach of security in later years. The Alabamians sipped cocktails in the Blue Room while awaiting the President. A second round had been served before Kennedy joined us. Lunch was in the State Dining Room, where the William Cogswell portrait of Lincoln looked down on President Kennedy in the center of the table. The menu wasn't chosen for an Alabama greens-and-grits palate: Oeufs Mollet a la Reine was followed by rack of lamb, lubricated by glasses of Almaden Cabernet Sauvignon. Liquid intake-gauge rising (not having been relieved since before 8 a.m.), by dessert I was more focused on my bladder than the conversation. Dad seemed at home—too much so in Mother's critique of the event. He aimed a large golden dessert spoon at the tiny neck of the golden compote sheltering the peach melba and paused, thinking: "Eli and Mildred wouldn't give me such a big spoon for such a small target." He directed the liveried waiter at his side, "Bring me a small spoon." Swiftly a smaller golden spoon was presented, an unheralded perquisite of dining with American royalty. And just about then, my bladder signaled intolerable choices: I could hold up my hand like a latter-day Forrest Gump, "Mr. President, I've got to pee," or just flee. I fled, met not by the protocol police, but by a helpful butler who took me down in the family elevator to the diplomatic restroom—whew.

Focus restored, I returned to the table. What I can remember of the points made by President Kennedy was that moderate blacks and whites should come together and lead in order to prevent black extremists from dominating the scene. With some justice, the publishers argued that it was unfair for Birmingham to be targeted for demonstrations just as moderate elements in the city had wrested control from Bull Connor's crowd. Grover Hall Jr. was memorable. His intervention at the time struck me as snide and disrespectful. Grover had succeeded his famous father as editor of the *Montgomery Advertiser*. Unlike the hard-drinking, Klan-baiting, Pulitzer-winning senior Hall, young Grover was a bit of a dandy. He wore a fresh rosebud in his lapel—calculating its dollar value precisely as the sum of all the cultivation, labor, and fertilizer that went into his garden. His intelligent, articulate insouciance alternately charmed and irritated. He would have been a brilliant agitprop chief of the Irony Party. In fact, he projected a passionless disdain for politics, though he was a friend and frequent adviser to Governor Wallace.

His nonchalant account of the luncheon appeared two days later on the editorial page of the *Advertiser* [see Appendix for the full column]:

WASHINGTON, D.C., May 14: So President Kennedy and a considerable deputation of Alabama newspapermen sat together at lunch in the White House to discuss Birmingham and all that embodies.

. . . Dessert was as long as Kennedy cared to wait and he bored right into it—Birmingham. He did not bark like Bobby; he wanted to converse.

He became visibly irritated but once—at the observation that the Revered Doctor King was a White House "pet"—and there could not have been a conference more correct and courteous on the part of all. The windbags were endured with no more chastisement than sly winks on the part of the victims. . . .

Grover's reference to "windbags" was meant to include Dad who had risen to address the President, lost his train of thought and hadn't made much sense. When he sat down, I patted his arm in encouragement and noted the sympathetic look on the face of the late Neil Davis, who was publisher of a progressive weekly in Auburn and Alabama's first Nieman Fellow at Harvard. Grover was extinguished a few years later by a cruel fate that attacked the core of his infuriating talent, a fatal brain tumor. Grover wasn't among the handful who visited the attorney general after the luncheon. Dad soldiered on, however. He didn't seem offended by Bobby's informality, chatting with his visitors in his shirtsleeves while perched on the front of his desk. Dad was grateful, however, when Bobby noticed that the late-afternoon sun was striking the older man uncomfortably in the face. Bobby hopped off the desk and briskly lowered the shades.

EVEN WHILE WE TALKED in Bobby's office, Burke Marshall was in Birmingham matching frustration with patience as he tried to build bridges between hostile strangers. Neither the white nor black community knew who, on the other side, had the standing and authority to negotiate an end to the demonstrations or to guarantee progress on the black agenda. Over the course of several days, Burke engaged in a shuttle diplomacy, talking to any and everyone with influence on either side. Finally, on May 17, he negotiated a truce that ended the demonstrations.

Despite the successful conclusion, the experience convinced him that federal legislation was necessary, that the tension between grievance and resistance could not be resolved by personal intervention, city-by-city, state-by-state. On the plane back to Washington, Burke and another senior Justice Department official, Joseph F. Dolan, talked about what legislation would be necessary to resolve conflicts that, while most obvious in Birmingham, existed throughout the country. Back in Washington, they went directly to Bobby's office. They found a sympathetic audience for their ideas. It was late Friday afternoon and Kennedy was scheduled to speak in Charlotte, North Carolina, on Saturday. He suggested that Marshall and Dolan accompany him and begin drafting the bill on the plane.

While the attorney general was speaking at the Charlotte hotel, Marshall and Dolan worked at a draft on the plane. Other Justice Department officials, including Lou Oberdorfer, assistant attorney general in charge of the Tax Division, joined them. The group reached agreement on the essential elements of the bill during the return flight. The broad outline of the bill sought to guarantee voting rights and prohibit discrimination in hiring and public places. The U.S. Attorney General would be given authority to sue where persistent violations of the law were proved. Upon returning to the capital city, Kennedy and the others went to the White House, where President Kennedy had independently concluded legislation was required. The president instructed the task force to put their concepts into a formal legislative proposal.

It would take more than legislative craftsmanship to alter the geologically settled views of the civilization then undergoing its death throes. Neither could unborn legislation divert the next turn of the onrushing social revolution destined to collide with demagoguery in the ever-moist Tuscaloosa air on June 11 at the University of Alabama. The Kennedy administration's continuing effort to build a climate of acceptance included a list of every company in the state with more than 100 employees for a member of the cabinet to call their CEOs personally. As part of that effort, Bobby met with Governor Wallace at the State Capitol. The transcript of that encounter reveals two bright, mentally agile men feeling each other out, boxers in early rounds probing for a weakness to sneak in a knockout punch. Neither man caught the other's guard down. Wallace could not be shaken from his assertion that he was not the lawbreaker. A tyrannical federal government was at fault by its insistence on forcing states to do things against their will. Kennedy maintained that the law of the land must be obeyed, sidestepping Wallace's evident desire for Kennedy to threaten him with an armed invasion by federal troops. "Well, I am planning and hoping that the law will be obeyed . . .," said Bobby near the end of their meeting. "Maybe somebody wants us to use troops, but we are not anxious to." Wallace's response forecast the conclusion of the drama that would be enacted on the afternoon of June 11. "I can assure you this," he said, "that I do not want you to use troops, and I can assure you that there is not any effort on my part to make a show of resistance and to be overcome."

When the fateful day arrived, the administration was on edge, remembering the tragedy of Ole Miss the year before, uncertain what the unpredictable Wallace would do, even though the governor had gone on the air telling everyone to stay at home. I was anxious as well, because I had written a story predicting that Wallace would back down. My story was slimly based on one source, the late John Vardaman, a highly regarded Anniston attorney who had been a member of a blue-ribbon group advising Wallace on how he should handle the situation. My story had been given front-page, banner-headline treatment in the Blue Streak edition of the *Houston Chronicle* and was carried by several additional Timmons Bureau clients.

I nervously slipped upstairs to the Press Club to watch the confrontation on TV. To my relief, the story held up in a scene that has been replayed a thousand times. The hulking, bent shape of Deputy Attorney General Nicholas deBelleville Katzenbach, arms folded. The rigidly errect Wallace making his constitutional case, concluding with a proclamation, "I . . . hereby denounce and forbid this illegal and unwarranted action by the central government;" Katzenbach, with mounting irritation, asking the governor to carry out the orders of the court, commenting rhetorically, "I do not know what the purpose of this show is." The deputy attorney general and aides then escorted the students to their dormitories. Vivian Malone by prearranged plan was greeted graciously by the housemother, went in to lunch and sat at an empty table where within thirty seconds several students, who had been prompted, joined her. A tense drama that had begun at about 10:50 a.m., Alabama time, requiring an anxious President Kennedy to sign an order nationalizing the Alabama National Guard, was concluded by 3:33 p.m. At that moment, General Henry Graham apologetically informed the governor that he must carry out the orders of the President of the United States. The drama was filled with high tension among all the players except for George Wallace, who knew how the play would end. It went off almost as if it had been rehearsed.

University President Dr. Frank Rose retold the story many years later over drinks in a sequence that could not have happened in the unitary way he remembered the day's events. Yet the story he told me is too funny not to repeat. The tale sketches a self-confident man, certain that the constitutional pageant would play out as written—more confident than he actually was at the time. This was his bourbon-inspired recollection:

He went to the university president's mansion about noon to repeat the routine that allowed him to summon the energy needed to run a state university. He had his usual vodka martini and cup of soup, and told the butler as he went upstairs for a nap, "I don't care if Jesus Christ or John Kennedy calls; don't wake me until 2." Frank put on pajamas and was soon fast asleep. Downstairs, the phone rang and the butler heard, "This is the White House calling for Dr. Rose." The butler answered politely, "I'm sorry ma'am, but Dr. Rose is not available." To which Operator Number One responded, "Perhaps you didn't understand. The President of the United States wishes to speak to Dr. Rose now." Unfazed, the butler answered, "Yes ma'am, Dr. Rose loves President Kennedy, and so do I, but when he went up for his nap, he said he don't care if Jesus Christ or John Kennedy calls, don't wake him until 2. And I ain't!" On being awakened, Frank asked if there had been any calls. "Yessir, President Kennedy called." Frank instantly dialed the White House and soon heard the President's distinctive Boston accent: "Dr. Rose, here we aaar in Waashington. We don't know whether to send the 101st Airborne, and there you aar in Aaalabaama, taking a naaap. But Dr. Rose, thank you for putting me in such good company."

If it had been true, that comedic scene on a day fraught with anxiety in the white-porticoed Old South mansion would have been one of the little jokes history plays on its actors. But the next event in the crowded civil rights spring and summer of 1963 was no low comedy. Before the March on Washington, President Kennedy had made a pledge he must redeem. On the night the University was integrated, in his speech to the nation, he said, "I shall ask Congress . . . to make a commitment it has not fully made in this century to the proposition that race has no place in American life or law." According to Arthur Schlesinger, the president's reason for believing legislation was needed is that it would inspire confidence in the black population and validate nonviolent leadership such as Dr. King over younger, more radical elements. Bobby agreed, but the White House political staff was solidly against sending a bill to Congress on the grounds it would endanger the rest of the administration's program. Nevertheless, a measure was drafted, more modest than the one that eventually passed.

My first inkling that the measure was being readied came in a telephone call from Jack Rosenthal, who later became editor of the editorial page of the *New York Times*. Reporters who regularly covered the department were summoned to Bobby's office for a briefing on the bill. Though its contents were measured, my Southern antennae signaled: *Radical! There will be tearing of hair, rending of garments, and gnashing of teeth.* I inquired, "Is there anything in the legislation that provides incentives for compliance?" Bobby gave me a look that said, "We haven't thought about that." But before he could speak, an older reporter joked, "You can pass out 'I' (for integration) flags." His suggestion was greeted with laughter and I felt foolish. Looking back now, I think the veteran reporter was cynical, and that I was too insecure and junior to play along with the joke but follow up on a question worth pursuing.

ON JUNE 19, 1963, President Kennedy sent the omnibus civil rights bill to the Hill. As expected, the bill had great difficulty in the swamps and bogs of Congress. Senator Sam Ervin's Constitutional fundamentalism moved him to declare the bill "as drastic and indefensible a proposal as has ever been submitted to this Congress." Ervin's stance on civil rights was not the full measure of the man, as the country was to discover during the Watergate hearings. He also had the Southern gift of courtesy and charm, which he exhibited one afternoon in debate with Senator Paul Douglas of Illinois. The liberal Democrat, white-haired and bent, prowled the floor like a wounded bear. Ervin, as bright and merry as a country squire, asked, "If the distinguished junior senator from Illinois would yield." Douglas growled assent, which gave Ervin the opening for a down-home metaphor. "My good friend, you put me in mind of an old probate judge down in Bertie County. When a case came before him represented by attorney, he would turn to the lawyer and say, 'Son, I'd appreciate it if you would make no argument in this case. I find that when I hear two sides of a story it tends to confuse me.'

The bill was going nowhere. As we know, the March on Washington that August did not dislodge it. Momentum for passage came only after the national tragedy of the murder of President Kennedy, his succession by Vice President Lyndon Johnson, and the statesmanship of Senate Minority Leader Everett Dirksen. The Senator from Illinois was a force of nature. His voice was so big, so deep that when he personally answered a call I made to his office, I thought I had dialed the wrong number and was connected with the Almighty himself. Jack Rosenthal remembers a sweaty July when the "Wizard of Ooze" (the press corps' affectionate nickname for Dirksen) emerged from a conference committee meeting on the Civil Rights Act to brief hot, sullen reporters. "Well, here we are," he rumbled, gesturing to his fellow conferees, "fake pearls—surrounded by real swine." Nick Katzenbach, however, believes Dirksen gets more credit than he deserves for his role. He attributes delays in getting the bill out of committee in the Senate to "making endless revisions to satisfy Dirksen and his colleagues." Katzenbach said, "Burke and I spent endless evenings doing that—mainly to satisfy Dirksen that it woldn't have much if any effect in Illinois." Grudgingly the former deputy attorney general admits Dirksen's role was "a key to enactment."

A people ashamed and mourning after President Kennedy's assassination seemed prepared to take the final step to correct what all through our history had divided the nation—the legal status of the black man. The legislative maestro, President Johnson, teamed with Republican leadership—unthinkable in the corrosive climate of partisanship that has poisoned our recent politics—and the bill was signed into law on July 2, 1964. Alabama and North Carolina were paired again as opposite bookends. The Act conceived in the streets of Birmingham had drawn its first breath on an airplane trip to North Carolina.

I HADN'T BEEN PRIVY to the legislation because it was crafted below periscope depth, but as a Justice Department regular I followed from the beginning the build-up to the celebrated March on Washington. Bobby Kennedy strenuously opposed the March. With ghastly images of Birmingham and Ole Miss haunting him, he feared what might happen in the largely Southern city of Washington. District of Columbia Delegate Walter Fauntroy reported weekly estimates of the rising number of marchers to a Justice Department team Bobby had appointed to oversee the event. One member of the team was the decorated Ole Miss veteran and Boston Irish good ole boy, U.S. Chief Marshal John McShane. When Fauntroy's final estimate reached 300,000 marchers expected to descend on the city, McShane posed a politically incorrect question that revealed cultural kinship between South Boston Irish and Alabama Redneck, "My God, 300,000—how'd you like to have the watermelon concession."

In my little rabbit warren of reporters at 1253 in the Press building, I anticipated the August 28, 1963, date only as "one helluva story." A down-the-hall neighbor, *San Francisco Chronicle* correspondent Richard Reston, son of *New York Times* editor Scotty Reston, and I decided to cover the event together. We had a tip that American Nazi Party leader George Lincoln Rockwell would stage an early-morning counter-demonstration and Richard and I agreed to meet on the mall before daylight. Memories of that long, long day are so vivid that I see them in present tense, just as I wrote it [see Appendix for the full story]:

> They came as if to a picnic, with their songs, their hard-boiled eggs and fried chicken—and their demands for freedom and jobs. Then, almost magically, they were gone. The vast body of the 210,000 marchers—hot, dirty, bone tired—was gone by 9 p.m.
>
> . . . If you saw the march on television and think you know its sounds and smells, and its meaning, you are wrong. The television lens is orderly but cold. Its view is no more accurate than an Admiral in the Pentagon moving ships of a fleet on a board. The sailor has no sense of the movement of the fleet but he is the only one who knows the meaning of the battle. I was there. From 5:30 a.m. until late in the afternoon I was on the grounds of the Washington Monument, at Union Station and finally at the Lincoln Memorial.
>
> . . . On the steps of the Lincoln Memorial, no more than a dozen

feet from Dr. King, I wondered about the predictions of violence as the speeches droned on. I hadn't even seen any shoving. I wondered about drunks. I had looked hard but couldn't find any.

My interest and the crowd's mostly responded to the singing. Peter, Paul and Mary were the best. The crowd also cheered the biblical oratory of Martin Luther King "I have a dream . . ." He is a good speaker but I had had enough of speeches.

Then it was over. By 4:30, the sea was draining away. As they left, their discards were exposed. There were no whisky bottles, but there was 400 tons of rubbish to clean up.

There is much more to tell about their going, but this is the central point: They went away from their Capital feeling the strength and unity of their numbers. For one unreal day they heard the demand, "Freedom," from every throat.

Now they are home in the real world. Their demands are not heard so clearly there. They will try to make them heard and there will be trouble for a long time.

The *Star* carried my report as a full-page feature. It drew no notice from family or hometown friends, but years later a black preacher told me, "We read what you wrote, and we knew you'd be different."

6

Meanwhile, Back Home . . .

Two years before the March on Washington, there were a few men back home in Anniston who gave evidence that the civic ideal spawned by the founders still had a detectable half-life. The bus-burning events on Mothers' Day 1961 had shocked the civic conscience of white business and religious leaders. Blacks had an organized entity, the Anniston Improvement Association, whose members, like blacks throughout the South, drew hope—the trigger of action—from the ever-expanding series of TV and newspaper pictures that showed Fortress Segregation crumbling. In the time between the wars, when there seemed little possibility the South would accept Jefferson's promise that "all men are created equal," an immobilizing fatalism froze black leadership. But now there was an organized reason to hope change would come, and where there was hope, men and women—in Birmingham, children too—were roused to action. The roll call of progress at the time read: 1954—*Brown v. Board of Education*; 1955—Montgomery bus boycott; 1957—Little Rock Central High School; 1960—lunch counter sit-in movement; 1961—Freedom Riders; 1962—Ole Miss. Though black citizens felt the momentum of the gathering storm, when they approached retail businesses and City Hall seeking better than custodial jobs, their efforts were stillborn.

Local black leaders, however, sensed a wise and decent heart in Phil Noble, the pastor of Anniston's First Presbyterian Church. Meeting him face-to-face was a breakthrough for the pastor of New Haven Methodist Church, the Reverend Bob McClain, who had been rebuffed in earlier attempts to meet with white Methodist colleagues. McClain and the city's most prominent black leader, the Reverend Nimrod Quintus Reynolds, pastor of 17th Street

Baptist Church, came to Noble's church office. They were impressed with his Christian attitude. A few days later, Reynolds called to suggest a meeting at 17th Street Baptist among black and white ministers "to talk." Symbolic of the gulf that divided the two communities, Phil Noble didn't know the location of Reynolds's church, a few blocks west of the main drag. At the meeting, the Reverend George Smitherman, pastor of Mt. Calvary Baptist Church, joined Reynolds and McClain, and Noble was accompanied by the Reverend Alvin Bullen, minister of Grace Episcopal Church.

Those meetings must have been a revelation to the two white ministers. Phil Noble put it this way in his memoir of the times: "It was during this period of time that I grew by leaps and bounds in my understanding of the problems faced by blacks and the relevance of the Christian faith to them." For the first time, these two white Christians saw firsthand what it was like to be sealed in a segregated tomb. Maybe they were struck, as I was at the time, with the realization that something so mundane as an overnight automobile trip was a major, potentially perilous enterprise: "Where can we buy gas and use the restroom safely? Where will we spend the night—in the car?" At any rate, as a result of those early interracial meetings the white and black ministerial associations "merged" and began to speak out, their views carried by the *Star* to the community.

Newspaper stories flavored with the Holy Gospel were at first as effectual as Christian Muzak. They raised no Christian soldiers to fight for truth and justice. The white community did not and does not follow its preachers. It follows power—money power. James Tinsley put it this way in one of the biracial committee meetings at the YMCA in the early 1970s, "You white folks sometimes criticize our preachers. Now, they may not be much, but in the black community, they're all we got. It's too bad you folks don't follow men of God, like Reverend Martin here [Charles Martin, white, then pastor of Parker Memorial Baptist]. You all follow . . . the Chamber of Commerce, the iron fist in the velvet glove."

In Faulkner's Yoknapatawpha County—in all Southern communities—there are the Sartorises and the Snopeses. Where the Sartorises (small-town aristocrats) are not too fragile and wan from grieving over the Lost Cause and can gin up a little entrepreneurial spunk, they are more than a match for the Snopeses (racist thugs). One such family lived in an Italianate house at the crest of Sunset Drive. Its veranda overlooked the city in the valley below. Leonard and Ann Roberts were a handsome couple: old family and old wealth. Leonard owned textile mills, served on the boards of Alabama Gas Corporation, the State Chamber of Commerce, and a local bank, and was related to the British literary and scientific Huxley family. Ann was the city's arts doyenne as president of the Knox Concert Series. They were favorites of my family and were the first grown-ups to encourage me to call them by their first names.

Men such as Leonard Roberts and Miller Sproull, with connections to banking, hardware, and industrial supply, were inheritors of the founders' mantle. They were the Great Validators. The question likely to greet any new venture was: "Where does Leonard stand on it?" If he was for it, the scheme would more than likely succeed. There were others: Marcus Howze at Commercial National Bank, Marshall Hunter at First National, attorney and UNC graduate Charles Doster, WDNG radio-owner Tom Potts, who was new in town, and cast-iron pipe magnate Charles Hamilton, rough and influential but no civil libertarian.

Dad had been one of them. Among civic, educational and political leadership posts he had held were de facto chairman of the State Board of Education and state governor of Rotary International. (An example of the ironies by which yesterday's radicals become today's establishment was an effort to create the city's first Rotary Club. Dad and Dr. George Lang, a professor friend with doctorates from Berlin and Edinburgh, made calls on the town's leadership cadre to introduce the idea of a local Rotary Club. Some of the older merchants and bankers grumbled about "the young Bolsheviks attempting to organize the community.")

Dad was not a dominant leader in the sixties; little strokes were beginning to confuse his thinking. Local leaders of the day, however, read the papers and could see the progression from *Brown* to Montgomery to Little Rock. They remembered the disorder and shame of the bus burning and knew another storm was headed toward Anniston. They talked at Rotary and at parties about the gathering storm. "We didn't want the city to get a bad name," explained Miller Sproull some forty years later.

Through an industrial haze far to the west of the Roberts' veranda, an outline of the kingdom of the Snopeses could be seen. Theirs was a cul-de-sac kingdom ruled over by an otherwise genial Negrophobe named Kenneth Adams, co-owner of Adams Oil Company. His domain was a dark heart in the center of two communities of decent, hard-working, church-going middle- and working-class neighborhoods, Eastaboga and Wellborn. The dementia which took hold of Kenneth Adams and his fellow Snopeses, pushing them over the edge of violence, was not much more prevalent in his own neighborhood than it was in the eastside precincts of the city's elite. In a 1962 race won by incumbent Sheriff Roy Snead Sr., 14,514 ballots were cast. Adams got 1,890 votes. His core following was much smaller, all known to the FBI. But they were mean, persistent and noisy enough to give the impression of an army.

The freedom buses had come on Mothers Day 1961, and the Snopeses had come howling out of their caves. The founders' "Model City of the South" became better known as "the town that burned the bus." There had already been talk among participants in the Ministerial Association and separately among the Great Validators that a biracial committee should be established. The Mother's Day tragedies were a spur to action. Miller Sproull determined to run for the City Commission and courageously pledged in his campaign literature the creation of such a biracial committee. In the Democratic primary on April 10, 1962, he was elected finance commissioner; Claude Dear was elected mayor; and Jack Suggs, a devout segregationist, police commissioner. There was only a shadow Republican Party at the time and so the three took over City Hall on October 1, 1962—the day following the Ole Miss riot.

The gathering storm had broken. George Wallace had touched down everywhere in his tornadic quest for the governor's office and everywhere he struck, he was a lighting rod of anti-government demagoguery. "States' Rights" was a constitutional fig leaf covering the unspoken, naked scream: "Nigger! Nigger! Nigger!" A plaintive echo of that scream rose from a disoriented people. *We have to hate somebody, because our lives, every common thing we have known is whirling, out of control. You have turned my universe upside down, you liberals and Niggers. So I will hate you, you, you . . . Communists!*

IT WAS A TIME when a proposal as bland as a biracial committee was tanta-mount to defaming the sacraments. It was a step toward erasing the mutu-ally understood social and legal line that had kept the two cultures apart. Miller Sproull knew where Jack Suggs stood, but he wasn't sure about the mayor. Why Claude Dear took the stand he did, he couldn't articulate on his eightieth birthday in 2002. Was it an innate sympathy for the underdog? Or a shrewd sense that history was altering old political calculations? Whatever the reason, he allied himself with the Sartorises and against what appeared to be the more numerous Snopeses. Their chief, Kenneth Adams, led one branch of the many-limbed Ku Klux Klan. He also was allied with the even more rhetorically violent National States Rights Party and its repugnant leaders, Edward Fields and J. B. Stoner.

Adams had served time as one of the white men who jumped on stage at Birmingham Municipal Auditorium during a 1956 concert to assault Nat King Cole. Back home, Adams was leader of a small, motley Ku Klux Klan cell that met on the third floor of an old building on Wilmer Avenue. Its members were drawn there by a combination of pathological racism and competition by blacks for the hot, dirty, but good-paying jobs in the city's many pipe shops. Anniston then was known as the "World Soil Pipe Capital," after the kind of cast-iron pipe that was part of the infrastructure underlying housing and commercial developments in the post-war boom. There was even a short-lived radio station (competing with Dad's WHMA) whose call letters were WSPC (for World Soil Pipe Capital), celebrating the ironic fact that more sewage passes through pipe made in Anniston than in any other city in the world.

Klan leader Adams was an anomaly, a genial, good-natured man to his close friends but with a twist in his character that would breed tragedy for him and the larger community. He was a good provider for a loving fam-ily as co-owner of Adams Oil Company, which included service stations. Though small, he had been a star high school center for the Oxford Yellow Jackets football team. He continued his interest in youth athletics as a booster of the athletic program of the Wellborn community. Many young baseball and football players owed their uniforms to his company. But he had a phobia about blacks, which would violently disrupt the community and isolate him in a dead end of septic passions.

His oldest daughter, Wanda, now a retired RN, was isolated by those toxic passions as well. She grew up penned in a poignant, lonely, mental chamber that had three sides: conflicted feelings for the only father she knew—a typical dad doing dad things such as coaching little league teams but who became a frightening stranger when the chemistry of alcohol and racism pushed up dementia as the controlling force of his character. The third side of her lonely prison was shame: knowing the community, even neighbors in Wellborn, despised her father and all of his works. As an adult, she tried never to reveal who her family is, or was.

In 2010, Wanda spoke about her life to Theresa Shadrix, managing editor of Josephine's magazine *Longleaf,* for an unpublished segment of the *Star*'s special on the fiftieth anniversary of the bus burning. Wanda has childhood memories of looking out her window at night and seeing the spooky wizard peaks of Klan hats at gatherings in the family's yard. She would watch as her father's personality, fed by alcohol, morphed into another person capable of running Klan activities and making midnight hate calls. J. B. Stoner was a frequent houseguest, a fat, ugly little man who in a dream of masculinity boasted that "JB" stands for "Jersey Bull." His actual role was attorney for the National States Rights Party. When Stoner visited, Wanda slept on the couch, and Mrs. Adams was assigned the demeaning role of washerwoman for the Great Man's underwear.

Theresa said that as Wanda talked on in their interview, laughing at some obscure past discomfort borne in the name of the Klan, she could feel that talking relieved the very Southern burden of isolation and scorn she felt. Wanda surely deserves a healing time as a silent survivor.

While Kenneth's disgruntled dozen or so Kluxers met semi-secretly (the FBI had informers), Anniston's civic and political leaders were publicly moving toward a demonstration of civil common sense. Unavoidably, the minds of Anniston's leaders were haunted by the all-too-vivid images from Birmingham during the first week in May. There, hundreds of black students had surged around Kelly Ingram Park, met by Bull Connor's police and fire departments, who accommodated the movement with police dogs lunging at children and high-pressure streams of water from fire hoses sending them tumbling like fallen leaves.

E. L. Turner Jr., a pillar of Anniston's First Presbyterian Church, had been in Birmingham on business when the melee took place. Returning home, the tall, soft-spoken church elder with the authentic old-world manner told a meeting of the governing body of the church, the Session, about conditions in the steel city and asked that the elders be led in prayer that Anniston would avoid Birmingham's tragedy. After prayer led by the Reverend Phil Noble, further discussion led to a motion that the Session endorse establishment of a human relations council for the city. The local church leaders felt that the chaos in Birmingham was a calamity for Alabama, but those pictures of snarling police dogs and buffeting fire hoses also were instantly projected to the nation and the world and were an incalculable contribution to the civil rights movement. They weighed on decision makers on the Anniston City Commission and in the Kennedy administration.

The immediate cause of preventive action came on Mother's Day, May 12, as an echo of the violent Mother's Day in 1961 when the bus was attacked and burned. Phil Noble recalls that the tranquility of the holiday was interrupted in late afternoon by a phone call from Miller Sproull.

Sproull asked: "Have you heard the news?

Noble answered: "No, what news?"

"The homes of two Negro families and the St. John's Methodist Church in south Anniston were fired into this afternoon by white men using shotguns."

Noble immediately inquired: "Was anybody killed?"

"Fortunately," Commissioner Sproull said, "no one was killed or injured." Then he added, "We are ready to appoint the biracial committee. Can you meet the mayor and me at City Hall tomorrow morning to talk about it? We want you to be the chairman."

Noble paused, his mind scanning a region where city after city had rejected biracial committees because of inflamed white opinion. Without saying he would accept, he asked what time and hung up. Phil and his wife Betty talked it over, weighed the risks and then came to the only conclusion they could after having advocated such a body for some time.

At the same time that President Kennedy was hosting the May 14 White House luncheon Dad and I attended—one of many attempts to encourage responsible leadership of the civil rights crisis—the Anniston City Commission was meeting for the same purpose. Commissioner Sproull announced that the Chamber of Commerce had voted to establish the Human Relations Council. Two letters were read endorsing its creation, one from the rector, wardens, and vestry of Grace Episcopal Church, and another from the Anniston Ministerial Association. There was no word—for or against—from the largest congregation in town, Parker Memorial Baptist. Dad still taught the men's Sunday School there, the Baracca Class, but had not attended 11 o'clock services since being denounced from the pulpit for editorially supporting legal sales of alcohol. On Thursday, May 16, 1963, the Commission appointed a nine-man Human Relations Council of five whites and four blacks with Phil Noble as chairman. It included such validating names as Marcus Howze of Commercial Bank, textile magnate Leonard Roberts, and the *Star's* executive editor, Wilfred Galbraith, who was also an attorney. Black members included prominent ministers Nimrod Reynolds and William McClain and businessman Raleigh Byrd.

The founding ideal was showing resilience.

If not unique, the official blessing of City Hall for biracial discussion and negotiation was rare at that moment in the South—most assuredly, a favorable contrast with its bigger sibling, Birmingham, which only days before had been the epicenter of chaotic racism. Anniston's decision was rare enough to merit a letter from President Kennedy, which Miller Sproull read to the Commission. The president wrote,

> It seems to me this is a most significant action by the city government and one that offers great hope for permitting legitimate racial problems to be identified and considered in a calm and orderly manner. I hope that the Council will provide the city of Anniston with a means of communication between the races and that its efforts will be fruitful. Your action is a sensible one, and one that should serve as a model for the United States.

By coincidence, these actions were taking place not many months after the tense days of the Cuban Missile Crisis. The prayers of a thousand towns like Anniston were answered. The Soviet ships did turn back. A call to prayer issued by a biracial committee, endorsed by the mayor, had a quiet hidden meaning—that the fires of nuclear holocaust would be equal opportunity killers, incinerating black and white Americans equally. That whispered sentiment, however, was drowned out by the sounds of Negroes marching in the streets, countered by sweating politicians and preachers shouting Biblical verse that they interpreted as ordaining black subjugation. The old segregated civilization was coming apart, noisily, with great difficulty, its pillars moaning under stress. All around, the old way was dying and an unfamiliar, frightening new civilization was emerging.

THE MORNING OF SEPTEMBER 16, 1963, began like all the Sundays before. Four Sunday School girls were primping before class in the basement of Birmingham's Sixteenth Street Baptist Church. A normal Sunday, until a deafening sound and instantly the girls died in a hail of flying brick, wood and glass. The dynamite bomb collapsed a corner of the church. The four girls were Denise McNair, eleven, and Addie Mae Collins, Carole Robertson, and Cynthia Wesley, each fourteen. A shocked nation contemplated what species could be so depraved as to murder little girls in Sunday dresses. (The act also fixed in the gut of recent law school graduate William J. Baxley, then twenty-one, the burn of long-lasting indignation. Elected Alabama attorney general in the New South wave of 1970, the young, long-haired lawman set forth on a hunt for the bombers. On November 17, 1977, Baxley's indefatigable investigation—with little help from the FBI—paid off: a jury of nine whites and three blacks found Robert "Dynamite Bob" Chambliss guilty of murder. In 2001 and 2002, Thomas Blanton Jr. and then Bobby Frank Cherry were also convicted of murder. Long-awaited justice was served.)

For some time, Anniston's Great Validators, knights of noblesse oblige, had quietly been making progress on the agenda of the Human Relations Council, persuading some white doctors and businessmen to eliminate separate waiting rooms and restrooms, erasing "white" and "colored" signs on drinking fountains, and desegregating some lunch counters. It does not seem so momentous looking back on it, but it was no small thing to eliminate the signposts of an apartheid civilization. There was agreement among the HRC members, the library board and a majority of the city commission that a logical next step would be to quietly integrate the city-owned Carnegie Library. Board chairman Charles Doster years later recalled that Dad was not in favor of the idea when it was first mentioned. "I don't know why, maybe it was a question of political timing," said Doster.

When the decision was finally made, they unknowingly chose a fateful day, the very afternoon of the Birmingham bombing, September 16, 1963. The plan developed with a tight seal of secrecy because of the volatile environment and the omnipresence of Kenneth Adams's irregulars. Accounts differ on police protection. Some recall the police were supposed to be there for protection and others say the police were to be there but out of sight to avoid drawing unwanted attention. Police were informed, that much is certain, and sympathetic friends of the Adams tribe within the police force must have leaked the plan to his gang. As it turned out, not having a visible police presence was a mistake.

The two ministers who were to make the symbolic entry, Nimrod Reynolds and Bob McClain, had no sense of foreboding. Reynolds vividly remembers:

> We were riding down the street right after church and we were talking about what happened in Birmingham saying, "What an awful thing." We parked the car right in front of the library. I was driving my car. We got out and started up the walkway. You had to walk a good distance to the place, and all of a sudden folks came from everywhere. I ran into one of them [he was struck on the head by a chain] and fell to my hands and that's how I got stabbed in the buttocks. They were constantly stabbing the buttocks. They had already cut up the car and jammed it with two cars where we couldn't get out.

Somehow Reynolds and McClain made it back to their car. The crowd surged around them as they tried to maneuver the car away from the mob, but the car was blocked in. A single shot was fired, shattering the window on the driver's side. Inside the library, the gunshot and the noise of the mob could be clearly heard. Patrons started for the door but Doster blocked the exit to prevent them from potential harm in the pandemonium outside. One man insisted on leaving. "Mr. Doster, I have a thirteen-year-old daughter waiting for me in the car. I'm leaving." Doster stood aside. Meanwhile, fearing for their lives, McClain and Reynolds scrambled back out of the car. Reynolds continued, "So we started up the street running and Mrs. Dolly Hughes picked us up and carried us to the hospital. Of course, they wouldn't admit me because they were frightened about what might happen to even the hospital, so I came home."

A shocked but calm Commissioner Sproull called Phil Noble and suggested that the two of them, Mayor Dear, and Charlie Doster meet at Sproull's house. There, Doster suggested that President Kennedy should know about the situation and placed a call to the White House. He was told that the president would return the call. The four of them then went by police car to Reverend Reynolds's house, which was surrounded by armed black men. City attorney Bob Field arrived. As Phil Noble recalls, he had just suggested a word of prayer when a policeman informed them that the president was trying to reach them. The white leaders' instinct was to race back to Sproull's house, but the mayor said, "We're not in such a big hurry that a prayer would do any harm." Phil Noble led a brief prayer and the men then departed. Back at Sproull's house, they placed the call and Operator One connected them to President Kennedy. He said he expected things would calm down in Anniston but to let him know if they didn't.

The group unanimously agreed that the integration of the library would be accomplished the next day. As Phil Noble put it and Doster emphatically agreed, "We had to make crystal clear to the citizens of Anniston, and especially to the hoodlums, that the city was not going to be run by hoodlums!" At 3:30 the next afternoon, the reverends Bob McClain and G. E. Smitherman were the first blacks issued library cards. Miller Sproull, Phil Noble, Charlie Doster, library board member Carleton Stern Lentz, and a substantial police presence escorted them.

Two other incidents had marred that violent Sunday in Anniston, and tension continued at the library. Five Negro teens, enraged by what had happened to the two ministers, attacked a white man who had missed a bus in west Anniston and was walking toward his home on Christine Avenue. He was treated and released at Memorial Hospital. Later that evening three shotgun blasts were fired into a black café, without any injuries inside. Police Commissioner Suggs, an avowed segregationist, nonetheless vigorously sought arrests in all of the September 16 incidents. A seventeen-year-old, who admitted to being enraged over the library beatings, was charged in the mugging of the white man. Four white men accused in the library assaults were bound over to the grand jury on charges of intent to murder. All were associates of Kenneth Adams. One, Mike Fox, 44, had been charged with Adams in the 1956 assault on Nat King Cole.

Bob Field recalls an unusual defense from one of the defendants. "Mr. Field, I don't know why they got me charged with anything," he said, "I don't care who goes in that library. I can't even read or write."

Monday morning in Washington, the horrifying Birmingham church bombing story had virtually erased any mention of events in Anniston. At the Justice Department, Burke Marshall surprised me when, in his quiet way, he said, "I'm sorry about what happened in Anniston." That was how I learned about what we now call "the incident at the library" in a morally neutral shorthand phrase that Bob McClain repeats with some bitterness and Nimrod Reynolds quotes with resigned irony.

Violence at the library, I thought when Burke told me the news. The *Library?* Not Carnegie Library. That's where we (white children) went to gawk at the bird collection and stare respectfully at the Egyptian mummy. That's the dark, quiet place where starchy sweet, ageless Miss Mildred Goodrich read to (white) children in "The Poet's Corner." Yet it had happened, and the dimensions of the shock sent out waves of complex feelings. To the black ministers, it is a knotted memory of fear and hatred. For the good (white) people who so lovingly used the library, for the chosen, the leaders, Validators, it was a crime against civilization. A temple to the civilization the Sartorises hoped to conserve had been violated. The barbarians had defiled a hallowed place.

The Snopeses kept up a threatening presence at the library for a few days, one that ended with a comic epilogue. Doster and a police officer kept a vigil, noticing that rough men—obviously not library patrons—would parade through the tables and stacks. From the KKK perch on the third floor of the Woodmen of the World building diagonally across from the library, they kept up a menacing surveillance. Doster hit on a stratagem to separate legitimate patrons from the undesirables—insisting on possession of a library card. Doster picked an older man whom he knew to use as a physical demonstration of the new policy. The officer asked for the man's library card, which he could not produce. He then escorted the gentleman to the door. Next, Doster called Police Commissioner Suggs and asked if he could stop the Klan from spying from their roost, spying which made library patrons and staff uneasy. Doster does not know how Suggs did it, but the Klan's presence evaporated, and Doster went back to his law office. Later, he ran into the gentleman he had caused to be symbolically evicted. "Mike," he said, "I have an apology to make . . ." The Mike that Doster had summarily removed from the library was Colonel Mike Halloran, former commanding officer of Ft. McClellan. Halloran took the news with good nature, "Charlie Doster, you old son of a bitch, I've been thrown out of bars and whorehouses, but I've never been thrown out of a library before."

Tensions did not go away with the integration of the library; the dying civilization was thrashing violently. From the black community came words appealing for calm. The Ministerial Association issued a prayerful call for racial calm. On November 13, the *Anniston Star* reported:

> Anniston Ministerial Association members Monday called on area residents to meet any school integration crises with Christian standards of responsibility and obedience to law and order. Gov.-elect George C. Wallace and all state officials were called on to provide the leadership toward avoiding the sort of violence that erupted this fall on the campus of the University of Mississippi.
>
> Their measure followed a similar call for civil obedience issued last weekend by the Trustees and Alumni of the University of Alabama where the next college integration crises may come soon. The unanimous call for peace and civil observance of laws came in this resolution:

"The Anniston Ministerial Association by this resolution respectfully requests that the Gov.-elect George C. Wallace, and all state authorities seek to avoid the tragedy of Mississippi repeated in any part of the state of Alabama . . ."

The resolution went on to spell out a litany of steps that would bring about comity in the state and community.

All those brave words debated, weighed, edited, approved, and finally published surely had some effect, at least locally, but the appeal would not be answered in full for many years. It is astonishing to look back from the twenty-first century and see how Lilliputian was the scale by which progress was measured in the early 1960s. Domestic terrorists had attacked and tried to kill two men who thought access to books—our common language—need not be segregated by race. The stealth and drama and peril and pain that it took to integrate the lending and reading of books in Anniston was a baby step but it was seen at the time as a great stride forward. And so it was.

7

Coming Home as Strangers

The violence and intensity of feelings in Anniston in those troubled years did not reach South Glebe Road in Arlington, Virginia, where Josie and I lived in a roomy, corner one-bedroom apartment, and only the major news reached me on the twelfth floor of the National Press Building. Our thoughts were locked on Washington, on our professional and social life there. Home, when I thought about it at all, was a pleasant collection of childhood and adolescent memories. We did not know that we were about to find ourselves in the eye of the storm.

Shortly after the March on Washington, on vacation at the family's favorite Florida resort, Ponte Vedra Beach and Club, Mother told us about Dad's declining health. It was time to come home, she said. I didn't want to go. It was too soon. Next year were political spectacles I yearned to see and write about, the two party conventions and the presidential election. I would be stuck in Anniston. But Josie and I dutifully packed up and headed south. Josie had down-to-earth thoughts about what lay ahead—finding a place to live, fitting into a charming, demanding, difficult family. I was a bit full of myself, anticipating the pleasure of parading before old friends and colleagues my status as a romantic figure—an authentic in-the-know Washington correspondent.

We were a young couple, ready for life's next turn, pretty much oblivious to the fact that we were heading into a war zone where some old friends and many *Star* readers would regard us as foreigners—or worse, traitors. Was I slower than most, or is everybody's life a series of jack-in-the-box surprises, being blindsided by people and events you should have seen coming? What neither of us knew was that when we left Washington and turned south, we were driving into our own past. We had forgotten that Alabama was on Old South Time, with Old South values. My thinking had been conditioned by the articulate statesmanship of two superior Southern governors, Hodges and Sanford, and by the Kennedys. Our version of conventional thought and opinion came from our friends, colleagues, the accomplished people a Washington correspondent meets on the job, and by the New York and Washington papers: the *Times*, the *Post,* and the *Star.*

What we needed was a wise old uncle to advise us: "Listen, you two, you're young and bright, you'll get along just fine, but remember you've been in a pretty advanced culture: an alien culture to most folks in Anniston and the South. Set your mental clock back a few years. Remember what you, and just about everybody you knew, thought about race relations. Remember the way you talked, the jokes you told. The separate waiting rooms, bathrooms, and water fountains are still everywhere in Alabama, though a little progress has been made in Anniston. Don't be too shocked by the way things are. They're just as they had been when you all were growing up, but nowadays our (white) folks feel their way of life is under threat and they are pretty upset about what's happening. Don't be too quick to judge or take offense. Folks need time to adjust, and in time they will."

WE DIDN'T HAVE SUCH a sage to shield us from culture shocks and collisions. We entered unarmed into Alabama journalism and the social life of Anniston. Our main cushion was the perfect little house Josie found overlooking the back nine of the country club golf course: a three-bedroom, mustard-colored house with white trim, an inviting sun porch looking out on the golf course, even a white picket fence. I set out from 501 Keith Avenue on my first assignment, editor of the family's first outside purchase, a weekly paper in the northernmost limits of what came to be the family's near-flung empire of dailies and weeklies in northeast Alabama. The *Piedmont Journal* was culture shock number one for this romantic Washington correspondent. It was located in a small-cinder block building, a few feet from the railroad track, filled with clutter and dust almost as old as the ancient press. No longer would the dashing young man be having martini lunches at the Sans Souci with White House aides and congressmen. He'd be having the vegetable plate and sweet tea at the Little Gem Cafe, diagonally across the tracks from the paper. It was there on Friday, November 22nd, that I heard the shattering news: JFK, the president who defined for us the limitless possibilities of youth, was dead.

Josie and I retreated behind our picket fence, our gloom unrelieved except for one moment of black humor: The TV camera framed a sobbing Senator Ralph Yarborough, a Texas Democrat but no friend of Lyndon Johnson. Josie managed a laugh at my remark, "You'd cry too, if your worst political enemy had just become president of the United States." That whole weekend, we stared numbly at our black-and-white television set in the bedroom, grieving alone, alone because we had already experienced the first social ambush that told us we were people apart, strangers in our hometown.

Shortly after returning home, we'd been invited to a party at the Glenwood Terrace home of a charming couple, Clare and Lelie Draper. Clare was a handsome, conservative, courteous executive in his family's window and door fabricating business, and Lelie was a sweet and lovely adornment in any venue. It was good to see my boyhood friend, George Kilby, there with his svelte wife, Houston. Houston was not a favorite. She had tongue-lashed me for calling her Houston in a story for the *Star*, instead of Mrs. Kilby, and I thought her pretentious for calling George's grandfather's place "The Estate." I've forgotten what provoked her at the Drapers'—probably a Kennedy anecdote—and neither Josie nor I recalls exactly what she said. We only remember angry words. My shaky savoir-faire left me and I responded hotly. George naturally came to his wife's defense. Our hosts' faces registered distress. We left, still angry, and sadly contemplated the distance that would have to be maintained between many in "our crowd" and us. I regretted the estrangement from George, an inseparable presence in my childhood memories. And, though we never had an opportunity to repair the breach with Houston, we were distressed to learn several years later that she had been struck with cancer. From a distance, we admired the grace and exemplary heroism with which she fought and managed her final illness.

My job was not much more uplifting in the first year back home. We found somebody to run the *Piedmont Journal* and I was installed in temporary quarters in the conference room of the *Star,* where I was to be a co-conspirator with executive editor Wilfred Galbraith in editing Dad's increasingly confused editorials. It was a sneaky, hateful job—especially painful when he caught us at our cowardly craft. In his final year, Dad adopted our beagle pup, "Frère," whose profile could be seen alongside his in the backseat of the black Chrysler as he was driven to work. The puppy's teething marks could still be seen on his desk, which now supports my professional clutter, until a refinisher couldn't resist an artist's need to obliterate what he thought of as blemishes.

The mist deepened around Dad. Within months, he gave up the pretense of reading the paper and retreated into his inner world. In September of 1964, a terrible stroke sent him vaulting over the banisters. He landed on a chair by the hall telephone table, smashing the chair but not breaking a single bone. That night at the understaffed, city-run Anniston Memorial Hospital, he was agitated, incoherent, thrashing about on the bed. Josie and I were distressed, but Mrs. Scott, the starchy, thin-lipped head nurse, didn't share our alarm and did nothing. Dad never went home. He spent his final weeks in a calm, deep silence at a local convalescent hospital. The last response I got was after an Alabama-Georgia football game at Legion Field, where he had first taken me with the grown-ups as a boy: a Southern Protestant bar mitzvah. It was getting dark outside as I held his warm hand. I leaned down and said, "Dad, we whipped hell out of Georgia." He smiled and squeezed my hand. A few nights later, Josie and I were there when he gently took one last breath.

The funeral packed Parker Memorial Baptist Church and Governor Wallace was among the mourners. I do not remember a word from the funeral homily, but I keenly recall what the separation meant to me. He could have been that sage to guide Josie and me, offering advice as we tried to fit attitudes formed by the progressive Upper South and Washington into the reactionary politics and culture of Alabama. But he was gone. I missed much in having an autumnal father—he had been fifty when I was born. We never fished or hunted together. And when I needed his guidance most, that autumn of 1964, he had gone.

If Josie and I had had an older adviser, and we had had the sense to listen, one piece of wisdom missing the year Dad died was the warning not to take a political detour that led directly to burial in an electoral landslide.

I accepted an invitation to join a slate of presidential electors pledged to support President Johnson, if he should carry Alabama. We were bastard surrogates for our two able U.S. senators, Lister Hill and John Sparkman, who never publicly claimed to have fathered us, expendable troops to test the strength of Governor Wallace. Our opposition in the statewide race was a slate of unpledged electors prepared to do whatever Wallace asked them to. I was chosen for our slate, probably because people might think Dad was the candidate. Nevertheless, I was determined to do my best. The first time I uttered a speech in public was at a northwest Alabama political rally at Crossville High School atop Sand Mountain, at the foot of which legend says there used to be a sign: NIGGER. DON'T LET THE SUN SET ON YOU HERE.

If the sign was there, we missed it, but joining Sand Mountain folks for the supper before the speaking began that cool April evening, we had the feeling we weren't on home turf. Josephine, by far the most beautiful and best-dressed woman there, wore a navy blue coat with white pinstripes over a navy dress. She was taken aback when one of the ladies fingered the coat's fabric and admitted, "I ain't never seen no cloth coat before." My maiden speech was a challenge, one that banished fear of public speaking for a lifetime. I followed, in order, George Wallace and Bull Connor. In the darkened backstage as I waited my turn to speak for our slate, I heard the crowd roar approval as Wallace shouted, "I have stood up for you in Wisconsin and Indiana. I have felt their spittle upon my face, and I have told them that Alabamians are just as educated, refined and patriotic as any other Americans!" Bull Connor, a candidate for the Alabama Public Service Commission, ran through all the offices he'd held in Birmingham, ending with a killer laugh line ". . . and custodian (pause) of the Po-lice dawgs." By then, I was certain that they weren't my crowd. I made my way to the podium with the inevitability of a prisoner walking the thirteen steps to the gallows. The crowd listened to my inept performance politely, registering one reassuring grin from a few when I described my dogged loyalty to the regular Democratic Party as being like Lincoln's dog, "He may not be much to look at it, and he ain't very fast, but Mister, he's hell on a cold scent."

There were other rallies and meetings; a high point for me was late in the campaign in north Alabama before one of our larger crowds. When I called the roll of other Southern states that were sticking with the regular Democratic Party and asked with some passion, "Why are we alone? Have we seceded from the South?" The large hand that belonged to the legendary six-foot, eight-inch former Governor James (Big Jim) Folsom struck my back. "Good talkin', boy," he said. But opposing George Wallace was so much futile energy. In the May primaries we stood beneath the avalanche. We carried only one of Alabama's sixty-seven counties—Macon, whose county seat is Tuskegee, home of the famous black university. Weeks later, Governor Wallace impeached my credentials as a critic of his politics in front of a group of journalists invited to observe how "refined" the state was. He told them, "Bran-dit ran for a little office and lost his own home box two to one." That was one of the few political mistakes I ever heard Wallace make—the actual vote was closer to four to one. His garbling of my name was deliberate. My name had come up in the company of some of his cronies during the campaign and the governor burst into the theme song of the TV serial "Branded." Wallace sang, "Bran-dit, scorned as the man who ran."

The vote in the elector race and the margin by which Barry Goldwater won in Alabama were measurements of the popularity of pro-integration advocates. Senator Goldwater, who had voted against the 1964 Civil Rights Act, carried Alabama by 69.5 percent, sweeping five first-term GOP congressmen in with him. He was the hinge by which the more dedicated segregationist wing of the Democratic Party swung to the Republican Party.

But the civic ideal that made Anniston's passage through the civil rights revolution smoother than in brawling Birmingham still had some energy. Different at birth, the two cities aged under polar influences. Anniston matured under the guidance of home-owned industries, mainly cast-iron pipe and textiles, whose owners—rough, some of them were—all lived in Anniston and thus were connected to the fortunes of the town. The light reins of the founding ideal guided them. In place of such anchoring ideals, Birmingham was driven by merciless men like the DeBardelebens, father and son, described by one writer as Ahabs crazed by pursuit of the black whale—coal. Birmingham's civic culture was also shaped by a procession of disengaged managers whose loyalty was to U.S. Steel instead of Birmingham, a corporation not a community.

Birmingham Police Commissioner Eugene "Bull" Connor, Wallace's popular twin at the Crossville rally, would have been a feared and familiar figure if he had been transported to the Union of South Africa. He had the bullet-headed, thick-bodied look of an Afrikaner caricature, a Bull Vandermerver who'd keep the kaffirs (niggers) under control, combining the roles of Minister of Bantu Affairs and Minister of Police and Justice. In the early 1960s the two emerging nations, South Africa and the American South, were two ships crossing each other in turbulent seas. South Africa was installing a twisted vision which sprang from the frightening brilliance of Prime Minister Dr. Hendrik Verwoerd. His "final solution" of apartheid was to lock the two races into black and white "homelands," separate and drastically unequal. The South was leaving apartheid behind, sailing in the opposite direction through fitful seas, dragging its anchor, with a mutinous crew and rioting passengers, but sailing away. Birmingham had its own version of Dr. Verwoerd: James Alexander Simpson, distinguished corporation lawyer, state senator, social acquaintance of my family, and a fierce advocate of Alabama apartheid.

Though still convinced that segregation was best for both races, by the time World War II was ending, Dad's native progressivism made him begin to question the denial of voting rights to Negroes. He expressed to his friend Simpson the concern that Simpson would invoke racial fears in his 1944 campaign to unseat U.S. Senator Lister Hill—whose New Deal credentials had won him the honor of nominating FDR at the 1940 Democratic National Convention. Simpson, an anti-New Dealer, answered Dad that he would not employ "the Negro question" in any way except to illustrate the evils of federal intervention. However, Simpson's campaign was not so subtle. Dad wrote a mutual friend that the Simpson forces wanted to "Talmadgeize Alabama by making the defenseless Negro a whipping horse on which to ride into office."

Among Simpson's campaign propaganda was a tabloid which had a front page photo: "Nigger of the Week." According to Diane McWhorter's mammoth *Carry Me Home*, a typical anti-Roosevelt headline in the tabloid

read, "Eleanor Greets Nigger Again!" Simpson's son, Henry, has said the
tabloid was an anti-Semitic sheet with no connection to the campaign. But
the campaign obviously was aware of the hate sheets and his son did not
say that his father renounced them.

Simpson was a strong candidate, stamped with leadership qualities of
intellect and a countenance of unsmiling granite—plus ill-disguised racism: a formidable combination, but not quite enough to unseat Dad's close
friend, Lister Hill, who prevailed by 55 percent of the vote. That was close
for an incumbent. Dad worried that Simpson's strong showing would encourage others to exploit the race issue. A few days after the primary, Dad
stung his friend Simpson in a May 7 editorial criticizing him for mixing
politics and race in a desperate campaign which soiled the state with "a flood
of propaganda by means of scandal sheets, public harangues, whispering
campaigns, etc., the equal of which we never before had." He went on to
advocate publicly for the first time equal voting rights for blacks, arguing
that the ballot box was a powerful antidote to race-baiting.

The next year Georgia's progressive Governor Ellis Arnall took a step in
the direction of voting rights by winning repeal of the poll tax. He paid for it
in 1946 when he was defeated by Eugene Talmadge's demagogic campaign.
Dad mourned the silencing of another voice of reason in the Deep South,
as did his own father. My grandfather, Dr. T. W. Ayers, an eighty-eight-
year-old retired Baptist medical missionary living in Atlanta, expressed his
own frustration in a letter to his publisher son:

> The clouds are hovering low all over Georgia today, for on yesterday
> the voters of this state nominated Eugene Talmadege for governor over
> one of the best men in the state. I can't understand why so many people,
> many of them men of intelligence and good citizens, could support a man
> with the record Talmadge has. In the nomination of Theodore Bilbo of
> Mississippi and this man in Georgia, on the race issue, shows that our
> people are possessed with racial hatred.

Simpson was Alabama's Talmadge in Brooks Brothers clothing. He is
portrayed in McWhorter's epic as a forbidding puppet-master who cre-

ated Bull Connor to maintain Alabama apartheid. An earlier threat to the Simpson-Connor order had been posed in 1938, when many of the South's most distinguished citizens went to Birmingham under the banner of the Southern Conference for Human Welfare. The defining flag of the conference—bold for the 1930s—was raised in the keynote speech by University of North Carolina President Frank Porter Graham: "The black man is the primary test of American democracy and Christianity."

That was as far as Southern leaders got in trying to work out a gradual and voluntary way for the two races to live together in harmony as equals. The next day Birmingham's then freshman police commissioner made certain the delegates were firmly, legally separated. In a famous malapropism Connor laid down the law: "Whites and Negroes are not to segregate together!" "Old Bull" had been a popular ticker-tape, play-by-play baseball radio announcer—a la "Dutch" Reagan. He made an art of amiable buffoonery, but he had the heart of an Afrikaner bully, and though he had no legal authority in my hometown, his Thou Shalt Not Segregate Together was law in Anniston just as surely as it was in Birmingham.

THE LAW WAS FIRST challenged by a mechanized assault, the "Freedom Riders"—a marker in the minds of city leaders telling them that the Snopeses' advance would have to be beaten back to preserve what was left of the unwritten civic ideal. The "bus burning" became a trigger for quick reaction to each civil rights era challenge. Josie and I were still in Raleigh in 1961, and to us the news of the events of that day seemed unreal, as if they had happened to some place neither of us knew. Read years later, accounts of that day by Taylor Branch, Diane McWhorter, and in the *Star* convey some of the shock of immediacy felt by people who were there at the time: flames, screaming mobs, terror, pain, and the deep, deep shame that those things had been done by our people, in our place.

Additional facts later uncovered soften somewhat Branch's judgment of police indifference at the Greyhound terminal in Anniston. Chief Lawrence Peek had released the police for lunch when the overdue bus hadn't arrived. The officers were quickly recalled, pushed back the mob, dragged two men from under the bus, and cleared a path for its exit. The authorities didn't know that the men under the bus had been slashing its tires. Pursued by a caravan of cars, the speeding bus fled west on U.S. Highway 78 until the deflating tires forced it to pull over on John Hardy hill (later the site of another civil rights crime).

In the midst of the melee, an incongruous thing happened, recounted by the *Star*'s photographer on the scene, Joseph "Little Joe" Postiligone. Little Joe wanted an interior shot of the burning bus, but his five-foot, four-inch frame wouldn't reach a window. He asked a nearby thug, mindlessly whipping the side of the bus with a heavy chain, for a lift. Apparently, the request was so brazen that the man complied. He dropped the chain, hoisted Little Joe up to a rear window to snap a couple of shots and then gently cushioned his descent. Having done his good turn, he picked up the chain and resumed his previous task. Injured passengers were ferried to Anniston Memorial Hospital and Lttle Joe's picture of the burning bus was ferried round the world.

An irony probably lost on the thugs who burned the bus was that they provided a significant victory for Soviet propaganda, ironic because Kenneth Adams called our newspaper, "the Red Star," probably unaware that the Soviet Army newspaper had the same name. A Radio Moscow broadcast said of the attack in Anniston: "Advocates of racial intolerance attacked a bus touring the South of the United States carrying thirty-two passengers, both white and black, participants in a campaign to abolish racial segregation." Tom Potts in his WDNG "audiotorial" the next day noted, "This very minute Moscow is having a propaganda hey-day . . ." Though he would cringe if accused of liberality, Tom's passionate good-citizenship won him credibility with black and white leaders. His commentary was an example:

> The real fault rests squarely on the shoulder of our citizens—you and me. It is our fault for allowing a mob to take over every time a race problem arises. WDNG Audiotorial suggests it is time for the decent people in Anniston to stand up and be counted . . . It is up to each of us to see that it does not happen again.

Little Joe wasn't present when a Trailways busload of Freedom Riders arrived, an hour behind the Greyhound contingent. Branch's reportage of police indifference to vicious assaults on passengers there stands, unsoftened. It is some small consolation that there was no active collusion between police and the Klan. In Birmingham, as recounted by McWhorter, police officials whispered to the justly famed Eastview Ku Klux Klan that its action squad would have to do its "work" in fifteen minutes and then the police would intervene.

As the events of that day unfolded, Sid Smyer, a gruff real estate lawyer and one of the feudal lords of Birmingham's status-quo ante, was in Japan. He was attending an International Rotary convention, assuring fellow Rotarians that all was well in Birmingham, when *Post-Herald* photographer Tommy Langston's pictures of white men in sports shirts beating blacks sprang from the front page of Tokyo newspapers. Scorned then by his Rotary peers, the incoming president of the Birmingham Chamber of Commerce underwent a conversion.

All these things and more were happening in Alabama, pulling at the shape and psychology of my state and hometown, but I wasn't there and so these events were not part of my fabric of memory when we returned for good. Anniston for me was still an idyll of remembered Saturday afternoons, the deadness of the mummy at Carnegie Library, the fumbled kiss I gave Lyda by the fig tree and the time Lloyd and I chased and spanked her in the backyard, the ocean of red clay where the new hospital was rising, the redness of the club's clay tennis courts where old Mr. Godwin taught generations the game, the hateful swish of corduroy knickers, the pint of bootleg bourbon furtively purchased from a bellman at the Jeff Davis Hotel, the porch light blinking 10 p.m. curfew at auburn-haired Marian Huey's grandparents' house—jumbled scraps of remembrance which held hometown firmly, immutably in place.

In reality, the picture of Anniston was only as immutable as a postcard, a picture of a place that was but is no more.

8

Stranger's Return
to a Familiar Place

I t is true, that feeling Thomas Wolfe had, you can't go home again. As strong as the pull calling you home may be, it is not the same place you left; either it has changed—or you have. Strangeness has entered to separate you from the remembered place, home. The place you left was governed by an over-soul of oneness. Everyone thought alike, spoke alike, the seasons turned as they always had, the same order of service was followed at Grace Episcopal and the same lively Baptist hymns were sung every Sunday at Parker Memorial, undisturbed by such distant abstractions as social revolution. But in 1964 and 1965 a historic election, racial tension, and violence signaled epic changes in my hometown, the South, and also in me.

Anniston had not changed visibly when Josie and I started our lives together there. The same four movie houses marched up the west side of Noble Street and downtown merchants ("the boys") still gathered for breakfast and mid-morning coffee at Gus Nicopolous's Sanitary Café—the white tile floor giving emphasis to the virtue its name advertised. They were the same good men who chaired the Chamber of Commerce, the Community Chest, and the Boy Scouts. But I had changed. I had seen more than I could understand of history on the march. Its advance guard had entered Alabama generating noisy headlines that were unsettling to "the boys." I could not join in the banter at the Sanitary's corner round table, conversation made easy by their knowing each others' loyalties, prejudices, and peculiarities for decades. Their casual disparagement of my iconography (the Kennedys) hurt and their racial jokes offended.

Revolution and counterrevolution were to disturb "the boys" and the quiet of good old Noble Street, which looked the same on the surface but was already altered in ways that stabbed the returning native with nostalgia. The soda fountain and tables were gone—collateral damage from the civil rights movement—from Scarborough Drug Store where so many afternoons at the movies had ended in the comfort of a familiar place and familiar faces.

Fears that the civil rights storm would enter and wreck their businesses affected even the sweetest, most generous souls. A friendly haven and the best restaurant in town, The Annistonian, was owned by Alfred Caro, a courtly German Jewish refugee with old-world manners. I have never tasted better, fresher grilled shrimp than Alfred's, which was a favorite luncheon order for me. On July 2, 1964, President Johnson signed the Omnibus Civil Rights Act guaranteeing equal access to all public places. I went to lunch early that day at Alfred's and was surprised to see that little RESERVED signs had bloomed overnight on each table. Alfred was sheepish about the signs and by the end of the week they were gone. The few blacks he eventually served drew objections from white employees of Sears and Roebuck, across the street. But a boycott by whites ended quickly, because it inconvenienced them more than it did Alfred. He questioned their logic, asking, "If you serve them as customers, why not eat with them?" Thus did a momentous passage in the life of the American South come to Anniston, virtually un-noticed. The front door—closed to African Americans for centuries—was now open. The revolution was almost finished. Legal racism was near death.

But there were more immediate and frightening signs that revolution and its counter force would trouble the peaceful city even into the 1970s, and test the inheritors of its founding ideal. The rest of 1964 was packed with tense moments in the contest between change and resistance.

ONE CAUSE OF ALFRED CARO'S nervousness about the public accommoda-tions act was civil rights pickets in downtown Anniston. The local black leader of the time, Nimrod Reynolds, chairman of the Calhoun County Improvement Association, recalls going through Dr. King's moral checklist of negotiating before demonstrating. "We went to the Chamber and begged them to try and deal with this business of hiring practices in their stores."

After two weeks of picketing in March, the Human Relations Council intervened. The executive committee of the Chamber of Commerce had already met with Reynolds. Mayor Dear attended the Chamber meeting and blamed intransigent merchants for the pickets. The picketing went on for thirteen weeks that year, achieving small victories with jobs at Wakefield's department store, Kitchin's discount store, and Berman's fashion store. But by September, the patience of the black leadership was near exhaustion just as hope of a significant breakthrough was rising. On Sunday, September 13, the Improvement Association published a full-page ad headed, "Anniston Manifesto," signed by Reynolds as president, the dentist Dr. Gordon Rogers Jr., first vice president, and two members of the Human Relations Council, Reverend Smitherman and businessman Raleigh Byrd.

The Manifesto asserted, "We have Negroes capable of being secretaries, clerks, managers, policemen, firemen and filling any other position. Are demonstrations, protests, pickets, etc., the only way the Negro can be integrated into our city?" The document's tone was a mixture of appeals and demands, appeals to conscience, to American ideals. It also struck ominous notes: "It has been said that 'It is better to die in the streets than to die on your knees.' We have been on our knees for one hundred years, yea, nearly 350 years. We want equal representation in jobs and accommodations, and we want it now . . ." It was a long, long expression of hope mixed with frustration.

A week later the Snopeses gave their answer—a dynamite bomb exploded outside Miller Sproull's hardware store in west Anniston, cracking the office wall. Miller paid a price for his heroism as a local pioneer in race relations. The Klan harassed his house, and a torrent of abusive, threatening phone calls led him to hire for protection Ted McLaughlin, a Chapel Hill graduate who had played football for Carolina until sidelined by an injury. Armed with a revolver, Ted stayed with Miller and his wife Barbara until the calls and harassment abated. Fortunately, the pistol never had to be fired.

In the Klan's terror campaign, the bombing was followed on October 20 by a series of "white man's rallies" sponsored by the extremist National States Rights Party. Bonfires lit the west Anniston sky as J. B. Stoner, Connie Lynch, and the ubiquitous Kenneth Adams entertained with racist rants under the 10th Street viaduct over the railroad tracks that we used to cross as teenagers to hang out at the Anniston Sandwich Shop. A racist rally there seemed radically out of context. Before the small crowd scattered to escape a shower, the rally organizers hanged in effigy local FBI men Clay Slate and Joe Landers, J. Edgar Hoover, Bobby Kennedy, and James Farmer, chairman of the Congress of Racial Equality (CORE). As a final flourish before leaving town, NSRP leaders presented the city commission with its formal answer to the Manifesto, "Petition for the Redress of Grievance to the Mayor and City Commissioners . . ."

My little band of four or five $85- to $100-a-week reporters and I, then managing editor, did not feel the tension so much as we were fed by it. We were young, indestructible, immortal, and things were popping. It was a helluva story, bigger than we were but we managed to get at least a surface account in the paper. And, being young and stupid, we could not resist the lure of danger. One of my reporters was a close friend from childhood, John McCaa. We were at his house with a mutual friend from Florence, Bobby Lemay, when Johnny Mac got a phone call from a high school acquaintance who was a Klansman and FBI informer. He had a tip for Johnny Mac and they agreed to meet behind Woodstock School. Just in case something went wrong, Bobby and I, armed with revolvers, hid at the entrance to the Kilby property, diagonally across from the rendezvous point with the Klan double agent. He never appeared, thank God. If something threatening had occurred, Bobby and I might have shot each other or Johnny Mac. I should have been fired for behaving so irresponsibly, but I couldn't fire myself. Besides, mortal danger was something that happened to people we wrote about, not us.

Civil rights leaders and good lawmen such as Reynolds and city attorney Bob Field had a more realistic and respectful acquaintance with fear and danger. "I guess all of us were scared," Reverend Reynolds recalled years later. "I was scared a lot of times, no question about that. You could die in a minute; you knew that. These crazy folks didn't care who they killed— either white or black. We weren't fearless but we knew something had to be done, regardless of what happened we knew we had to break through some of the barriers."

One of the people Reynolds and his allies feared was Police Commissioner

Jack Suggs, which surprised me. I liked Jack. I didn't agree with his views on race, but I found his soft-voiced sincerity appealing—and appropriate for the city's top lawman. To all appearances, he enforced the law equally to black and white offenders, an impression that Charlie Doster shared. Apparently, the police commissioner's soft voice and surface fairness masked a private Jack Suggs, a different, forbidding face he revealed only to a few, and only privately. Reynolds thought, "He was a snake." Bob Field also saw a threatening side of Suggs's character that would reveal itself in a bizarre incident the next year.

BY DECEMBER 1964, IT was clear that the public accommodations section of the Civil Rights Act had some bite. Six black men who had been refused service by Anniston business owners filed a federal suit in Birmingham. One of the men was Wedzell Escott, a minister who had been refused service at Adams's service station. Adams told the *Star* he'd been expecting the suit and was quoted by the Associated Press as refusing to talk to city detectives and the FBI. "I don't talk to them boys," he said. "We treat them just like Negroes and tell them to go to . . ."

Adams and his boys had a difficult choice to make in the presidential election of 1964. George Wallace was running his first third-party campaign—red meat to the Adams gang. But that came to an end in July. From then on, the Snopeses were Goldwater men. Senator Barry Goldwater of Arizona, the Republican nominee, was the darling of white voters in the Deep South. He had broken with the Senate Republican leadership and voted against the Omnibus Civil Rights bill. The rock-jawed, wavy-haired senator was no racist, but his far-right conservative principles rejected federal enforcement of civil rights. Further, he knew where the votes were and where they were not. As early as 1961, he had told Southern GOP activists in Atlanta that the party was "not going to get the Negro vote in 1964 or 1966, so we ought to go hunting where the ducks are." Adams was among the Goldwater ducks in Alabama and the Deep South. Goldwater carried Alabama by 77 percent of the white vote and swept the white vote in the rest of the Deep South by a similar landslide, 71 percent.

The hinges of history are hung backward in the Deep South. The doors opened inward to Goldwater in South Carolina, Georgia, Alabama, Mississippi, and Louisiana, welcoming him into the Balkans of America with its never-forgotten history and prejudices. Everywhere else but Goldwater's native Arizona, the doors opened outward, the whole continent welcoming President Johnson and his sense of the rights of man. Unwittingly, Senator Goldwater led a motley parade of White Citizens Council members, Kluxers, and generic racists out of the Democratic Party to install racial prejudice as the founding core of the Southern Republican Party. "It still is," Jimmy Carter agreed on a recent visit to Anniston. "It has been; it always has been, ever since 1964. That's right. I agree completely." The former president and Nobel Laureate spoke with some heat of the 1966 defections to the GOP in Georgia, adding with evident satisfaction, "Four years later they were all defeated, by the way, which is gratifying."

The front page of the *Star* on Wednesday, November 4, was a poster for the opposite paths taken by the nation and the Deep South. The lead story detailed the historic Johnson landslide and the off-lead story was about five Democratic congressmen caught in the Goldwater riptide. Among them was our own congressman Kenneth Roberts, who would have chaired the House Commerce Committee in the new Congress. Roberts contributed to his defeat by a desultory campaign and infrequent visits to his district. The victor was billboard advertising executive Glenn Andrews, who had been a lonely, good-natured GOP pioneer in the days when two votes for the Republican Party in Calhoun County raised suspicions of voter fraud. Andrews was a nice man of moderate views who died in September 2008, just short of his hundredth birthday. He demonstrated moderation in his campaign by sending a signal to the black community that he'd appreciate their vote—though his messenger wasn't exactly a civil rights pioneer. Isaiah Wilkins, country club chef and brother of our family's all-purpose retainer, my pal Eli, brought me a letter endorsing Glenn. I told "Ike" as he left my office to tell the candidate that I said, "You country club Republicans are all the same." To his credit, Glenn got and enjoyed the joke. He served only the single term and was defeated in 1966 by a conservative Democrat, Bill Nichols.

Alabama gained a new majority party but lost national influence and prestige. The conservative prairie fire fanned vigorously by George Wallace had already consumed Congressmen Carl Elliot of Jasper, author of the National Defense Education Act, and Albert Rains who, absent the race issue, might have contended for Speaker of the House. Though the temper of the times meant that white Southern voters regarded the national Democratic Party as a euphemism for forced integration, the winning Republican candidates were not bad men. Jack Edwards in Mobile became an able and progressive public citizen, chairing the University of Alabama trustees. He later recalled with bemusement that his efforts to facilitate black voter registration in his district "were registering votes to defeat me." In Birmingham, the victorious GOP candidate was a liberal-minded Baptist preacher, the Reverend John Buchanan, who later became a leader of People for the American Way. Jim Martin, who became a statewide conservation and environmental leader, filled Rains's old seat in the neighboring industrial city of Gadsden.

The state Republican chairman, Dr. Thomas A. Brigham, gave Governor Wallace credit for the Democratic rout. "Wallace helped mold the people's thinking to oppose the Democratic national party." Everybody knew what that meant. A week after the vote, the *Star* did the numbers, and I wrote a somewhat shell-shocked editorial, "What Have We Done?" In sum, it read, "We have sent five anonymous men to Washington. They will play minor roles in a further diminished minority. We have defeated . . . three men who made our delegation effective, balanced and admired." To back the claim, I quoted a publication of vestal non-partisanship, *Congressional Quarterly*, "Raines, Elliott and Roberts were among the most admired members of the House, influential with both Southerners and Northerners."

Never again would national publications write so admiringly of Alabama's contribution to the nation. We would close out a volatile year as we had so many before, and would so often in future years—in the embrace of our fetish, defeat.

1965, THE YEAR OF Selma and the Voting Rights bill, marks the beginning of the largest social construction project in American history—a bridge from the Old South to a newly discovered and undeveloped land. It spanned a canyon river where the collision of civil rights, civil resistance, and the violent throes of a dying civilization created vicious crosscurrents. Five years later when progressive governors were elected throughout the South the span was secured at the other side of the canyon: a wholly new civilization stretched out ahead with new assumptions and possibilities. The signal achievement of the New South would be the end of legal segregation—a feat that had frightened the Founding Fathers, which even Civil War could not achieve. Southerners, to their amazement, discovered they were mostly comfortable with the new arrangement. In time, there would be a fabulous sprouting of cities, new wealth, a black middle class, cookie-cutter suburbs dotted with MacMansions, as well as failing inner-city schools and traffic congestion worthy of the older industrial cities of the North and West.

But 1965 was just the beginning, a year of promise and portent, which would seize the imagination of the nation and test the mettle of the local knights of noblesse oblige. It was the first year of the emerging Republican majority in the South, founded on old segregationist beliefs. And it was the year a fire lit in Watts triggered a black urban rebellion which, when merged with anti-war protests, destroyed the liberal consensus that had guided the country so effectively, and with such admirable civility.

Who should be the local ringmaster of the circus of grotesques dominating the year but that personable psychopath, Kenneth Adams. The first week of February, Kenneth organized Klan and National States Rights Party pickets of Kitchin's discount store. Claude Kitchin had accepted appointment to the Human Relations Council and had been among the first to hire a black sales clerk. Several members of Kenneth Adams's unruly gang were arrested on orders from Police Chief Lawrence Peek when they refused to halt their loud and threatening march around the store.

Shortly after police broke up the lawless demonstration, Commissioner Suggs called the chief to his office. "The conversation was just one of the craziest I'd ever heard in my life," former city attorney Bob Field recalled. "He told Lawrence that he had instructed him previously that, before they used any force at all on any of these things, he'd have to consult with him. He said something like he had a gun on him and, just in case Lawrence was planning on shooting him; he had a gun, too, and would shoot. The chief protested, 'You know I didn't come here to shoot anybody, and it's my job to maintain law and order out there. I thought I was just doing what I was supposed to do.' Suggs suspended Lawrence and when the chief left, Suggs said to me and Miller Sproull, who also was in the room, 'I want you to be a witness to this because if he does anything like this again, I'm going to fire him.' Miller said something to the effect, 'Well, I'm glad I was here, too, because as far as I'm concerned you're not going to fire him. All he was doing was doing his job. I hope he keeps on doing it.' That's the way the conversation ended." Field's story left me with the impression that underneath Suggs's quiet, competent exterior was a mind that had dark and turgid twists.

Kitchin's was targeted again on March 17, when a man later identified as Billy Mack Quick, a local outlaw, released a tear gas canister in the store. In response, the store, the city, and the *Star* offered an $850 reward for the attacker's arrest and conviction. Mayor Dear called it "a cowardly act . . . not in keeping with the manly, level-headed spirit of this city." The next afternoon's *Star* editorialized, ". . . this community heard an expression from one individual who would make of Anniston another Selma—with all of the loss of dignity and good reputation that would come in such an event."

"Another Selma." Selma had been seared into my consciousness, as it had been to the nation and much of the world on Sunday, March 7. That was "Bloody Sunday," the date that Alabama state troopers and mounted sheriff's deputies set upon peaceful marchers with a level of brutality that was to make the Edmund Pettus Bridge a battleground as memorable as Chateau Wood or Guadalcanal. It was the starting point on March 21 for the march from Selma to Montgomery—a trek which in distance was dwarfed by Mao Zedong's Long March but which would make a similar impact on its society. Five months later on August 6, President Johnson signed the Voting Rights Act of 1965. It was a death sentence for legal racism and the more blatant variety of Southern demagoguery.

At the paper and among community leaders in those solemn days, there was a determination that carried an undertone of controlled desperation: We can't let *that* happen here. What united us was not so much a conviction that we occupied a higher moral peak as it was fear of the disorder and shame that would be visited on our hometown. Ten days after news of the tear gas bomb at Kitchin's, civic soldiers stepped forward to counsel calm acceptance of the Civil Rights Act. A front-page editorial on Sunday, March 20 (the day before the start of the second, successful Selma-to-Montgomery march), called attention to a full-page ad on page 5A. There, row after row of more than five hundred well-recognized local citizens, Josephine and me among them, signed the ad. Under the headline, WHERE WE STAND!, the copy said that the ". . . community must react to this new situation confronting us in a responsible, realistic and thoughtful manner . . ." and concluded, "Communication must be maintained between the races within the community."

The *Star's* rare front-page editorial, at the top of the page under the nameplate, said the advertisement asked only one thing: "That is a chance to avoid the tragedy that has overtaken other Southern communities when only the voices of the extremists speak."

EVENTS CROWDED THAT YEAR, practically stumbling over each other: On April 2, U.S. District Judge H. H. Grooms issued an injunction requiring Kenneth Adams and three other businessmen to serve Negro customers. The others were Jimmy Gardner of Gardner's Bakery and Cafeteria, Lee Backus of Lee's Drive-In and Victor L. Robertson of Vic's Café. Adams said he would comply, "I don't want to go to the federal penitentiary." At the end of the month, City School Superintendent J. Reavis Hall announced plans for the desegregation of Anniston schools by the fall.

In the tug of war between reason and reaction, reaction would have its day: Mother's Day again, when the Klan used Anniston to stage a rally, march, and recruiting drive—to the intense, worried irritation of community leaders. A reluctant city commission granted permission for a march downtown and a rally in City Auditorium. I watched with a sparse crowd at 10th and Noble as the line of more than a hundred white-robed Klansmen, most from other cities, strolled in unmilitary imprecision up 10th Street and turned left onto Noble Street, their peaked wizard hats incongruous against the familiar Victorian buildings. There was an air of unreality about the silent marchers, as if they were playing themselves in a movie. But they were there all right, and they joined with others, many women among them, in a standing ovation at a post-parade news conference for their leadership,

Imperial Wizard Robert M. Shelton of Tuscaloosa and Grand Dragons Robert Creel of Alabama and Calvin Craig of Georgia. Presiding at the meeting was W. O. (Bill) Chappell, who later would become a successful inventor and cease his Klan affiliation. A more persistent racist was guest speaker Dr. Edward Fields of Birmingham, representing the National States Rights Party, and the only speaker to use the word, "Nigger."

Shelton had done my family a courtesy during Dad's declining years. The state's chief Kluxer was at his usual post in the lobby of the Stafford Hotel in Tuscaloosa when Dad entered, accompanied by his black driver. Dad ordered two single rooms for himself and the driver, and they both went to their rooms, Dad calm and the driver nervous. Downstairs, Shelton called the *Star*. He got general manager Ralph Callahan. "Mr. Callahan," said the Imperial Wizard, "Colonel Ayers has just checked in with a Negro driver. Now we respect the Colonel and wouldn't want any harm to come to him, but I can't control all my men. It would be best if you could persuade him to come home." Ralph thanked Shelton and immediately called Buford Boone, publisher of the *Tuscaloosa News*. Mr. Boone said he would alert the Tuscaloosa police but agreed that the prudent thing was for Dad to return home. Ralph called Dad's room and invented a problem at the paper that required Dad's personal involvement. They then left the hotel for the drive back to Anniston, Dad completely unaware that their car had an escort, front and back, of Tuscaloosa detectives until the caravan reached the Jefferson County (Birmingham) line.

A less benign presence three days after the Klan rally shattered the bucolic calm of the small cluster of rural houses aptly named Friendship Community. A bomb exploded in the sanctuary of the Pine Ridge CME Church, which black members of the rural community had built eleven years before with hands-on devotion. "No, I'm not really fine," said one of the members, Mrs. Hattie Adams, correcting herself. "I could just scream, scream, scream." Again, community leaders immediately met violence with action. Within twenty-four hours, $2,000 had been raised for repairs to the church—the first $600 coming from the board of the Committee of 500, publishers of the "Where We Stand" statement. The *Star* added $250, and among three front-page stories was a box suggesting where donations should be mailed. The two radio stations, Dad's WHMA and Tom Potts's WDNG contributed $100 apiece as did nine local industries.

The bombing of that little church, the second certainly Klan-related bombing, coming on the heels of the rally, made me angry—which might explain such extensive coverage of an incident in which there were no injuries—anger which fired the response of local leaders. Birmingham might have been spared what amounted to racist carpet-bombing if it had had a more proactive civic leadership and newspaper. Diane McWhorter's history of 1960s Birmingham detailed dozens of bombings there.

IF ANNISTON'S LEADERSHIP NEEDED a scourge to keep its focus, Kenneth Adams was happy to wield it. On June 11, his gang gathered in front of Anniston High School to insult the school board. But later that summer, the community's leadership faced its severest test and most grievous shock.

On Wednesday July 14, other National States Rights Party members joined Adams for two nights of "White Man's Rallies" on the courthouse steps. My reporter friend John McCaa covered the opening rally. Johnny Mac was a descendant of the founding Noble family. We had grown up together in Grace Church, built by the other founding family, the Tylers. If fate had better matched his early desires with opportunities, Johnny Mac would have been a fine Episcopal priest. His background may have influenced the way he chose to begin his account of the opening rally: "Standing before some 110 persons assembled Wednesday night at the courthouse steps, the Reverend Connie Lynch greeted his audience 'in the Name of Jesus Christ' and advocated the murder of Negroes." Joining the Reverend Mr. Lynch were the omnipresent Kenneth Adams; Charles Keyes, publisher of a local racist news sheet; and J. B. Stoner, attorney for the NSRP, whom we would meet again in another venue. A sample of the Reverend Mr. Lynch's dementia, which ignited dangerous passion in members of the audience, are these highlights: Politicians who give concessions to blacks will be hanged when the NSRP seizes power; the Negro should be deported or exterminated; the streets will soon "run red with blood." He reiterated his desire to murder Dr. King and later told the *Star* (I was listening on an extension): "If it takes killing to get the

Negroes out of the white man's streets and to protect our constitutional rights, then I say, yes, kill 'em.'"

In the crowd Thursday night was Damon Strange, a 25-year-old employee of Kenneth Adams, and his 28-year-old friend Jimmie Glen Knight, there with his wife Betty. The young man with the strangely poetic name, Damon (a symbol of selfless friendship in Greek mythology) became increasingly intoxicated with visions of Aryan power. He had fallen under the influence of Adams and his crowd, Betty Knight told *Star* editor-at-large John Fleming in 2009. "He had to prove he was worthy to be a Klan member," she said. "They didn't exactly put him up to it, but the let him know he had to do something to be a member." The decisive moment for Damon came the night before the rally at a bull session in one of Adams's gas stations. The lights were out, the pumps were turned off, they got to talking to him, telling him he had to prove himself."

Next night when the Reverend Mr. Lynch ran out of inflamed rhetoric and the rally broke up about 10:20, four black laborers had finished their shift at Alabama Pipe Co., and headed home in Jeremiah Adams's 1957 black Pontiac Chieftain. Among them was 38-year-old Willie Brewster, a complete stranger to civil right leaders, whose hobby was tending his vegetable garden. Adams was driving when the working men stopped for gas at the Tenneco station on West 10th Street. As they paid for $3 worth of gas and a quart of transmission fluid, three young white men in a dull yellow 1955 Chevrolet with twin exhausts and no front bumper pulled up and parked near the station's office. The driver was Johnny Ira DeFries, 25. In the front passenger seat was Clarence Thomas Lewis Blevins, 26, and Damon Strange was in the back seat. All three had been at the rally. The black Pontiac's owner, Jeremiah Adams, complained of aching feet and Brewster volunteered to drive the rest of the way. It was a fateful courtesy.

When they left the station the dull yellow "hot rod" followed. Four miles west of Anniston on Highway 202 at approximately 11:30, a few feet west of Forsyth's Store, the rear window exploded, peppering the men in the back seat with glass. Henry Beavers was knocked to the floorboard, slightly injured. The 48-year-old worker wasn't aware that a second shot had been fired. The heavy deer-hunting slug tore a three-quarter inch hole in the center of Brewster's back, severing his spine. Brewster called out "I'm shot, I'm dying, take the wheel," and slumped over. The Pontiac veered to the left as a third shot from the hot rod missed. The gunmen's car turned sharply right on a county road, tires squealing. Jeremiah Adams took the wheel from Brewster, guiding the Pontiac to a stop. He woke people in a nearby house, called state troopers and an ambulance.

At about the same time, Jimmie Knight was finishing a six-pack with his brother-in-law Bill Rozier and their wives at Rozier's house on Eulaton Road. The six-pack finished, Rozier and Knight decided to get more beer. As they were getting into Betty Knight's station wagon, Johnny DeFries drove up, his souped-up Chevy so hot it was smoking. "We shot us a nigger," said Johnny and took a double-barrelled, hammerless shotgun from the rear floorboard. "Find those empty shells," he barked to the occupants. Johnny asked Bill if he could leave the car there but Bill said he didn't want to get involved. Johnny headed home alone.

Knight followed in his station wagon with Bill, Damon, and Lewis Blevins to Johnny's house where he put the Chevy in the garage. Johnny got in the back seat with Damon and Lewis and said he wanted to go out to the scene of the shooting. Jimmy asked where, and from the back seat came "John Hardy Hill." As they drove west on Highway 202, Jimmy heard from the back seat, "Damon put a punkin' ball in a nigger's head." Damon added, "Yeah, I had to lean halfway out the window to get a shot at him." Jimmie asked, "How many did you get?" and Damon replied, "I know I got the driver 'cause the car veered to the left, I believe it went into a ditch." Soon, they came to the black Pontiac with the shattered rear window. In front of the car, Willie Brewster lay dying. "Don't stop, don't stop!" the back seat passengers called out together. Jimmie drove on to Coldwater Road, turned off and headed for Sparks Drive-In. There, he got out, ordered five beers and flirted with the waitress, Brenda Hamm. They downed their beers before Jimmy dropped off his passengers, picked up Betty and drove home: An anti-climactic ending to the Snopses's big night out.

Brewster's 31-year-old wife Lestine learned what had happened when Jeremiah Adams came to her door. He was carrying a box of groceries that Willie had bought for the family. The box was covered with blood.

Two front-page stories Friday afternoon reported the assault and detailed the modest life of the man clinging to life in Anniston Memorial Hospital. Deep anger mingled with a wave of anxiety for my hometown when I heard the news. I sensed the approach of the great ship Controversy, packed with sincere and hardened, professional protesters, bristling with media paraphernalia, its giant propellers boiling the streets of our little city. When I sat down at my manual Royal typewriter to do the lead editorial, the words just flowed:

> Do we start it now, Anniston? Do we stand back silently and let the whole ugly box of racial violence open up? Do we do nothing and invite into our city the unwanted and unneeded ranks of the contestants who can take over our town and make of it a nationally watched battlefield? Anniston can have it—right now, another Selma, another Bogalusa! Think about it. Think about your children. Think about your personal safety in your own home. Think about the future of your community. Do we start now?

Friday afternoon, when news of the nightrider assault reached the community, the phone rang in my newsroom cubicle office. It was Dr. T. C. Donald, an internist and founder of a clinic which drew the most talented specialists in the city and inspired spiteful gossip from some older practitioners of the healing arts. His voice conveyed anger and urgency, "We've got to do something." We decided to meet that evening at 6 at his house, the highest point of Hillyer High Road overlooking Choccolocco Valley. Our plan was to raise pledges toward a $20,000 reward through a telephone pyramid—each calling three who agreed to call three, who in turn would call three others, and so on. By midnight, the hours whirring by in a blur, we had collected almost three hundred pledges who also agreed to sign their name to a full-page ad in Sunday's *Star*.

Sunday morning a story at the top of Page 1 called attention to the ad on Page 5-A. There, a headline in 96-point Railroad Gothic blared in all capital letters: $20,000 REWARD! Four long columns of instantly recognizable names declared:

We, as a community, are determined that those who advocate and commit secret acts of violence will not control this community.

We are determined to fight with the weapons of law to retain the dignity of this community and to punish those who struck down a respectable and industrious citizen.

Therefore, we, the undersigned, pledge the sum of $20,000 to the person who supplies information leading to the arrest and conviction of those responsible for the shooting Thursday night of Willie Brewster."

Sunday's editorial, written when I thought Brewster might live, said to Willie Brewster ". . . that he is not alone at this moment, that the persons who brought him to the point of death, who have crippled him, are not just his enemies. They are enemies of us all, and we stand together in opposition to them."

Lestine took the children, Katrina, 5, and Willie Jr., 6, to see their father. As Willie held his Dad's hand, the elder Brewster told his son he would have to be "the man of the family." His wife then took the children to stay with friends and family and kept a vigil at his bedside for two days. She was there Sunday afternoon at 5:15, when he died quietly. Monday afternoon's editorial, "In A Man's Dying," reflected my bitterness. "A modest man," it began,

. . . known and loved only by family and a small circle of friends, had become a martyr, a symbol:

We have had our generals and our gallant heroes. Now we have our Willie Brewster.

We have had our scientists, our statesmen, our men of industry and commerce. Now we have our Willie Brewster.

We have built our schools and churches. We have extolled our past and sung glad songs of our future.

And we have made a society which produced the murderer of Willie Brewster . . .

In later years at professional meetings, during discussions about objectivity in journalism, I had to admit we weren't objective in our crusade to "get" Willie Brewster's murderer. There isn't a good answer to the question: "What is the objective view of racist nightrider murder?" The crusade began right away. A page one graphic told potential witnesses to the crime how to secretly give information and get the reward, raised Monday to $21,000 by Governor Wallace's offer of $1,000 from State funds. I penned the graphic on a lined page of a reporter's notebook. It read: "John Doe did it. Signed XYZ123." An accompanying story explained that the informer should keep a copy of the code he used in giving information to law officers or executives of the *Star*. Later in the week, on the advice of investigators, the front-page graphic became more detailed: "I saw John Doe in his 2-door, blue, 1965 car speeding west on Hwy 202 at 11:45 Thursday night with another man in the front seat. He was all fired up after the rally. Signed: XYZ 123."

There were no breaks in the Brewster case, as far as we knew at the paper, as July turned to August. In reality, the case had already been pretty well wrapped up. Jimmie Knight had been a paid informer for FBI agent Joe Landers and so Landers thought Knight would know something about the shooting. He talked to Knight, who told him enough to make the case interesting. Landers passed along what he knew to the state investigator, a good one, Lieutenant Harry Sims. Sims had been in Mobile the night Brewster was shot but was summoned home by Trooper Capt. B. R. (Billy) Bishop. Sims talked to Knight shortly after returning to Anniston on Friday. After news of the $20,000 reward hit the paper, Knight's civic conscience was awakened. Investigators found him powerfully motivated to tell what he knew, and he knew a lot. Sims and the FBI agree that it was the reward that solved the case. On a Saturday, less than a month after Willie Brewster died, Jimmie Knight gave Sims a detailed account, which he signed on the second floor of the Calhoun County Jail.

The nights were pleasantly cool, averaging in the mid-60s, during that summer in Anniston. On one of those evenings in the first week in August when the family was dining at Mother's house, I got a telephone tip that there may have been a break in the Brewster case. The police were holding Larry Kissinger, a pleasant young man who helped bedridden older people. He was one of the simple people who were easily manipulated by the force of

Kenneth Adams's personality. Kissinger was telling state investigator Harry Sims, city attorney Bob Field, and city detectives everything he knew about plans to kill a black person. He didn't know a lot of specifics but had good, helpful background information.

Evidently, he knew enough to worry Kenneth who had some friends sign a bond to get Kissinger out of jail. The young man was afraid and didn't want to leave the jail. Field told police sergeant Bill Morrow that the bond was not legal until it had Kissinger's signature, and he wouldn't sign. That set up another confrontation with Police Commissioner Suggs. Field recalls an angry phone call threatening "heads would roll" and demanding, "They are down there with a good bond. I don't want to be putting up with that kind of stuff!" Field stiff-armed Suggs with, "You don't have to be putting up with anything. The bond is no good until the defendant signs it. He's got to sign it, too, and he doesn't want to sign it."

At about the time bail was rejected, I arrived downtown. An event was going on in City Auditorium so there was no parking place on the block leading to the police department and jail on 12th Street. I parked on 11th and began to walk the long, dark block to the jail. As I walked north on the deserted street, I saw three men walking toward me. It was Kenneth Adams, accompanied on either side by rough-looking men. We met in the middle of the block. I was scared, but also conscious of how I would look in any future account of the altercation. Putting up a brave front, I said, "Okay, Kenneth, there are three of you. You can whip me, but you better do a good job of it, because I'll be after you again tomorrow." I didn't have time to savor that scene in the future movie—courageous editor spitting in the face of danger. Kenneth's reply ruined my melodramatic moment, "Aww, Brandy, we're not going to whip you. You'll holler and scream, and get us in trouble." Deflated, but grateful to be in one piece, I made my way to the police station. Sergeant Morrow was polite but incommunicative.

Behind the scenes another comic charade was being staged, starring J. B. Stoner. Kenneth and his allies were increasingly anxious about what Kissinger might reveal and unaware that Jimmie Knight had talked. They wanted to get Kissinger away from the authorities. Stoner represented Adams and company in a habeas corpus hearing before Circuit Judge Robert Parker, a tobacco-chewing, country-talking rookie judge whose liberal credentials (if he had any) were well-camouflaged. Country he might be, but he was also fair and smart. Before the hearing could be held, a squadron of FBI agents came to City Jail and spirited Kissinger away. Prior to the formal hearing, Judge Parker called Field. "Have you got him?" the judge asked.

"No, sir," answered Field. The judge wanted to know where he was. Field, not knowing if he was flirting with contempt, said, "I don't really know. I think he's in the Cleburne County jail."

The judge, broadly hinting, told Field he had the perfect defense. "What's that?" asked Field, not yet sure of his footing with a new judge.

"The defense is, you don't have him. There is no answer to that. That's it."

If Field was wary of Parker, the judge was unsure of how the FBI regarded him. The federal agents, he thought, might believe he was sympathetic to Adams because he had defended him in an assault case.

At the hearing, Stoner derided Police Chief Lawrence Peek, "You're the police chief and you don't know where he is?" The chief replied, "All I did was follow instructions. I was told to turn him over to some FBI agents and that's what I did." Judge Parker dismissed the writ of habeas corpus.

Adams and his gang had good reason to worry. Kissinger was telling the FBI everything he knew. On August 5, an "urgent" teletype to FBI Director J. Edgar Hoover reported that Kenneth Adams had told Larry Kissinger "we have some work to do," blowing up the *Anniston Star* and the Reverend Dr. Phil Noble's First Presbyterian Church. The FBI dispatch explained that the *Star* "has been recently carrying articles and editorials criticizing the segregationist policies of the Adams group," and that Phil Noble had been chairman of the local Human Relations Council. Local FBI agent Joe Landers didn't tell Phil or me about the bombing threat, but he did tell me that I had made it to the top of the Klan's hit list. Surprised and flattered by the honor, I was also concerned and asked Joe if there was anything I should do. He said, "No, we keep a pretty close watch on them, but I wouldn't have a couple of beers after work at one of those dives out on Highway 202." I think he was referring to Sparks' Café. I took his advice.

As it turns out there was reason to be concerned. An arsenal of ninety-eight sticks of dynamite, thirty-one blocks of TNT, hand grenades, and ammunition were stolen by James Willie Roberts and his son-in-law from a bunker at Fort McClellan one night and delivered to a building behind Adams's house. Adams warned the men, including James Leroy Price, to keep quiet about the theft. On Friday, August 20, Adams was arraigned and jailed on federal charges in connection with the theft. Roberts pled guilty, but Adams was found not guilty at his trial.

MEANWHILE, AS PROSECUTORS BUILT their case against Strange, the countdown began to September 2 when city schools would be desegregated under the Freedom of Choice system. On a warm, partly cloudy Thursday, September 2, Anniston and Calhoun County schools were quietly desegregated—eight politically and legally contentious years after voluntary integration in three North Carolina cities. It was not known how many African American children actually attended that first day, but 20 had registered in the county system and 50 to 75 in the city system. That very evening, Governor Wallace met with the State Board of Education and released a statement advising schools to halt desegregation unless specifically ordered to go forward by a federal court. The board noted that the legislature in regular session had urged a freeze on integration until a constitutional test of the orders had been resolved. An "unnamed" local school official (an irritated Superintendent J. Reavis Hall) fumed, "Desegregation plans had to be in the hands of the Office of Education by June. They've known that and they're just making it difficult." Score one more act of futility in Wallace's and Alabama's obsessive devotion to defeat.

Calamity would be avoided by Anniston three times in as many months, surely through Divine compassion. I was reminded of the passage from Jonah 3:10: "When God saw what the Ninevites did, how they turned from their evil ways, God changed his mind about the calamity that He had said He would bring upon them; and He did not do it."

The forces of disorder were aligned perfectly to make Anniston the next civil rights battleground—a three-TV-network contest between, on one side, the SCLC, NAACP, and CORE; arrayed on the other side would be the NSRP and the KKK. The scenario would play out like this: Damon Strange would be tried for Willie Brewster's murder and found not guilty.

It was a rarity for a white man in the South of that time to be convicted of murdering a black. SCLC would start demonstrations, Kenneth Adams's boys would do something crazy and the whole civil rights/media apparatus would descend on our small town, turning everything and everybody topsy-turvy. My heart sank contemplating what might lie ahead as the trial date neared. The distance between appearance and reality were so close that to do the honest thing might well appear to outside observers to be racist or weak. If we were honest, the paper couldn't condemn a not-guilty verdict because the state had no physical evidence and no eyewitness. Neither could we say there was justice in targeting Anniston as the whipping boy for civil resistance. We would have to say that was not fair and the paper would look mealy-mouthed—at best.

As the trial was about to start, old friends from the national media arrived, among them Gene Roberts, then Atlanta bureau chief of the *New York Times* and Jack Nelson of the *Los Angeles Times*. Gene deepened my anxiety by repeating a conversation with the flamboyant Atlanta civil rights warrior Hosea Williams: "The one thing the movement needs that it hasn't had in a long time," he told Gene, "is a good ass-whippin', and there are some mean folks over in Anniston that can give us one." The marches were already planned, the protest leaflets printed, and neatly stacked at Nimrod's church. *That's just great*, I thought with bitter irony when I heard Hosea's message. *Anniston's Armageddon starts now.*

The first near-calamity followed the indictment and arrest of Blevins and DeFries by the August grand jury, which had been recalled Friday, August 27. Damon Strange was also indicted but he wasn't jailed until Kenneth Adams brought his employee in early Monday morning. All three were out on bail September 14, and they were deeply suspicious that one of their friends, probably Knight, had turned state's witness. That afternoon Jimmie went to their old hangout, Sparks Café on Hunter Street. As he nursed his beer, Damon Strange and his brother, Richard walked in. Instantly, the air was charged between Knight and the Strange brothers. A fight broke out and Jimmie got a nasty gash across the face. He heard one of them threaten, "We're going to kill you," and saw Damon draw a derringer. Jimmie drew his .22 pistol "faster than I've ever seen a gun pulled before," a witness said.

They fired simultaneously. Jimmie hit Damon in the chest and Damon grazed Jimmie's hand forcing him to drop his pistol. Damon went down. Richard picked up Jimmie's gun as the state's key witness vaulted the bar and fled out the back door. Richard followed, steadied his aim on the door frame at the zigzagging Knight and pulled the trigger: Click. Click. Click. There had been only one bullet in the chamber.

Damon recovered, and the trial began Monday, November 29, under tight security from state troopers and sheriff's deputies before the rookie judge, Robert Parker, who was a model of firm fairness. During jury selection, defense counsel J. B. Stoner objected to the presence of two black men in the venire. Judge Parker allowed them to be seated after asking if their association with civil rights organizations would prejudice them and they had answered, "no." Kenneth Adams, who employed Strange and DeFries, sat at the defense table as if he were co-counsel. The judge asked him to take a seat with the other spectators.

Another calamity threatened when a trial juror, Jacksonville truck driver and city councilman Olin Deason, fell ill. State law required a mistrial if any juror had to be replaced during the trial. Deason had a miserable time of it, dogged by nausea all week but hung on through the trial's end Friday.

Spectators in the balcony of old Courtroom One, and on the wooden benches below, were miniaturized by its vaulted walls and cathedral-sized windows. High above the judge's dais, a portrait of white-haired John C. Calhoun stared down with an expression of wild urgency on the spectators: a mixture of suits and coveralls, cheap dresses, and, here and there, a smattering of designer-clothed ladies. Watching wordlessly from the balcony was Willie Brewster's widow, Lestine, a slight figure in the huge courtroom.

Careful, low-keyed Circuit Solicitor Clarence Williams built a strong case with a number of witnesses who placed Strange and the co-defendants at the white man's rally and at the service station where Brewster and his co-workers stopped for gas, and he pumped the state's star witness Jimmie Glen Knight for every detail he had given in his statement to investigator Harry Sims. Stoner hammered away at Knight, but couldn't shake his testimony. In later assessments, Judge Parker, Sims, and one of the defendants, Bill Rozier, agreed that Stoner was a sub-par lawyer. Justice achieved by stealing a man's brains. Regardless, it was a confident, even cocky Stoner who rested his case. In the foyer, Josie struck up a conversation with the short, pudgy NSRP lawyer who boasted, "J. B. stands for Jersey Bull." She was struck by his "good-natured, courteous avowals of hatred and bigotry." Propped against a courthouse wall, he chuckled and tried to shock her with: "The only thing I find wrong with Hitler is that he didn't exterminate all those six million Jews he's credited with." Her interview was a page one feature Sunday, unsigned for security reasons. She had been followed during the trial two days in a row to our house on Keith Avenue. The following car, which had no official markings, paused until she entered the house, then drove off.

The jury was composed of foreman Brandon R. Rigney, owner of Rigney Typewriter and Repair, a bank officer, a farmer, a retired fireman and nine others, who started their deliberations Wednesday afternoon at 1:30. Two hours later, Dr. Jerre Watson was called to attend to poor Mr. Deason, threatening a mistrial yet again. Stoner confidently predicted an acquittal or "the worst we can get is a mistrial." He wasn't far from being right—in the beginning. The first vote was eight for acquittal and four for conviction. The next tally was a six to six tie; that mysterious process in which the desire to conform dissolves bit by logical bit was underway. The tie vote held until they were sequestered for the night. By noon Thursday the vote tilted toward guilty as the foreman's poll showed only 2 for acquittal. At 2 p.m. the ballots were unanimous and the jurors debated the severity of the sentence for the next hour and ten minutes. At long last, they agreed on murder in the second degree. It had been a close thing, rare for the South of the time.

God had done for Anniston what he did for the Ninevites, changed his mind about the calamity he was poised to deliver. J. B. Stoner was shocked and Hosea Williams was deflated. If the "movement" was depressed at losing a new battleground, I was grateful. My Sunday piece reflected relief, with a touch of hyperbole:

> These twelve . . . stood in the white hot glare of controversy and brought in a decision. No one who did not stand there with them can fault them for that decision . . . It was an historic decision, and by their decision law and order stands higher, the South stands higher, we all stand

higher. But no one in the South stands higher today than these twelve good men and true.

EPILOGUE: WHEN DAMON STRANGE washed windshields at Kenneth Adams's gas station, customers noted the fingers of his right hand were tattooed: L . . . O . . . V . . . E. No one will ever have a chance to untangle the Freudian knots in Strange's head because, among other shortcomings, he was a lousy shot—in a fair gunfight.

He was also a serial outlaw. In March of '66, while his conviction was on appeal, Damon and a brother, John, came upon a white textile worker sitting in a car with a black man at 15th and Glen Addie. The Strange brothers made the 42-year-old man get into their car, drove him to rural Buttermilk Road, and beat him—for the mortal offense of casual conversation with a black man. The Strange brothers were charged with assault with intent to murder. Released on a bond signed by Kenneth, the next week Damon was in jail again, in Guntersville, charged with driving while intoxicated. (It is a Southern thing that Kenneth Adams and I were on a first-name basis.)

Weeks later, Damon lost his last gunfight—with auto mechanic Billy Claude Clayton in the parking lot of a favorite hangout, Sparks Café on Hunter Street. Clayton shot Damon in the chest and finished him off with two bullets in the back of his head. Twenty-one years later, Clayton's stepson gunned down his stepfather with shotgun blasts outside Clayton's garage on Highway 202, a road with scar tissue of history. The Snopses devour their own.

Forty years after his father's death, following a career in the Army and a good job at Anniston Army Depot, with children of his own, Willie Brewster Junior's anger had cooled. He told an interviewer soberly that he wasn't sure justice had been done, and asked the unanswerable question: why? Like his father, he takes pleasure in gardening, and broke into a wide grin when his wife, Doris, complimented his tomatoes.

Lestine Brewster was 71 in the spring of 2009 and drew some consolation from the thought, "I do believe, as bad as it was, that he did have something to do with making things better."

In 1989, Willie Brewster entered an archive of a violent era. In front of

Morris Dees's Southern Poverty Law Center—an incongruous institution in Montgomery, the Cradle of the Confederacy—thin sheets of water gently cascade over a nine-foot wall of black granite and across a thigh-high saucer. The monument, designed by the architect of the Vietnam Memorial, Maya Lin, is a legendary circle of forty civil rights martyrs. One of the names etched there is Willie Wallace Brewster.

Above left: Brandt Ayers in the side yard of his home, 818 Glenwood Terrace, Anniston, Alabama, ca. 1941. Above right: Portrait of Dr. T. W. Ayers wearing medals awarded by two Chinese presidents for his work in China, ca. 1924. Below: Dr. Ayers (right) with Col. Ayers (left) at Dr. Ayers's home in Atlanta.

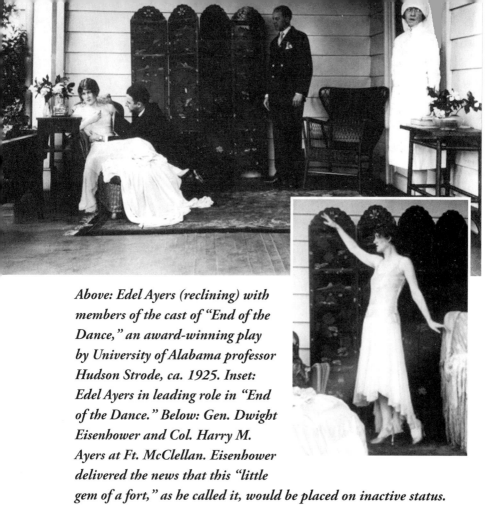

Above: Edel Ayers (reclining) with members of the cast of "End of the Dance," an award-winning play by University of Alabama professor Hudson Strode, ca. 1925. Inset: Edel Ayers in leading role in "End of the Dance." Below: Gen. Dwight Eisenhower and Col. Harry M. Ayers at Ft. McClellan. Eisenhower delivered the news that this "little gem of a fort," as he called it, would be placed on inactive status.

Above: Col. Ayers with Gov. John Patterson at a parade honoring Ayers, ca. 1960. Below: Col. Ayers receiving the "Ernie Pyle" award from Terry Sanford, future governor of North Carolina, ca. 1960.

Left to right: Sam Heyman, Bruce Kullman, Captain Brandy Ayers, Harry Hollins, Karl Voit, Mr. Wilson.

Above: Brandt Ayers as tennis team captain, the Wooster School, 1953. Right: John D. Verdery, Headmaster, the Wooster School, 1953.

Above: Ayers, John F. Kennedy, Mrs. Luther Hodges, and others (including Ayers' family friend "Loutoo" Johnson, far right) at a Kennedy stop at the N.C. Governor's Mansion, Raleigh, 1960. Below: Ayers (front right) at a White House luncheon for Alabama editors hosted by President Kennedy (center right), May 14, 1963.

Above left: Nimrod Quintus Reynolds, Anniston civil rights leader who was stabbed during the Incident at the Carnegie Library in 1963. Above right: James Tinsley, a Tuskegee Institute-educated tailor, was heavily involved in the Committee of Unified Leadership in Anniston. Below: John Nettles, whose house was fired upon during the Anniston riots in 1971.

Above: Bill Jones was recruited by interim police chief Gerald Powell (below left) to reform the police department during a tense time in Anniston. Below right: Willie Brewster and his wife, Lestine, in a portrait prior to Brewster's brutal murder by white supremacists in 1965.

Above: George Wallace visiting Ayers's office at the Anniston Star *during his 1974 campaign. Below: Chris Waddle, an editor, and Ayers confront protesters at the old Anniston Star building.*

Above: Josephine and Brandt Ayers at the medical school built by Ayers's grandfather, Dr. T. W. Ayers, Huanxian, China, 1984. Below: Ayers being greeted at a market day parade, Huanxian, China, 1984.

Above: Ayers over the shoulder of 80-year-old Gen. Giap, architect of the Vietnamese military victory, Hanoi, Vietnam, 1994. Below: Ayers with a delegation led by former ambassador to Germany Martin J. Hillenbrand (front right), Berlin, Germany, 1990.

Top: Ayers with Sen. Edmund Muskie, keynote speaker at the second annual meeting of the LQC Lamar Society, Atlanta, Georgia, 1971. Bottom: Delegation of editors to the Soviet Union. On the right is Lt. Gov. Penko of Irkutsk, Siberia where the meeting was held. Ayers, left, is flanked by James Hoge (at Ayers's left) of the Chicago Sun-Times, *and Lee Huebner of the* International Herald Tribune, *1975.*

Above: Ayers, trustee of the Southern Center for International Studies, with "Secretary of Everything" Elliot Richardson. Inset: Ayers visiting Margaret Griffis, his beloved first-grade teacher and lifelong friend, on the occasion of her 88th birthday, 1999. Below: Josephine and Brandt Ayers with former secretary of defense Donald Rumsfeld.

Above: Ayers (back right) remarking to James Schlesinger at the Southern Center for International Studies' 11th Report of the Secretaries of Defense. Amused colleagues of Schlesinger are from front left Frank Carlucci (1987–89), Schlesinger (1973–75), Caspar Weinberger (1981–87); from back left Donald Rumsfeld (1975–77), Harold Brown (1977–81), Richard Cheney (1989–93). Below: Ayers with former secretary of defense Melvin Laird (1969–73), Southern Center for International Studies, 1997.

To my good friend
Brandt Ayers
Jimmy Carter
10-14-17

Above: Ayers visiting President Jimmy Carter at the White House, 1977. Right: Letter from the president, 1979. Below: Ayers and former president Jimmy Carter meet at the Jimmy Carter Work Project, Anniston, 2003.

To Brandt Ayers

I want you to know how deeply I appreciate your thoughtful words of encouragement.

Your guidance has helped me set forth clearly such national goals as energy security, and will be important in developing the policies we need to meet these goals.

I look forward to your continued counsel as we act together to realize our vision of a strong, renewed America.

Sincerely,

Jimmy

It was good to hear from you & from

Mr. H. Brandt Ayers
Editor and Publisher
The Anniston Star
Post Office Box 189
Anniston, Alabama 36202

Jim Turner's barbershop - two good sources of sound advice - I

And some...

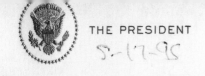

Dear Brandy—

Thanks for your last letter and the
editorial—we're talking more and more
about it—

On the chronology/paternity battle
between you and The Southern, you're right,
about the chronology and closer on paternity.
I had long felt we needed an MEC.—→

                    But— Bill

Above: Clinton note regarding Ayers as the originator of the idea
for an Economic Development Council, 1995. Below: Josephine and
Brandt Ayers congratulating the president-elect, Bill Clinton, Little
Rock, Arkansas, January 1993.

Top: Ayers; U.S. Representative, Alabama native, and civil rights hero John Lewis; and former Gov. John Patterson at Lewis's induction into the Alabama Academy of Honor, October 2011. Patterson was the governor of Alabama 1959–63 and opposed the civil rights movement. He later expressed regret and, with Ayers, sponsored Lewis's nomination to the Academy. Bottom: Ayers at the Anniston Star, *1998. A portrait of his father, Col. Harry M. Ayers, is behind him.*

9

Escape from the South

A fter the great 1965 thunderclaps of the civil rights storm—climaxed by the white man's rallies and the Brewster murder—Josephine and I knew we had returned to a very different place. The dreamy Arcadian endless Saturday afternoons of youth were myths from another civilization. We were soldiers in a war of civilizations that seemed as if it would never end—a civil centrifuge which would whirl for an eternity. An image of that time that I can't shake came during the 1966 campaign when Lurleen Wallace ran for governor as term-limited George's surrogate. A pickup with giant WALLACE posters covering the frame sides of its bed was parked right at the main intersection of 10th and Quintard. A crew of lean, raw-boned men in overalls, unemployed factory and farm workers paid to work in the campaign or Ku Klux Klan volunteers, were slapping WALLACE bumper stickers on nearly every car that entered the intersection. The scene filled me with anger. Those rednecks were raising an army of my own people, wearing the insignia of everything hateful about the South. The Wallace crew worked the intersection for hours and with every passing minute my isolation, my angry, lonely estrangement from my people was reinforced. I think I really and truly hated my beloved South in those days.

Even after passage of the Voting Rights Act in 1965, when the Old South began its five-year descent into history, it seemed as if my own private civil war would go on forever. The memory of racist rallies and Willie Brewster's killing were fresh. We almost became the next Selma or Birmingham and would have if Brewster's murderer hadn't been convicted. My war wasn't entirely with the South but partially with myself, with my ambivalent love for a place that harbored deadly men who also claimed to be Southern. The lonely war dragged on, relieved only by the excitement of the civil rights story. There was to be one year of blissful escape—at Harvard, of all places.

Dad once had mentioned something about a program for journalists at Harvard, but at the time such a tower of intellect seemed unattainable for a young Alabamian. However, when University of North Carolina President Bill Friday encouraged me to compete for a Nieman Fellowship, the prize seemed within reach.

My first try was a disaster. I was advised by a former Fellow, Ray Jenkins, then editor of the *Alabama Journal* in Montgomery, to have a couple of martinis so as to be loose and relaxed for the interview. If I'd met the selection committee right after lunch, I would have been articulate, funny, and at ease. Unfortunately, the interview was late in the afternoon. I got up from a nap, hung over, and left my wits in the hotel room. I began to awake to the downward spiral of the interview when I heard my sponsor, Gene Patterson, the much-admired editor of the *St. Petersburg Times*, his voice rising, "What *do* you believe?!"

Next time, I was cold sober. Ted Sizer, then dean of Harvard's School of Education, told me I won the committee not by the acuity of my journalistic judgment or brilliant command of Southern politics, but with my sense of humor. A wonderfully blunt publisher, the late Bob Chandler of *The Oregonian* in Bend, Oregon, asked a curious question, "Mr. Ayers, would you explain to me just what reason there is for Anniston's being?" With rising panic, I calculated how to answer a question phrased that way. "Mr. Chandler," I replied, "is that an economic . . . or a moral question?" The committee laughed and I was in.

THOUGH I APPROACHED THE highest peak of American intellect with awe—I was a miserable lump of Alabama red clay, fearful that opening my mouth would release all the pent-up ignorance of my region—the year was just as perfect as everyone said it would be. There was one big surprise. Hodding Carter had advised me to get out my civil rights speech because I'd be courted and lionized as a heroic Southern liberal. That was not to be. The academic year was 1967–68. I painfully discovered that no one was interested in anything but the Vietnam War. At a party to welcome new members of Quincy House, the residential house to which I had been assigned as a senior fellow, I wandered into the Junior Tutor's library where

I expected the undergraduates to treat me as an icon of truth and justice. Instead, they peppered me with informed questions about Vietnam. I had dumped the war in a back-of-my-mind box labeled "containment," giving total concentration instead to George Wallace and the civil rights movement. The encounter with the Harvard students was an intellectual lynching, and I was the guest of honor. When I finally escaped, Josephine took one look at me and asked, "What happened to you?" I replied, "Can't you tell? I'm covered from head to toe in dove do-do."

Needless to say, my views on the war evolved during that year and found a comfortable place between doves and hawks—the pro-military, anti-war owlish posture. The Harvard experience also brought me a mind-expanding insight related to the course of study I had set out for my Nieman year, "The consequences of extremism in American political life." Seeking guidance for the project, I invited constitutional history professor Robert McCloskey to lunch. When I told him the title, he said, "You've only got half the question." I was taken aback at first. But when McCloskey went on, "You want to explore the values and consequences of extremism," I felt the pleasant smack of a new insight, a new way of looking at things. Of course, he was right. Every act of extremism from Shays' Rebellion on has its roots in one or more underlying causes that are often obscured by journalistic focus on the actors, and the means through which they act out their grievances. The civil rights movement and anti-war protests were cases in point. The relative value of U.S. extremist movements from past to present might even be measured by a moral bell curve: At one end would be Shays' Rebellion, the civil rights movement at the apex, and at the other end would be the bombers of Birmingham, Oklahoma City, and the World Trade Center.

Oddly enough, this insight made me more rather than less tolerant of George Wallace and his supporters. It also deepened my sense of the tragedy of his misapplied talents. He held out to his people the futile hope of escape from a strange and upsetting life-predicament. It was the very futility of Wallace's reign of excess that set in my stomach a lifelong knot of bitterness at the mess he'd made of governance in my state and at the psychological hangover he left behind: a sense of victimhood, of angry resignation. Wallace was so needy he pandered to the crowd and luxuriated in their adoration—political autoeroticism. His anti-government philosophy grew willy-nilly, not from a carefully crafted vision, but piece by piece in reaction to each of the predestined defeats he suffered. For his people, gulled again by a demagogic politician, he was the leader of another lost cause—another episode in the Deep South's sad love affair with defeat.

In another time, before the racial revolution, Wallace would have been allied with a great man and teacher who had entered my and Josie's lives in the 1960s, U.S. Supreme Court Justice Hugo Lafayette Black, a native of Ashland, Alabama (the town's daily newspaper is the *Star*). Wallace's early alliance with Big Jim Folsom and the non-racist character of Wallace's first gubernatorial campaign had demonstrated his allegiance to Black's New Deal wing of the Democratic Party. The two charismatic leaders could have been connected to each other through the strain of Southern liberalism that championed the "little man" over the moneyed interests. In the 1920s, when Black was first elected to the U.S. Senate, they would have been allies. They would also have been linked by the Ku Klux Klan which Black joined, thus posing the dilemma: How could a great civil libertarian belong to such a de-mented organization? Support for the "little man" over the moneyed interests is the consistent theme that explains that contradiction. Most members of the 1920s Klan were different in character from the KKK bombers of the 1960s. They were aging Populists and free-silver William Jennings Bryan supporters or sons of that generation. Most were neither sadists nor anti-Catholic, nor obsessed with racism (submissive segregation being the norm). They joined a mysterious order, the fraternity of the common man, maybe because the exotic rituals were an exciting contrast with their drab lives and because they felt at home in the company of men who lived similarly hard lives. Among Judge Black's explanations for joining the KKK was advice from Jewish supporters that it would help his campaign, a habit of joining any group who could vote and who would have him (he told Josie and me a hilarious saga of joining the lowly Civitan Club in Birmingham because he'd been snubbed by Rotary, Kiwanis, and Lions). Finally, he explained that the KKK was the liberal wing of the Democratic Party on the dominant economic issue of the time—specifically, it was anti-railroad.

Dad, who poked fun editorially at the KKK as "grown men in bedsheets," originally was a Black supporter. Dad had advised his great friend Tom Kilby that he had been too good a governor and had spent too much political capital to be elected to the Senate. Both Black and Dad told me the story of their separation in the 1926 campaign in virtually the same words. Dad was attending a Black campaign strategy meeting in Birmingham when a call came through for him. When he returned to the room, he said, "Hugo, Tom Kilby has just announced for the Senate." Black responded, "Harry, I know he's a great friend and a fellow townsman. That means you'll have to support him, but Harry, knowing you're a man of integrity, I expect you'll hold in confidence everything you've heard in this room today . . ." Dad was about to reply with an equally graceful speech when Black went on, "Because, Harry, if you don't, we've got plenty to use on you."

Most of the state's political money was drawn to the campaigns of Kilby and John Bankhead Jr., whose political legacy and coal-mining fortune made him the man to beat. But before television, money didn't mean as much in politics as did energy and an issue. Black had those. He had two campaign cars, one for north Alabama and one for south Alabama, which he road in a cyclone of dust into every town, hamlet, and branchhead he could reach, quizzing folks in the general store about their needs, beating the village checker champion in the town square. He campaigned as the champion of the common man. Black put it this way in a letter to a distant relative the previous December: "I am personally of the opinion that there have been so many millionaires and corporation lawyers in the United States Senate that the people rarely ever have a representative. It is my ambition to give them one."

Bankhead and Black sucked the political oxygen out of the state, leaving Kilby gasping for support. Since the 1880s, a Bankhead had represented Alabama in Congress as Speaker of the House and then Senator. John Hollis Bankhead I died in 1920, and John H. Bankhead II wanted to succeed his father in the Senate. He would three years later, but in 1926 he was no match for Black's oratorical fireworks and a campaign so energetic it wore out two automobiles. The results were Black's 71,916 votes to Bankhead's 49,841. Black carried 42 of the state's 67 counties.

Black couldn't have won with such a substantial margin without support of the Klan. That support embarrassed the newly appointed Supreme Court justice in 1937, when Paul Block, the acidic, anti-New Deal Republican publisher of the *Pittsburgh Post-Gazette,* assigned investigative reporter Ray Spriggle to uncover Black's Klan connections. The old story—with fresh documentation—stirred a raging controversy. On September 30, on all three networks, Black addressed a national radio audience, said to be the largest since Edward VIII's abdication. In deliberately undramatic language he expressed devotion to the Constitution and its beating heart, the Bill of Rights, pointed to his Senate service as proof that he was innocent of racial or religious bigotry, said he joined and then resigned from the Klan and concluded by offering his public life to constant inspection and judgment.

Until his career lengthened and the press saw the fully drawn picture of a first-rank civil libertarian, the Klan story would be the subject of suspicion by, for instance, the *New York Times.* The story had a long half-life because the Klan is an incendiary noun, made so by media focus on its demonstrable excesses. But, as the mind-altering insight Robert McCloskey had given me, the 1920s Klan to me was a working-class gargoyle pushed up by the geologic heaves of an amoral decade. Acquisition, greed, and excess were the Trinity of the time, the flapper was its High Priestess, and bathtub gin its communion wine. The Ku Klux Klan was a kind of Moral Majority of its day—hyper-patriotic and super-Christian. Gatsby's circle wasn't in touch with that class because his class didn't go to church and didn't invite blue-collar families to their houses except as gardeners and servants. The working class didn't find a friendly face in the White House either. Presidents Harding and Coolidge weren't exactly liberal friends of the common man. They proclaimed laissez-faire economics, which translated: "Leave the railroads alone to make excessive profits. The government should never interfere with the right of the working man to be exploited in his productive years or to be penniless and sick in old age."

The Klan was a false friend, however, flawed in its philosophy; killing itself by its own excesses. By the middle of Black's first term in the Senate, the Klan was almost impotent. With the coming of the terrible leveling power of the Depression, the optimistic grin of Franklin Roosevelt, and the friendly hand of the New Deal, the reason for the Klan's existence as a mass movement vanished, absorbed into the New Deal as the Populists had been by the Progressive Movement of the teens, when Kilby and Dad were campaigning.

On the Court, as he had in the Senate, Black continued a lifelong habit of study in his library at home, perhaps to fill intellectual gaps left when he bypassed undergraduate studies to enroll in law school at the University of Alabama. He had been an ardent supporter of Roosevelt's New Deal, and so FDR, assured that Black's speech had calmed the storm, stuck by his appointment. Later, Roosevelt named to the Court another loyal friend, Felix Frankfurter, the brilliant Harvard Law School professor. Roosevelt could not have predicted that these two appointees would engage in a bitter fight for leadership of the Court.

Frankfurter was a worldly scholar, adviser to presidents and cabinet officials, and friend to Supreme Court giants such as Oliver Wendell Holmes and Louis Brandeis. He was an agnostic for whom the Law was religion, the Court its temple, and Judges its priests. To Frankfurter, the Divine Tablets were created in the Magna Carta, refined by British judges, and handed to us in a state of perfection so great that only the slightest alteration should be permitted. He had the understandable beliefs of a Jewish immigrant that the Law, the Court, was the only reliable refuge when the unpredictable tides of public opinion were whipped into angry waves by passing fears and passions. If courts and judges were strong enough, they were barrier reefs against the inevitable pogroms.

Black was a self-taught scholar. As a freshman U.S. Senator he annotated the works of Jefferson, studied Aristotle's *Politics* and the economic theories of Veblen and Adam Smith. He was a Southern Baptist who knew that God did not wear black robes. His philosophy was formed by a rural background and law practice in Birmingham in the 1920s when working men and small merchants were virtual serfs to the great corporate interests. Thoroughly American, he believed that the Revolution freed us from British law so Americans would have greater freedoms through the Bill of Rights than British citizens had.

The Alabamian led the Court in protecting the individual from abuse of power through the novel theory that the Fourteenth Amendment meant that the Bill of Rights applied to the states. To do so, he had to match wits with the unbending Frankfurter, who cautioned: Go slow, not so fast, an inch at a time. The issue which provided the country lawyer from Alabama an opportunity to take a majority of the Court away from the internationally celebrated Harvard intellectual was a free speech case. Harry Bridges, a radical California longshoreman's union leader, was fined for contempt after he sent telegrams to the Secretary of Labor and several newspapers criticizing the judge and threatening a strike if the court's decision against his union was not reversed. The *Los Angeles Times* had also been found in contempt for a series of editorials virtually ordering a state judge to stiffen the punishment of two Teamsters union members. At first the lordly Frankfurter, who tended to treat his colleagues as law students, had a majority in favor of upholding the contempt citation, based on two centuries of British reverence for the dignity and power of judges. With an assiduous application of charm, humility, and close reasoning, Black took the Court away from Frankfurter. Writing for a five-judge majority, the warm and wily Justice Black wrote: "No purpose in ratifying the Bill of Rights was clearer than that of securing for the people of the United States much greater freedom of religion, expression, assembly, and petition than the people of Great Britain had ever enjoyed."

He had written a declaration of independence from British jurisprudence. Bitter enemies at first, the two titans pursued their divergent interpretations of the law with intellectual rigor. In time, they were drawn together in respect and affection. It was a judicial rapprochement on the scale of the reconciliation between John Adams and Thomas Jefferson. Black and Frankfurter both saw the law as a bastion against any threat to liberty—Frankfurter believing that greater protection for courts and judges would achieve that end and Black emphasizing that American freedoms could be secured through greater protection for peoples' rights. As the two men grew in years and wisdom, they saw that they agreed on ultimate ends and became affectionate friends in their twilight years—just as Adams and Jefferson did.

When Frankfurter died in 1965, Black wept.

Judge Black was an awesome figure in my mind, and so I was delighted to read that he prized friendly visitors from his home state—especially since the Court's civil rights opinions had made him a lonely Judas figure in Alabama, where an eruption of highway billboards, repeated throughout the South, shouted, IMPEACH EARL WARREN. On a trip to Washington, I called Black's office and he invited me to visit him at his home in Alexandria.

On my first visit, he led me from the dark interior of the two-story brick house out to the garden. He pointed to a row of green leafy plants and asked, "Do you know what they are?" Being a city boy, I was clueless but took a chance and guessed, "Turnip greens?" It was a lucky guess and the Judge seemed pleased at my faux horticultural expertise. He then insisted I cram myself into a set of Hugo Junior's tennis clothes and hit with him on his backyard court. Nearly eighty at the time, the slight little man on the other side of the net didn't put much steam on the ball, but it kept coming back, deep. Later that afternoon he told why, after being courted for years, he consented to give the Carpentier Lectures at Columbia School of Law. During a game of doubles with the Law School dean and Mrs. Earl Warren, Black's second wife, Elizabeth, who seldom did any harm to a tennis ball, launched an overhead squarely in the dean's eye. To make amends for the dean's shiner, Black did the lectures. The judge both forgave and marveled at the power of his non-athletic mate. She had been his secretary whom he married after the 1951 death of his beloved Josephine. Elizabeth was from a good Birmingham family and the couple made each other very happy as the light of a brilliant career began to dim.

As friendship between teacher and student ripened, the judge invited Josie and me to sit in the family box at the Court on an Opinion Day, Monday, May 23, 1966. The Judge gave the opinion for the Court in the case of *Mills v. Alabama*—a First Amendment case by the Court's First Amendment champion. The case involved an editorial written by *Birmingham Post-Herald* editor Jimmy Mills on Election Day urging voters to throw out the Bull Connor-dominated city commission in favor of a reform slate. Alabama law prohibited "electioneering" on Election Day. Justice Black, for the Court, ruled that the state law violated the Constitution because, "Suppression of the right of the press to praise or criticize governmental agents and to clamor and contend for or against change, which is all that this editorial did, muzzles one of the very agencies the Framers of our Constitution thoughtfully and deliberately selected to improve our society and keep it free."

The next September, on our way to the Nieman year in Cambridge, Josie and I stopped in Washington and went out to dinner with the Judge at the Army-Navy Club. That evening he entertained us with the story of his first case in Birmingham, when he was a Clay County country boy come to town. The intellectual leader of the United States Supreme Court gave a detailed accounting of a dispute involving the ownership of a sow and a litter of pigs. From little acorns . . . The dinner-table atmosphere turned serious when the question of the war was raised. Though he and Elizabeth were affectionate friends of President Lyndon Johnson and his family, the Judge was very doubtful about the necessity for the war and its outcome. As a not-yet-reconstructed hawk, I was surprised and troubled by my hero's views.

Driving home for Christmas, we stopped again for dinner with the Judge. On the drive to Alexandria, armed with one semester of Constitutional history, I asked a cheeky question. "Judge, you've been on the Court for over thirty years. Surely you have a different view of the institution now—and regret your support in the Senate for Roosevelt's notorious court-packing scheme." With tolerance bred of handling generations of know-it-all Ivy League law clerks, he replied, "Funny you should ask that question. I had some of those old speeches out the other night. I couldn't find anything in them that I could disagree with. Of course, I might have purified the language some." He went on to explain that there was no Constitutional commandment that the Court be a certain size. In fact, it historically had been sometimes larger, then smaller. He had been reviewing those speeches in preparation for a memoir—which he never finished.

The last time we saw the Judge and Elizabeth, we had drinks with them in his upstairs library at their home in Alexandria. Josie took a snapshot of him holding our one-year-old daughter, Margaret. That was on a weekend, the last of June 1971. I had to go home for some urgent and now forgotten task, but the Judge talked Josie into staying over until Monday, June 30, when he would deliver an opinion for the Court that he said she would find "interesting." She and Elizabeth sat in the family box to hear the Judge's last great opinion, a 6 to 3 decision against the Nixon administration and for the *New York Times* and the *Washington Post* in the Pentagon Papers case. The administration had gotten an injunction against the papers to cease publishing what amounted to the government's only accurate accounting of the Vietnam War. In Judge Black's mind the issue was framed: Government versus Truth and an Informed Public. In his powerfully worded opinion, laden with history, he wrote, "And paramount among the responsibilities of a free press is the duty to prevent any part of the government from deceiving the people and sending them off to distant lands to die of foreign fevers and foreign shot and shell." His doubts about the wisdom of the war that had surprised me in my state of uninformed hawkishness had found their fullest expression. More importantly, he had written another declaration of independence, this one freeing the press from prior restraint by the government. What no one but Elizabeth knew was that the line "foreign fever . . ." came from a "Yankee" taunt, a Dixie folk melody, "I Am a Jolly Rebel," sung by his generation and mine when feelings of "Dixiefilia" were intense. It went something like this: "I am a jolly Rebel / Oh yes, by God I am / And for this Yankee freedom, I do not give a damn / A hundred thousand Yankees died of Southern fever, of Southern shot and shell / I wish there were a hundred thousand more / I'd damn their souls to Hell!"

In another comic aside during that historic occasion, Elizabeth took Josie "backstage" to congratulate the Judge for his landmark decision. She was introduced to that magnificent-looking mediocrity, Chief Justice Warren Burger, who was modeling a judicial robe for a trip to a legal conference in London. "How do you like my drip-dry robe?" he cheerily asked Josie. My love is swift of wit, and so it was a dangerous moment. She instantly thought, and did say, "What can you do with basic black—other than a string of pearls?" Justice Burger laughed. It was for her a funny and exhilarating moment—a rich last memory.

Within three months, the Judge was dead. He and his philosophical opposite but cherished friend, Justice John Harlan, both lay dying that summer in Bethesda Naval Hospital. Judge Black went first, at 1 a.m. on Saturday, September 25. Josie, whom the Judge adored, and I went to the funeral at the National Cathedral, honored to be on the bus and seated with his "family" of former clerks. Before the service began, I thought of his story about attending the last rites of a not-so-dearly departed colleague when a breathless friend arrived late and asked, "Did I miss anything?" The Judge responded, "No. Counsel for the defense is just summing up." The cathedral was filled with a congregation of celebrities, headed by the Court, minus Harlan, and President Nixon, who would have the appointment that Judge Black had not wanted to give him, but who would be out of office himself in two years. The service was triumphal. Vigorous country Baptist hymns rang out under the vaulting arches of the great cathedral. It was filled with the great language of the classics, passages the Judge had underlined, read by his friend and Unitarian minister, Duncan Howlett. Dean Sayre read Black's favorite Bible verse, I Corinthians 13, "and now abideth faith, hope and love, these three; but the greatest of these is love." As we departed for the burial in Arlington Cemetery, the cathedral bells tolled eighty-five times—once for each year of his life.

WE COULD NOT HAVE guessed in 1968 how little time Judge Black had left. Neither were we prepared for the two great shocks to the placid life of the mind that spring in Cambridge. On Thursday, April 4, we were having one of the regular Nieman dinners at the Signet Society when word came that Dr. Martin Luther King Jr. had been assassinated in Memphis. The evening dissolved into private grief and thoughts about what such a terrible event meant for the country. By Saturday in Anniston, the *Star*'s editorial page worried that radicals might seize the mantle of leadership. "The grim prospect for America now is that Dr. King's assassination has removed from the scene a major, and possibly the most effective, proponent of (nonviolence) who might have won the ear and the heart of Negro America away from the incendiaries." The biracial Human Relations Council was more anguished in a statement published in the *Star* that Dr. King's murder "is a blow to all those working for improved race relations. But more than that, it is a blot on the character of our nation . . . We urge every person in this community and in the nation at large to stand openly and firmly for a social structure that knows no lines of color or creed." Simultaneously the black Interdenominational Ministerial Alliance planned a memorial service which was held Monday at the 17th Street Baptist Church, where Dr. King had once preached. A crowd of 1,500 heard speakers urge an Easter boycott of segregated downtown stores. From his pulpit, Dr. Reynolds said, "Those who sit in the seats of power must do something. City Hall, the mayor and the Chamber of Commerce must give concessions." The signal had been given for direct action on the sidewalks of Noble Street.

The April 11 *Star* carried in its readers' "Speak Out" column a kind of moral homily to a broken nation divided over the war and grieving the loss of a great leader. It was written by one of the virtually anonymous, plain people, a Mrs. Lillar Skinner. She wrote: "Think back to the times you added fuel to the fires of hate by saying, 'I'll be so happy when old Johnson is out of office and old King is dead.' Just how happy are you today . . .? If we are not gathering, we are scattering . . . Be sure you know you are right, then speak out when a right cause or a good man is being persecuted. I learned years ago the way of the cross leads home. Will you accept yours?"

Bobby Kennedy was even more deeply and directly affected by the news. His Indiana presidential campaign schedule called for him to speak the night of April 4 in the bleakest heart of Indianapolis's black ghetto where people had not yet heard of Dr. King's murder. His police escort peeled off when Bobby's entourage penetrated the depth of the ghetto. He climbed on the back of a flatbed truck and when he told the crowd the news it was greeted by a shocked gasp. Then Bobby spoke to the crowd, spoke from the hurt and healing heart of a man whose brother also had been murdered by a white man, who fought through the pain and saw hope again. Incongruously, he spoke about an ancient Greek poet, whose words written centuries ago struck home to that crowd of stunned, poor blacks. "My favorite poet was Aeschylus. He wrote: 'In our sleep, pain which cannot forget falls drop by drop upon the heart until, in our own despair, against our will, comes wisdom through the awful grace of God.'" On Tuesday night, June 4, after winning the California primary, Bobby was shot dead taking a shortcut through the kitchen of the Hotel Ambassador in Los Angeles.

On the following Wednesday morning in Cambridge, Josie and I awoke ready to make preparations to leave Harvard and return home. We turned on the TV and the news was like a physical blow. I wheeled and slammed a fist against the closet door, so stunned I didn't feel the pain. Thursday evening the

Anniston Star began its editorial on a note of unbelief, "Shattering violence once again has brought grief to a family too burdened already with grief, and numbing disbelief to a nation which has seen too much violence." The next week, an urgent call from home informed us we had been invited to attend the funeral and ride the train bearing the senator to Washington for burial. There was no way to get the official invitation to us in time, only a telegram informing us we'd been invited, but we flew to New York anyway. A crowd had begun forming around St. Patrick's Cathedral early Friday. Saturday morning, we made our way through the dense crowds to a side entrance where we were told invited guests would enter. The service in that majestic place was a moving experience. Josie was right at home with Catholic mass—even defying the ban against non-Catholics taking communion, though I declined. The surviving brother, Senator Edward Kennedy, spoke movingly, his voice catching only once. A family friend, Andy Williams, sang "The Battle Hymn of the Republic," after which we were instructed to go to a waiting fleet of buses that would take us to Pennsylvania Station to board the funeral train. Marshals on the buses checked invitations, which we didn't have. We were about to be turned away when a friend, Louis Oberdorfer, saw us and waved us aboard. Lou had been Bobby's assistant attorney general in charge of the Tax Division, a Birmingham native, close friend to and former clerk for Judge Black.

That journey was long and lugubrious. Ethel Kennedy made a stoic walk the length of the train to thank each one of us, followed by Ted Kennedy and Bobby's son, Joe, who also greeted each of the passengers. Josie was in the aisle when Ethel came through our car and sat in the nearest available seat, next to Dr. King's widow, Coretta Scott King. The two women noted Mrs. Kennedy's bearing in the face of tragedy, a poignant moment for both women, and as women do, Josie inquired about Mrs. King's children. Somber crowds gathered at every stop, Cub Scouts and Boy Scouts in full uniform. One image is locked in my mind. From a distance, I saw a man walking quickly up a hill toward the moving train. He crested the hill as we came alongside. He was a working man, blue work-shirt sleeves rolled up over muscular forearms. In his big fist was a bright yellow bouquet of late jonquils with which he saluted the train.

That New Jersey man looked no different than the men pasting the Wallace stickers on bumpers in Anniston two years before. Were they alike in some strange way—an answer to the mystery posed by Bobby Kennedy and Wallace carrying some of the same Indiana counties? The author of a six-volume series of books on the states, Neal Pierce, and I talked about Wallace's appeal beyond racism, an attraction that many working-class people outside the South felt for his racial polar opposite, Bobby Kennedy. I put it to Neal this way, thoughts I later shared with Wallace himself in a fateful meeting in my office:

It's the problem of the 65 percent majority. In Anniston, as in any other city, you have the Chamber of Commerce crowd who represent 1 percent of the population, but about 80 percent of the wealth. They are organized, articulate, well-funded, a group with a strong sense of mission and an ability to draw public attention to their agenda. Then you have the black community, which in the 1960s developed similar mechanisms and which represented 34 percent of Anniston's population at the time. That leaves the other 65 percent who are most of the resistance. Some are racists, out and out. But cumulatively a host of other problems outweighs racism. The highway department removes a traffic light from a blue-collar community, and there's a series of serious accidents, but it seems impossible to get the bureaucracy to restore the light. Despite the sanitary hazard of an overflowing drainage ditch in a working-class neighborhood, the residents don't seem to get anybody to listen or do something about it. The 65 percent begin to feel: Nobody seems to understand the conditions of my life. Hell, I know I'm the majority in this country. I built it with my own hands. The only person who understands me is George Wallace, who knows what I mean when I say I'm so pissed at those bureaucrats, chamber types, sneering journalists and black leaders I see on TV and in the paper, I'd like to punch one of them in the nose!"

STILL, IT WAS HARD at the time to think of George Wallace and Bobby Kennedy paired in any way as we returned to an almost bare apartment on Harvard Street, subdued by the experience and sad to be leaving our idyllic retreat from Alabama reality. Momentary downdrafts of depression accompanied thoughts of returning to George Wallace's Alabama, to again be branded as traitor to class, race—and the memory of our Confederate dead! But distance and insights from the Harvard experience had widened and softened my understanding of the culture to which we were returning. It was still a somewhat alien culture, but it was home, too, and you can't reject home and live there. That way lies madness. Strangely, thinking back about going home, amidst the jangling mental pictures of conflict, angry faces, threats and accusations, softer memories, of a funeral for an old woman swam into focus.

How many summers has it been since Mrs. Gardner died? I don't remember precisely. No matter, her death was only an incident in a long life, a life, which in many ways symbolizes the Southern continuum. She carried in her blood that perfectly irrational sense of being Southern, a way of seeing and experiencing change but somehow remaining the same—a distinctive sub-culture, shaped by living through an un-American history.

Mrs. Minnie Bell Gardner was born into and departed from the Old South before it, too, died. She was very different from the rootless, disconnected people Vance Packard wrote about in "A Nation of Strangers." She moved only once. That was when she married Mr. Gardner, at eighteen. She lived the rest of her life in the context of one place, Anniston, Alabama, until she died, much mourned, at the age of ninety-six. At some distance, Mrs. Gardner witnessed her nation at war five times, saw the election of twenty presidents, and lived through almost incomprehensible economic, technological, and social changes.

But at the funeral the pastor and pastor emeritus of Parker Memorial Baptist Church didn't talk about presidents or armies or other abstractions; they talked about the fifty-eight years she had taught Sunday school. Those two Southern Baptist preachers put things in their right order because Mrs. Gardner's Sunday school class affected her more directly than technology or elections or even wars. Year after year, every Sunday, for nearly six decades, the faces changed in Mrs. Gardner's class, but for her they were the same. They were sons and daughters of sons and daughters whom she knew and who knew her.

She was rooted, touched by the place she was in and the people who lived there. Being connected to people and place, she knew and cared. She knew those changing faces before her, when to worry about them and when not to, in a way that is beyond the skills of academic medicine to teach. It is knowledge that comes only from attending so many baptisms, weddings, and funerals.

Thinking of Mrs. Gardner, an icon of normality, was something like counting sheep for the insomniac, it calmed anxieties about returning to what had been a cockpit of controversy, and reminded me of the great journalistic oversight—the uncovered story of any time—the ubiquitous, permanent, context-framing presence of normality.

10

A New Civilization Aborning

Ordinary lives of the vast majority of people are lived as placidly as the sea, which from time to time is roiled by a momentary squall but is eternally governed by the deep swells and monotonous tides of normality. Only when the squall passes do we recognize just how big normality is. The UNC sociologist John Shelton Reed recalled an observation about one famous civil rights conflict that, squeezed into the frame of a TV screen, seemed to engage the entire city of Little Rock, Arkansas: "During Little Rock's troubles 124,500 of the city's 125,000 citizens went about their business, then went home at night and watched the other 500 on television."

On returning home to Alabama from the refuge of the Harvard fellowship, not only was there a renewed sense of ubiquitous normality to give perspective to the controversies of the time, but there were real signs of change. The glue that held the old, segregated civilization together, which binds our society today, is the sameness of everyday life: workaday rituals, habits of civility, conformity to the norm, ambivalence, indifference, and resignation. There were bitter-end haters, but it is remarkable how light was the hold of the haters on the rest of us. The South had been engaged in a war of civilizations that was fought with hate-hot intensity, or so it seemed to front-line combatants, but most Southerners looked on with no more than a slow burn of irritation. Its active-duty soldiers had been told blood would run in the streets, and martyrs there were, a small number that seemed larger because of the demonic spirit revealed.

One of those martyrs was Jonathan Myrick Daniels, an Episcopal divinity student who volunteered to work in Selma. Arrested with others protesting denial of voting rights, he and his companions were unexpectedly released from jail in the tiny Black Belt town of Hayneville in Lowndes County. As one of the black protesters, sixteen-year-old Ruby Sales, approached Cash's Store for a drink of water, a man armed with a shotgun cursed her. Sensing imminent danger, Daniels pulled her to him and turned around to shield her. He took the shotgun blast in his back. He was one of forty-four who died in the civil rights movement.

Only forty-four. Forty-four martyrs, yes, but for a war of civilizations, the casualties were light—fewer than the number killed by lightning in the same period. (In another democracy, India, during a single month of 2002, hundreds of Hindus and Muslims died—183 were burned alive—as tens of thousands of Hindus in Gujarat State rampaged through Muslim quarters.)

To those who fought against the haters with the greatest intensity, it seemed as if war were a permanent condition, that victory would be forever beyond reach. Yet, as in all wars, there was a beginning and an end. The "hot" war lasted sixteen years (1954–70). Between the Voting Rights Act of 1965 and the election of a class of progressive Southern governors in 1970, old attitudes, along with the civilization that supported them, plummeted to an obscurity beyond the easy reach of memory. When I graduated from the University of Alabama in 1959, 72 percent of white Southerners objected to any school integration. In 1969, the year after returning home from the Nieman Fellowship, only 21 percent objected to sending their children to a school with (some) blacks.

"The statistics cannot be evaded," Hodding Carter would say later when asked if there would be a "new" South. "It is useless for Southerners to pretend that the region we love is not identical with the region whose faults and needs have been so thoroughly tabulated. But the past does not endure even when men insist that it is unending. The Southern legacies are not eternal and need not be accepted when reason suggests their rejection . . ."

Some legacies do endure. It would be silly to say that the South is no more—as foolish as proclaiming an end to history. The South is its history. Yet times were a'changing. It was in 1969 that I received a letter—from a man I'd never heard of, Dr. Tom Naylor of Duke University—which was to put me in touch with a network of young Southerners who had similar views. Just four years from the last racist rally on the courthouse steps, from the night Willie Brewster was murdered, from the day mounted state troopers charged into the peaceful protesters on the Edmund Pettus Bridge in Selma, word came that my sense of isolation was not total, that there was an army of pallbearers somewhere out there who were willing to carry off the body of the Old South in a Georgia pine box.

On August 25, 1969, a second letter came from Dr. Naylor on the letterhead of the L.Q.C. Lamar Society, in old-English type, inviting me to a meeting at the quaintly named Quail Roost, a University of North Carolina conference center. The letterhead also bore the name W. J. Michael Cody. Mike was a Memphis lawyer. He and Tom Naylor, a Duke economics professor, knew each other through a mutual friend. Mike and Tom were among those in our generation who had witnessed their parents' generation desperately try to maintain a dual society; we were children who at first viewed our color-obsessed society with mystified eyes but were in time led to the conviction, "This is wrong." Mike describes how their search for open-minded younger Southerners was launched. "I had talked to Tom back in 1968 when we [the Memphis firm of Burch, Porter & Johnson] were representing Dr. King during the sanitation strike." He and Tom talked about "the need for people like me in Memphis to share our experiences in matters of this kind with others in different areas of the South who felt as we did. We decided that there were common feelings and common problems that all of us were facing, but we had been isolated from each other and had little or no communication."

ORIGINS OF THE NEW South impulse, which focused the mind of the South for a season, actually date back to a series of conversations as early as 1966 between Tom Naylor and a young historian, Jim Leutze of Chapel Hill (later president of UNC Wilmington). As Tom reconstructed those talks, "We had observed with dismay the fact that an increasing number of young Southerners were choosing to leave the South after becoming frustrated by the intransigence of some of the region's political leaders in dealing with the South's more pressing socio-economic problems." Naylor and Leutze sensed "a feeling of utter hopelessness was driving many bright and energetic young Southerners out of the South."

Doug Cater of Montgomery put it this way: "In my day it was said

that if a young man had any get up and go, he got up and went." Doug
did, becoming valedictorian of the Harvard Class of '47, an architect of
the Great Society in Lyndon Johnson's White House, and co-publisher of
The (London) *Observer*. In their day, the two Carolina professors talked
dreamily of an organization of young Southerners whose common bond was
"not ideology, but rather a desire to see the South achieve its full potential."
Conversation was fleshed out in an action plan after an airport breakfast
meeting in Memphis between Tom and Mike. They got in touch with
Hodding Carter and Willie Morris (then the thirty-five-year-old editor of
Harper's), both of whom were enthusiastic about creating the network of
young progressives. A series of meetings in Durham, Atlanta, Memphis,
Jackson, and New Orleans expanded the net and a $6,000 grant (a hand-
some fund in 1969 dollars) from the Stern Family Fund made the Quail
Roost gathering possible.

None of us in that network was so prescient as to know that the old
order was crumbling, nor were we so bold in the beginning as to assert that
it was our duty to define a better civilization. Mainly, as Mike and Tom envisioned the fetal organization, we would come together "to get ideas and, in
a sense, comfort from each other." We had all come of age in a conservative
culture that was in love with the past. Thus, the Lucius Quintus Cincinnatus
Lamar Society, an antique name to disguise a liberal purpose. My original
guide back in the early 1960s to the medieval politics of Mississippi, former
congressman Frank Smith, then director of the Tennessee Valley Authority in Knoxville, suggested the name. He knew everybody, conservative
and liberal, and supplied Tom with many of the names in the initial list,
including mine. Our namesake, Lamar, had all the right transformational
credentials. He had been a firebrand secessionist before the Civil War who
was celebrated by John Kennedy in his Pulitzer Prize-winning book, *Profiles
In Courage*. Lamar qualified for Kennedy's pantheon when, in his maiden
speech as a newly elected U.S. Senator from Mississippi, he appealed for
reason and reconciliation, "My countrymen, know one another and you
will love one another."

Tom's earlier letter about "a proposed organization of progressive young
Southerners" had been widely circulated. His August letter reported, "From

the response we have received, it is apparent that the interest which you expressed is shared by a large number of other Southerners." He invited me to join the Lamar Society as a $200 founding member and to attend the organizational meeting November 21-23 at Quail Roost. The featured speakers were talented friends, Hodding Carter III and Willie Morris. I didn't know what to expect, but if there were a lot of Southerners with the same outlook and values as Hodding and Willie, I dared to think that the South's penance for its sins, its sentence to separation and scorn, might be coming to an end.

Quail Roost had once been the country residence of Watts Hill Sr., founder of Jefferson Pilot Insurance Company, a progressive business leader who was instrumental in developing North Carolina's Research Triangle Park with Governor Luther Hodges. The sprawling, colonial-style manor house was reached by a winding drive through a forest of pine and hardwood trees. Among the thoughtful and progressive men attending were a few Republicans and there were virtually no women. In addition to Mike and Tom, Hodding and Willie, Vernon Jordan was there as president of the Voter Education Project, the novelist Reynolds Price, John Ward, a top aide to Arkansas Governor Winthrop Rockefeller, Bob Eckhardt, a Texas congressman from a working-class Houston district, and representing the Southern Regional Council were Dr. Raymond Wheeler, Paul Anthony, Reese Cleghorn, and the late James McBride Dabbs. There were about eighty native Southerners, mainly in their thirties and forties, including presidents of two insurance companies, a university chancellor, attorneys, editors and publishers, businessmen, political activists of both major parties, professors, and state legislators. We came together with a sense of anticipation, discovery, and validation much as expatriates working in Saudi Arabia or Yemen might feel on finding other Americans who shared similar experiences and beliefs.

We were a band of brothers, happy to discover each other, neither opposed to strong drink nor without some talent for the art of story-telling, but not a soul equaled Willie Morris's fabulous capacity for drink or, except for Reynolds Price, his skill as a Southern troubadour. There were differences within the brotherhood over whether the organization should be activist or educational. We debated those choices the first day. Hodding seemed to be advocating a more activist position. That path would have launched something like a fourth political party in the South: tough, ideological, an organization to find, support, finance, and elect candidates for political office who mirrored its views. Hodding doesn't remember being such a strong spokesman for an activist role. Maybe I just interpreted what he said as advocating an activist political posture because of his astounding feat in Mississippi. He had defeated the Mississippi establishment in 1968, becoming co-chairman with civil rights leader Aaron Henry of an integrated delegation to the Democratic National Convention. I didn't have Hodding's gutsy, winning idealism. I did have the experience of being sent tumbling by the Wallace tsunami, and I calculated how effective the Lamar Society's endorsement would be against the force of nature that was the Wallace phenomenon, especially without the support of a national party or an incumbent president. At one point when Hodding's passionate intelligence seemed about to sway the group, I appealed to Bob Eckhardt to use the wily ways of congressional rules to delay or divert a decision. The laid-back congressman declined out of a belief that unfettered debate would reveal whatever flaws of logic lay in most arguments and eventually produce consensus. He drawled, "It has always been my belief that you shoot folly as it flies." (It being un-Southern to shoot folly on the ground.)

As the discussion continued, tepid pragmatism prevailed over hot-to-trot idealism. Almost subliminally during the afternoon of the second day, the focus shifted away from the hard line, but it was not until a temporary board of twenty directors was elected that the prevailing view became nearly unanimous. Mike presided over an interim board of directors and asked each of us at the round table to define our view. Only one spoke in favor of direct intervention in politics. Thinking about the meeting during the next few days and what it might augur for the future, I wasn't sure what the Lamar Society could mean to the South. I certainly did not feel a definite sense of release, of pardon from internal banishment. In my Sunday column, I wrote: "Hard skepticism is the safest mood in which to reflect upon the events of last weekend. Hopeful fantasies too often conceal the inevitable, despairing rock of failure. Yet, it is tempting to feel that something momentous began here last week." I thought I could see "a mosaic of purpose" forming through the board members' composite statements, characterized as practical, success-oriented, interested in building a regional alliance of men (no women?) attuned to the reality that a cadre of enlightened "movers and shakers" of the South will not lend their money, their validating talents, and prestige to a group which is not both respectable and pragmatic. I saw—or hoped I did—thousands of energetic, progressive "new" Southerners who'd devise strategies to head off urban problems before they overwhelmed us, who'd seek corrective action to the familiar problems of rural poverty, low per capita income, barely adequate educational systems, and the omnipresent issue of race woven through the whole policy agenda. I concluded with cautious optimism: "So, it is best to be skeptical. Yet, it is still tempting to dream of a progressive organization of diverse Southerners united by one overriding commonality—devotion to their native region."

MAYBE MY INTERPRETATION OF Hodding's position at the time was right. Maybe we should have worn our insignia proudly, liberal-minded Southern kamikazes diving against a rearming Republican establishment that would reemerge in the 1980s, a party whose core footings were formed by the White Citizens Councils who fled the Democratic Party as integration became the norm. In the main, the Southern Republican Party would devote itself to refined bigotry and selfishness—Trent Lott as totem of a new one-party South. Trent Lott was a big man in the 1980s and '90s, but in the new millennium, ahh, what a mighty fall there was!

The sad thing about Trent Lott's pathetic ordeal is not that he was humbled and neutered as a power in the Senate but, given what was revealed about his character, that he was not a better man for the experience. His downfall can't be classified as a tragedy—a great man brought low by events turning on a flaw in his character. Trent Lott is no Lear, Macbeth, or Hamlet. He is of my generation, a familiar Southern type I've known all my life: sentimental about the Confederacy, hankering for his segregated boyhood, uncomfortable around African Americans.

When he said that if Strom Thurmond had been elected president on the breakaway racist Dixiecrat ticket in 1948, "we wouldn't have had all these problems over all these years, either," it was no slip of the tongue. Lott was at the old segregationist's one hundredth birthday party; among friends, he clearly felt he could open the tightly sealed door to his inner self and utter long-suppressed sentiments from the depth of his soul. Deep in his heart, behind that sealed door, he and one wing of the Southern Republican Party truly believe: "We would be better off if we hadn't let these colored people push themselves into our schools, churches and neighborhoods. That's when all the trouble started."

Not all Southern Republicans feel the way Lott evidently does; not even all Mississippi Republicans do. "Mr. Southern Republican," Clark Reed of Greenville, and the state's senior senator, Thad Cochran, would never utter the words Lott did. They don't believe what those words say. But plenty in the Southern GOP do. A political aide in the Reagan White House, Lee Atwater, explained the appeal this way: "You start out in 1954 by saying 'Nigger, nigger, nigger.' By 1968 you can't say 'nigger'—that hurts you. Backfires. So you say stuff like forced busing, states' rights, and all that stuff."

The evolution began in 1948 when President Truman integrated the Armed Forces and the most extreme segregationist Democrats mounted the Dixiecrat rebellion, nominating Thurmond at their convention in Birmingham. Bull Connor and KKK thugs mingled with Southern governors and congressmen as former Alabama Governor Frank Dixon gave the keynote address. It was a fighting speech. He said the States' Rights movement would protect the South from a "federal Gestapo" and defend "against those who would destroy our civilization and mongrelize our people." Later, Governor Dixon muted the racial themes, elevating the debate to a choice between Big Government and States' Rights, putting a high-minded gloss on the Dixiecrat movement to attract allies from outside the South. In private letters, Dixon was more candid, lamenting, "The Huns have wrecked the theories of the master race with which we were so contented so long," and referring to blacks as "apes" and "gorillas." And so it went: in every presidential election more and more arch-segregationist Democrats swelled the ranks of the GOP, going for Ike in '52 and '56, Goldwater in '64, until even Southern Baptists Jimmy Carter and Bill Clinton couldn't carry the white South.

In my lifetime, there have been two Souths, cut in half by the civil rights movement. We were born on the far side to an extinct civilization, the old segregated South, but our best years have been on the New South side. My generation's claim to greatness is that we tore down the wall of legal racism, a wall before which the Founding Fathers stood silent and afraid, which even Civil War couldn't bring down. Against every step we took toward finally achieving the long-denied American ideal that all men are created equal, Lott and his allies staged a dogged resistance.

The senator's craven attempts to save his skin and his power, vowing to promote policies he never supported—such as affirmative action—mark him as an even more deeply flawed person. The Republican leadership could not afford to have Trent Lott as the public face of the party. Changing the face of the party one day could mean changing its heart as well. When elected in 2000, Governor Bob Riley of Alabama seemed to be a harbinger of a Southern Republican Party that was courageous, truly compassionate, and inclusive. He seemed more the spiritual heir of Virginia Governor Linwood Holton than of Trent Lott. In his 1970 inaugural address, Governor Holton promised to put the past to rest and to govern to solve problems rather than to be swayed by ideology. Riley stunned our lagging state in 2003 by presenting a package of tax reforms that would have raised $1.2 billion and vaulted the state's educational system and state services into the middle range of Southern states. Campaigning for the revolutionary package, he stressed its spiritual core, the unfairness of a system that begins taxing the poor with an annual income of $4,600. Of course, his plan fell to our fixation with defeat—2 to 1.

Inclusiveness was one of the hallmarks of the Lamar Society that I led as president beginning in 1971. It would have been more influential if it had had a clearer, crisper definition as a progressive leadership organization rather than one overly concerned with making sure that everyone was welcome: conservatives and liberals, blacks and whites, men and women, a gelded creature whose welcome was so universal as to make it meaningless. A black leader put it this way during a Lamar Society meeting in Dallas: "being for everybody is like being for nobody."

We couldn't see that in 1969, so absorbed were we with defining an all-inclusive South that would take the place of the segregated one that was disappearing. The 1970s for me were the happiest decade. I fell in love with my native land all over again. It was getting smarter, richer, and more tolerant. The national media began to speak of us with awed surprise as a newly discovered magical kingdom, "the Sunbelt." We were admired, felt good about ourselves. I loved it and it loved me back. Even Alabama in 1969 had a bright, progressive young governor, Albert Brewer, who as lieutenant governor had succeeded Governor Lurleen Wallace when that good lady died of cancer. I fooled myself into thinking that fickle Alabama had quit her bad old backward ways and I could brag about her unashamed anywhere on God's green earth. Of course, she would break my heart again and again, testing my love for her in ways that sometimes made me wonder why I even cared. But it was 1969, and I was infatuated with the whole blamed nation of Dixie.

Riding that happy bubble, Southern liberalism on the march, I could not hear the melancholy cellos signaling yet again the South's affinity for tragedy. To achieve racial integration, the federal courts set in motion a process that by the 1990s would result in an almost totally segregated, poor, and black urban school system throughout the South. But it was 1969, and in that school year, there were more than 7,000 students in the thoroughly integrated Anniston school system, more than 55 percent of them middle class, mostly but not exclusively, white. In time, we would learn that what we called "white flight" was in reality, the flight of money, civic commitment, and academic preparation, leaving behind a student pool that was poor, from single-parent households, and academically stunted by a segregated system.

11

The Opening Act

The opening act of the "new" New South was to be in Memphis, a packed two-day symposium on April 17–18, 1970, at the Rivermont Hotel, where a double room with a river view cost $21 a night. The Lamar Society and Southwestern College sponsored the meeting. The keynote speaker was chosen to set the right tone for the launching of a new organization in a region deeply suspicious of being ambushed by radicals and "outsiders." A moderate Republican, Arkansas Governor Winthrop Rockefeller, was the after-lunch headliner. His tailored, double-breasted suit only partially disguised his considerable girth, and his slow, unsteady gait revealed an unhappy fact: the governor was drunk, so drunk he uttered only one memorable line, "We've got what it takes to move. Southerners can control their own destiny." Fourteen floors below the penthouse conference room, the Mississippi River was a perfect accompaniment to the governor's speech, moving sluggishly, like a fat boy doing his chores, and hating them.

As it turned out, the two main speakers were bookends: buffoonery at one end and brilliance at the other. The brilliant other bookend was the LBJ speechwriter Richard N. Goodwin, who spoke eloquently that evening about "The End of Reconstruction." He spoke of a rootedness that his native New England shares with the South, as if they "are the only parts of America with a history." He believed that a South, which solved its own problems, could impart strengthening values to the nation:

> For what America hungers for is not more goods or greater power, but a manner of life, restoration of the bonds between people that we call community, a philosophy which values the individual rather than his possessions, and a sense of belonging, of shared purpose and enterprise. A South unshackled from distorted memories and present injustices can,

more than any other section, open new dimensions in American life and help shape the American future as it decisively molded the American past.

Goodwin's intoxicating words, the brisk intelligence of bright young Southern panelists addressing Southern challenges—from the creeping bleakness of the Black Belt to the growing ghettoization of the region's cities—the embrace of enlightenment from university deans and presidents, I could almost feel on my face refreshing breezes blowing away the dead, stale air of a South that was extinct . . . but didn't yet know it.

The *New York Times* thought it saw a region in the act of changing. On April 20, the paper carried Jon Nordheimer's report from Memphis:

> A new Southern Strategy, one devised by the natives instead of by Washington political theorists, took shape this weekend by the banks of the Mississippi.
>
> The L.Q.C. Lamar Society—a group of white liberals, members of the black elite and a few cautious conservatives—gathered in Memphis to ponder the problems and bugbears of a South in transition.
>
> What emerged was a common conviction that the South faces tragedy and eclipse unless ways are found to unite the racial and economic factions that are now divided . . .

From that April weekend in Memphis to the next April, there was a blur of activity. To make up for Winthrop Rockefeller's performance in Memphis, his staff gave the Lamar Society a block of time at the Southern Governors Conference in Biloxi that September. Georgia Governor Lester Maddox, ever the clown, masqueraded as a waiter, serving his gubernatorial colleagues. When economist and Lamar Society board member Ray Marshall addressed the governors on the issue of rural poverty, Maddox pulled the press away for an impromptu press conference. He had his say, the New South didn't. Even so, the year brought a cascade of good news. The primaries and general elections of 1970 for the first time in the South put on stage a cast of reasonable, thoughtful new governors, not a demagogue among them—except for Alabama, and even it had offered a moment of hope.

The slight, young lieutenant governor, Albert Brewer, elevated in 1969 to the governor's office on the death of Mrs. Wallace, was not a pre-possessing man. But as I listened to him speak to the Anniston Rotary Club, I felt a rising excitement. I don't remember what he said so much as the tone. It wasn't Alabama political boilerplate; he conveyed a vision of a clean, progressive, proud state. He was one of us, I thought. My enthusiasm was validated by the early polls, which in March showed Brewer ahead of George Wallace by as much as 19 points.

Brewer's campaign money worries were answered by a peculiar source: President Richard Nixon, who wanted Wallace eliminated. A much-admired former newsman, the late Bob Ingram, Brewer's finance director was picked to ferry the clandestine contribution from New York to Montgomery. Dan Carter in *The Politics of Rage* describes a comic encounter in the tiny Sherry Netherland Hotel lobby between a dour White House operative, Herbert Kalmbach, and Ingram, the Alabama boy, innocent to the dark world of money laundering soon to be made infamous by Watergate. The good-natured Ingram did see the ingredients of comic opera in the scene as it unfolded: code words; the Nixon operative stuffing stacks of $100 bills in a bag; waiters from La Petite Café looking on (friendly faces to Josephine and me when we used to stay at the hotel, but vaguely menacing to the man from Montgomery with $100,000 in a bag).

As the Democratic primary neared, I was excited and hopeful. My long, long endorsement editorial was reprinted as an ad by the Brewer campaign. Toward the end, it read:

> Wallace has given us turmoil and asked the man who works for hourly
> wages to pay the bill. Brewer has given us peace and a governor who is
> willing to work, really work here in Alabama to help solve people's prob-
> lems . . . He has given us more. He has given us a sense of the possible,
> a taste for a better future when Alabama is not 48th but—at last—on
> its way to first.

On May 5, Brewer finished a nose ahead of Wallace, 422,000 to 414,000, but the 180,000 won by other candidates would decide the race in a runoff. Racist fringe candidate Asa Carter—more about him later—got 15,000 votes, enough to have given Wallace a victory. When Wallace and his people saw a poll that showed rural and working-class voters worried that Brewer might be "soft" on the integration issue, they knew what they had to do. And they did it with a vengeance.

Wallace unleashed a turgid river of demagoguery. One broadside was headlined: WAKE UP ALABAMA! BLACKS VOW TO TAKE OVER ALABAMA! Another showed a pretty little white girl in a bathing suit surrounded by leering black boys, "This Could Be Alabama Four Years From Now. Do You Want It?" The copy for a Wallace radio ad read: "Suppose your wife is driving home at 11 o'clock at night. She is stopped by a highway patrolman. He turns out to be black. Think about it . . . Elect George C. Wallace."

As the Wallace mudslide oozed over the state, I called the Brewer campaign in mild desperation to find out why their campaign had stalled. I suggested that Brewer go on a "victory tour" with a band playing an upbeat, hopeful melody such as, "There'll Be A New Day In The Mornin'." Could that kind of a confident, optimistic expedition tap into the affirmative wave of reform sweeping the rest of the South? My idea was laughed off. Wallace surfed the wave of muck to a 30,000-vote margin in the run-off. Alabama had lost its last chance in the twentieth century to join the march of able, progressive Southern governors.

DESPONDENT AS I WAS, it would have been a morbid moment had I realized that I would be an alien to Alabama's political culture for the rest of the century. However, planning for the second annual meeting of the Lamar Society buoyed my spirits. My main task as chairman was to line up the headliner, U.S. Senator Edmund Muskie, then the front-runner for the Democratic presidential nomination in 1972. The senator, with whom I maintained friendly relations for the rest of his life, agreed in time for us to announce his acceptance in promotional material. At one of the last planning meetings at Tom Naylor's house in Durham, he had exciting news. Perhaps as many as four of the Class of 1970 governors would come to Atlanta. Some class it was. One after the other, each gave inaugural addresses that sounded—accustomed as we were to ranting demagogues—as if these new

Southern governors were returning mariners describing a fabulous new-found land. Virginia's new Republican governor, Linwood Holton, put it this way: "At the dawn of the 1970s it is clear that problem-solving, and not philosophical principles, has become the focal point of politics . . . old cliches have now blurred and old dogmas have died."

Three weeks before the April 30–May 1 symposium, with the announced theme of "The Urban South: Northern Mistakes in a Southern Setting," there were few reservations, which made us all anxious, but as the date neared, they came piling in. The old Biltmore Hotel was crammed with New South acolytes. For them, the headliner wasn't the main act, but the ballroom was packed to hear Ed Muskie. Josephine and I had drinks with Ed and his wife Jane in their suite before going down to the banquet hall. They were good company, comfortable, interesting, and the hour passed quickly. From their pleasant cell of serenity, we were plunged into the mad, mad world of celebrity: Television strobes and flash bulbs drowned us in light. Hands reached out to touch us. I gave a glancing touch to a couple of hands and said, "Hi. I'm Brandt Ayers. I'm nobody," which was greeted with rapturous expressions. Ed and Jane, accustomed to riding the rapids of celebrity, marched on smiling and nodding left and right until at last we reached the head table. In my introduction, I noted the irony of a small-town publisher chairing a symposium on urban affairs, claiming expertise on "rapid transit in the rural South." Max Frankel (later editor of the *New York Times*) in the front row laughed with the rest of the audience. The senator's speech lacked the soaring language former speech-writer Dick Goodwin could have given it, but it was solid, thoughtful, suggesting urban conventions to expose the problems and opportunities of emerging Southern cities before growth overwhelmed them.

In the ballroom the following afternoon, anticipation rose as four of the governors elected the year before took their seats on a panel chaired by former North Carolina Governor Terry Sanford, then president of Duke University. There was tall, angular Reubin Askew of Florida; handsome Dale Bumpers of Arkansas; lean, intense Jimmy Carter of Georgia; and four-square solid John West of South Carolina. These four governors were to appear together again and again, so often in fact that they began to refer to themselves as "The Dale and Jimmy and Reubin and John Show." What they said, what they stood for, was nothing less than the death of one civilization and the birth of another.

But that afternoon was the first group appearance for the four New South governors, Class of '70. Nobody really knew what they would say, although the mood was hopeful because of the campaigns they had run. The audience was not disappointed. Governor Carter, speaking without notes, put it most directly: "I think Southerners now have realized that the solution of our problems is our own and that we can no longer berate the federal government, the Supreme Court, or any other "outside group" for our own problems, our own needs, our own shortcomings . . . the obstacles we have to overcome."

Never in the twentieth century had so many Southern governors come together, standing on the same stage—facing forward—and saying plainly that the South must turn away from racial rhetoric and begin the serious business of problem-solving. For everyone in that ballroom in the old Biltmore, it was a Southern epiphany! An enormous weight, put on our backs by Cain himself, had been lifted. I was positively light-headed. There was a feeling that more was possible for this generation of Southerners than had been possible for our fathers and grandfathers. No longer would we have to be defensive because we bore the mark of a historic sin. No longer would the South have to starve its talent and imagination by feeding the retarding myths of the past.

On May 3, the *New York Times*, again by Jon Nordheimer, reported in a detailed story that began:

ATLANTA, May 2—An organization of young Southern progressives ended a two-day conference this weekend with a call for mutual defense against the greatest threats to Southern cities since the armies of Gen. William T. Sherman—urban blight, pollution and racial polarity.

Speakers at a symposium conducted by the L.Q.C. Lamar Society stressed the need for interstate cooperation if the South is to avoid the urban ills now resisting remedy elsewhere in the nation.

Nordheimer's account focused on the practical fruits that we hoped would emerge from the symposium, as one did. In his keynote address, Terry Sanford called for the creation of Southern regional growth boards to coordinate planning for the cities and states and to serve as a conduit for federal funds. I presided at the Lamar Society board meeting that voted to adopt Sanford's vision as our work program. As the newly elected president of the Society, I became vice chairman of the partnership between Duke and the Lamar Society, which would give the concept the flesh of reality. I thus earned for myself an asterisk in history—a fate awaiting anyone who became Vice to Terry Sanford's Chairman.

Sanford, as a student at Chapel Hill in the late 1930s, fell under the influence of the great regional sociologist, Howard Odum. Professor Odum's vision was similar to but more realistic than that of the Agrarians who once clustered around Vanderbilt University. The Agrarians tried to warn us what would happen. In their joint 1930 manifesto, *I'll Take My Stand*, they spoke to young Southerners who were succumbing to the lure of the industrial idea. "They must be persuaded to look very critically at the advantages of becoming a 'new South,' which will be only an undistinguished replica of the usual industrial community."

But where the Agrarians saw the romantic yeomanry in such pastoral creations as the crop-lien system, Odum saw wasted men and women scratching for cotton in fields of dead clay. He planted in the mind of young Sanford the idea that the South could be a laboratory to discover ways to make "a larger regional contribution to national culture and unity." Sanford became one of North Carolina's best governors in the early 1960s, but it wasn't until the 1971 Atlanta conference that Odum's values were projected into the realm of policy by his old student, then president of Duke University. In his keynote address he proposed the laboratory that Odum hoped to see in the form of an interstate compact, the Southern Growth Policies Board, chaired each year by one of the region's governors. The idea was to have a secretariat reporting to the regions' governors and legislatures that would help solve the riddle of unbalanced growth. It would seek a cure to the leukemia afflicting rural areas and small towns, and the cancerous growth in the centers of large cities—not just as a

Southern strategy but also as strategy for the nation.

By November, Terry had persuaded a majority of Southern states to join in a compact to create the Southern Growth Policies Board. Was this to be the fulfillment of the promise of the New South?

PROFESSOR ODUM WOULD BE disappointed, as I am sure Governor Sanford was, at what their dream became. The SGPB became for a while little more than a Dixie home-guard protecting the South against raids on the Treasury by Yankee units such as the Northeast-Midwest congressional caucus. The SGPB continues as an interesting meeting place for business, education and government leaders to discuss ideas, but it certainly hasn't cured rural depression or shielded the urban South from repeating Yankee mistakes.

Where was the South fifty-plus years after *Brown* and fifty-plus years after the passage of both old and new Souths? Taken as a whole, the half-century represents a strong assertion of democratic principles. We won a fight that frightened the founding fathers, that even Civil War couldn't achieve—the defeat of legal segregation.

However, the outcome of the issue that *Brown* sought to resolve is muddied by a persistent trait of human nature: If there is a hard thing to do, let someone else do it. Governors, senators, legislators and educators refused to put their hands to the difficult task of designing a unitary school system in which poor and middle class children of both races could achieve.

They let the courts do it. Courts, operating as they do through the distant and rigid arm of the law, are numb to elegant choices affecting race, ease of access, different opinions and levels of preparation. With applause from liberals like me, one of our heroes, Justice William Brennan, delivered an opinion that was the death knell of urban school systems in the South. In a 1968 Virginia decision, *Green v. County School Board of New Kent County*, the Supreme Court, in effect, struck down gradual integration under "freedom of choice" plans. Such plans had been drawing increasing numbers of blacks into previously all-white schools. In New Kent County, the Court said that the three-fold increase in black enrollment, from 35 in 1965 to 115 in 1967, wasn't good enough. Brennan's opinion pointed to the 85 percent still attending all-black schools. Under freedom of choice, there was a similarly geometric acceleration of black enrollment in Anniston High from ten lonely pioneers in 1965 to triple that number the next year. By the 1969–70 school year 45 percent of the 7,000 students enrolled in Anniston City schools were black. Then, there was still a chance to achieve maximum economic integration, a majority of middleclass achievers to poor underachievers that lifts the below grade-level performers without retarding advanced students.

Lower courts took their cue from the language in *Green* that gradual isn't good enough, and from *Brown* that segregated schools are "inherently unequal." So, instant and total integration would make them inherently equal? The logic didn't work. By the time the *Green* decision had been fully applied by the lower courts, the Anniston system lost 2,000 students, was 55 percent black, and mostly poor. In 2000, the system was more than 95 percent black, 84 percent poor enough to need meal subsidies. A majority of poor, socially and educationally unprepared children flooded systems from Birmingham to Boston, and middle-income parents—white and black—fled to avoid the deluge. In a rueful conversation with Anniston's civil rights veteran Nimrod Reynolds, he agreed that parental reaction would have been the same if poor white "redneck" students overwhelmed middle-income black school systems.

Integration became an end in itself, a value greater than education, or so it seemed. But more and more integration didn't translate into better and better education for either race. The result was more and more re-segregation.

A Southern statesman, William Winter, who would kick-start school funding in Mississippi as governor in 1982 had this to say about the double anchor of race and poverty: "Discrimination is not limited to race. The line that separates the well educated from the poorly educated is the harshest fault line of all. This is where we must begin. We must get the message out to every household and especially every poor household that the only road out of poverty runs by the schoolhouse."

But do the political and educational leaders of Deep South states, counties and cities have the will to travel the William Winter highway? On the fiftieth anniversary of the decision, *Brown* could still have had a brilliant legacy in my native Calhoun County, and systems like it throughout the

South. One or at most two consolidated city-county school districts could achieve a high level of economic integration, a majority of middle-income and high-achieving students in all or nearly all schools. There were examples of consolidated systems in Chattanooga, Louisville, and Raleigh, for instance, that guaranteed a majority of achievers in every school to pull up the disadvantaged without stifling more advanced students. In the consolidated Raleigh and Wake County system, no school had more than 40 percent eligible for free or reduced-price lunches, and no school was to have more than 25 percent testing below grade level.

This nationally admired and studied system was reversed in 2010 when conservatives of the tea-party stripe were elected to the school board and by a 5-4 vote it was decided to return to a straight neighborhood system in which wealthy neighborhoods had good schools and poor neighborhoods had bad ones. Creeping parochialism claimed another victim.

A solution similar to the former Wake system, voluntarily agreed upon, would be next to impossible in balkanized counties such as my county, which has five school systems. Why? Preponderantly white systems would say, disingenuously, "It's not about race. We just don't want bad schools exported to us." And the mirror argument would be voiced by Afro-centrists. "What makes white people think that blacks can't improve their own schools?" It takes rare courage to upset local conventions, loyalties and prejudices on behalf of even the highest ideals. Yet, in the absence of state action, exceptional local leadership or legal mandates, poor districts and their children throughout the South are doomed to perpetuate failure—generation after generation.

THE POLICY BOARD BORN in Raleigh in 1971 still exists as a useful meeting place where academic, business, and political leaders of the region come to know each other and share ideas. Under the chairmanship of then-Florida Governor Bob Graham, the board achieved one of its most significant policy initiatives—interstate banking among Southern states. Governor Graham's rationale was that unless the capital-poor South moved before national banking became a reality, Citibank or First Boston would suck up most of the capital and the South's capital deficit would be permanent. There should be a statue of Graham in downtown Charlotte, amidst the towers of national banks. But there was a downside to the South's sudden accumulation of wealth. Small towns throughout the South, and nation, were losers in the inevitable bank mergers. In Anniston, First National became SouthTrust (then Wachovia, then Wells Fargo). Local bank presidents cared about their communities. Instead a cascade of bank mergers left whole floors of local banks empty and their towns bereft of civic leadership; where there used to be local bank presidents, supreme commanders of civic armies, there now are merely managers, who take their marching orders not from community concerns but distant corporate headquarters. Corporate headquarters of giants such as Wells Fargo could give less than a damn about local communities, their peoples' problems or aspirations. If you had debt, the merged banks were bullies. If you sought help to back a marginally profitable civic venture, you would be regarded with benign indifference.

By a perverse law of social physics, creation of the SGPB signaled the slow death of the Lamar Society. In effect, we had helped midwife an offspring that would devour its parent. The SGPB had a public-private structure and financing which, in time, made the under-financed and less well-defined Lamar Society redundant. Looking back, Mike Cody reflected, "Once we brought the New South governors and their staffs into the picture, the networking and communications were taken over, and we lost our relevance and unique position." He added this benediction, "The mere fact that over thirty years later you and I, who had never heard of each other in 1970, are still friends, talking together, and worrying about the state of the South, is an indication that something important happened at Quail Roost."

THE HISTORIC IMPORTANCE OF those two days in Atlanta has been for me the specific date when we knew that Jim Crow was forever dead and gone, along with the civilization that had nurtured him. Racism, that defect of the human heart, did not die and I doubt it ever will, but Statutory Racism lay moldering in the grave. There was no doubt about his demise, after those elected Southern governors had given their homilies over the grave of the deceased.

We could now support a claim to being "The Second Greatest Generation," those who fought World War II being the "Greatest Generation," according to former NBC anchor Tom Brokaw in his book of the same name. Our claim to greatness rests here: We tried, hard, to make all men equal, and we created a new black middle class. We have seen the walls of legal racism fall and we have seen the end of the civilization that supported it. That bears repeating. Our generation achieved a victory over fear and prejudice which made the Founding Fathers balk and lose heart, a victory that even 620,000 dead in Civil War couldn't secure. We helped bring down the curtain on an entire civilization which existed as a denial of the Declaration of Independence.

The magnitude of what had been achieved in our time would dawn on us later, but meanwhile we busied ourselves at annual meetings in Birmingham, Jackson, and Atlanta, again, with spreading the new gospel of problem-solving to replace the old-time religion of race-baiting. Tom Naylor and I took on the task of pulling together an eclectic collection of thoughts about the New South. Our book, published by McGraw-Hill in 1972, bore the title of a speech I had given around the state at colleges and other safe havens after being flattened by the Wallace steamroller, "You Can't Eat Magnolias." The book lacked the classic literary merit of the Old South exegesis by the Agrarians at Vanderbilt, *I'll Take My Stand*. It did not have the scent of freshly turned earth or the arch cynicism of the Agrarian poets and professors. It had a practical, solid feel of pavement under feet and a hopeful, forward-looking spirit.

The book was no best seller, but it did get around in the right places and helped shape the thinking of our generation in the South. During a book promotion tour, I found myself in an awkward and funny pose in Nashville. I was doing my first televised call-in show. The host advised me to look into the camera so I would make eye contact with the questioner. I looked at the telephone before me on the coffee table, expecting it to ring. To my surprise a powerfully amplified voice descended from above—God, speaking in a nasal, redneck accent. I looked for the source of the voice and the viewers got a good view of my Adam's apple.

One morning during the tour, I received a call in my hotel room from the Reverend Dr. C. C. Washington, a former minister in Anniston. There is no record of Mrs. Gardner, my icon of normality, ever having met Dr.

Washington. They would not have met at a social occasion or even at a regular worship service, even though they shared the same faith and lived in the same small town for many years, even though Dr. Washington was one of the town's most prominent citizens. He was, of course, black, the pastor of the largest black congregation in town, Seventeenth Street Baptist. She was white. They might have met at a funeral, because there have always been some things in the South which ranked above segregation, and death is one of them. Another is that special mixture of feelings about place and people that make us refer to them as "home" and "homefolks," long after we have left.

Dr. Washington left Anniston before the glory days of the civil rights movement. He went up to Nashville to be executive director of the Sunday School Board of the National Baptist Convention, but he never forgot home. When he read that I was visiting Nashville to promote our book, he tracked me to my hotel room and insisted that I come by the board's publishing house for a visit. We reminisced for a good while. Dr. Washington spoke of good times back home and of good fights—disagreements with men he liked and respected, among others, Dad—all told with enormous good humor.

His visitor was white but, in the best tradition of the South, that didn't matter. In the blood of both was knowledge of a people and a place that touched them equally, knowledge not just of Anniston but of the South itself, of two peoples locked together in a history of loving and hating and caring, of enduring through defeat, insult, poverty, and injustice.

That "way of life" was the only one Mrs. Gardner knew. She was born at a time when water, sewerage, and transportation systems were essentially the same as the Assyrians used; she died before the last commuter rocket took off, before the World Wide Web both isolated and joined us to larger universes. Dr. Washington was born before Martin Luther King Jr., and outlived him, outlived even the civilization Dr. King was born to destroy. Yet, through all the troubles and changes they saw, neither he nor Mrs. Gardner was altered in any essential way. They were Southerners, members of a unique tribal culture.

The Lamar Society was born of that culture and died in it. But before the end came, when we still thought it had a vibrant future, we sought a permanent, paid president to be a charismatic spokesman and chief fund-raiser. Governors Askew and Bumpers agreed to co-chair a search committee, but before their staffs produced a list of candidates, a seemingly perfect candidate materialized. Frank Rose had retired as president of the University of Alabama and headed a D.C.-based consulting firm, University Associates. I called him and he expressed an interest. I flew up for talks at his house in Alexandria. Before he had finished his trademark Jack Daniels (black) on the rocks, he agreed to head the Society and give it space in his office. With some excitement I passed on the news to Reubin Askew and Dale Bumpers, who were relieved to be shed of a chore and agreed that Frank would be a good choice. The board validated the choice, and it was a done deal.

With Frank as president, and after three years as volunteer leader, I welcomed an arranged palace revolt. A talented friend and board member, Atlanta entrepreneur and attorney Edward E. Elson took over as chairman. Eddie's company had bookstores and sundry items in airports and Hilton and Hyatt hotels around the country. He would later sell his company, go on the boards of international corporations and cap a brilliant career as Rector of the University of Virginia, chairman of National Public Radio and a popular, imaginative ambassador to Denmark.

I was to be put out to pasture in 1974 at what turned out to be a final conference in Atlanta. At the luncheon that day, I was seated at Jimmy Carter's right. Small talk is not one of his talents and to make conversation I suggested that, after serving as governor, leaving office would be hitting a brick wall of inactivity. He assured me, "I have some plans." He did not elaborate, but within weeks it became obvious what those plans were. That evening, Frank presented me with an enormous plaque at the banquet, and Senator Edward Kennedy gave a dull foreign policy address.

I became an interested has-been, viewing from the sidelines the next phase of the organization. In the name of the Lamar Society, Frank mediated a potentially explosive school integration crisis in Louisville and conducted a study of the religious schools popping out all over the region which discovered that race was only one of several reasons parents were deserting public schools. But apparently Eddie and Frank weren't afire with determination to make the Lamar Society a permanent, prominent, influential, progressive voice in the region. Frank was at the end of his career, semi-retired and a little tired. The flame in the board flickered, and my own as well; our interest riveted by the rising success of one of our members in his campaign for president of the United States. Of the United States? A Southerner? We couldn't imagine such a thing but we hoped, held our breath, and watched with fascination. The Lamar Society membership roll was his first fund-raising list and a good many of our star members were absorbed into his administration such as Labor Secretary Ray Marshall and Assistant Secretary of State Hodding Carter. With a Southerner in the White House, we shrugged, "Well, we won the war," and went home. By the 1980s, the Lamar Society didn't meet any more. Another progressive voice in the South fell silent.

Its end wasn't dramatic. There wasn't a blinding nova ignited by collision with some fascist death star. It disappeared into the moist, fragrant Southern night as imperceptibly as the last firefly of summer.

OUR NEW SOUTH MOVEMENT suffered the same fate as a brave attempt in the 1930s to confront the region's historic dilemma—the short-lived Southern Conference for Human Welfare. On the evening of November 20, 1938, more than 1,500 delegates— 250 of them black—from all the states of the old Confederacy, filled Birmingham's Municipal Auditorium. Dad was there with liberal newspaper friends such as Jonathan Daniels of the (Raleigh) *News and Observer*, who many years later would give me a job. Barry Bingham and Mark Ethridge of the *Louisville Courier-Journal* were there, men who befriended me in my career. The Bingham family suffered a Lear-like tragedy when a dispute among the children led to the sale and decline of a great paper. Ironically, Barry Senior, a serious Shakespeare scholar, played the role of Lear, declining to anoint Barry Junior as his successor and thus, helplessly, watched the kingdom dissolve in sibling war. Barry Junior and his lovely Edie suppressed the tragedies that have cursed the family: the bizarre deaths of Barry's brothers, Jonathan in 1964, electrocuted while stringing lights for a party, and Worth, a fun-loving rising star with a bit of a swagger, whose spine was severed in an accident returning from the beach on Nantucket Island in 1966, and finally the cruelest blow—the loss of the paper to the mediocre Gannett chain. Barry and Edie were for years a charming part of the pageant that is Derby from the family's Italianate manse on the hill at Glenview until Barry's untimely death in 2006.

Barry Junior's elegant father and beautiful, smart, tart mother, Mary, turned heads, even in the assemblage of VIPs that November night in Birmingham. First Lady Eleanor Roosevelt and Alabama's own FDR, Governor Bibb Graves, were there. Among the academics of both races were Fisk University's eminent sociologist Charles S. Johnson and a future star historian, C. Vann Woodward, "Marse Vann" to my generation of journalists, civic, and political leaders who learned from him what it means to be Southern.

All are now ghosts that haunt histories such as the Pulitzer-winning *Carry Me Home*, by Diane McWhorter, but in 1938, they were in their prime. University of North Carolina President Frank Porter Graham's keynote address that evening was a shining moment for progressives in the audience. Blacks mingled with whites—an amazing effrontery to convention—as the Industrial High School choir sang the spiritual, "Deep River, My Home Is Over Jordan." Dr. Graham, mirroring the anthem spirit of the hymn, gave a cosmic altar call to his colored brethren, welcoming them "into the promised land." Then, a standing ovation greeted his assertion: "The black man is the primary test of American democracy and Christianity." Diane McWhorter quotes one giddy participant who felt as we did at the 1971 Atlanta meeting: "The whole South was coming together to make a new day."

Delegates filled with love and gratitude were doused with cold water the next day. The ludicrous face of the South appeared in the barrel-shaped form of the newly elected public safety commissioner of Birmingham. Eugene "Bull" Connor was there to enforce the law that upheld "our way of life," and it was there he uttered his famous malapropism, "White and Negro are not to segregate together." News stories of the event led with the resolution that all future SCHW gatherings would be integrated. Stories noted Bull Connor's enforcement of "the law of the land" and cast the event as a repudiation of segregation laws.

That was too much for many of the delegates, including Dad, who was still locked in the torturous contradiction of a New Deal liberal who earnestly wanted black equality—within a segregated system. The following Sunday, his editorial expressed admiration for Dr. Graham, respect repeated at dinner so often that the Tarheel educator became for me a hero-once-removed. In muted tones, Dad wrote that "instead of keeping the conference on the high level pitched by Dr. Graham, it was allowed to depart into channels that ran wild and thereby submerged thoughtful consideration." The editorial concluded: "This paper is willing to admit that the South is the nation's economic problem No. 1 . . . But our ills will best be solved by evolution rather than revolution, to which some of the recommendations of the Birmingham conference would lead if we sought to put them into effect at this time. We repeat, therefore, that education and not ill-considered agitation is the open sesame that we must seek."

Dad was never able to resolve his personal quandary, but the SCHW proved it wasn't the answer either. By 1948, it was a living corpse. Its financial lifeline was pulled by the labor group that supported it, the Congress of Industrial Organizations, John L. Lewis's CIO. Also, a red shadow had fallen over its energetic director, Joe Gelders. He was the son of a respected Jewish family who owned a popular Birmingham restaurant. His intellectual curiosity from boyhood led him to believe that communism was the cure for society's ills, thus lending credence to the Right's classic critique of liberals as "liberal-commie-pinkos." Gelders had been quietly separated in 1941, but the House UnAmerican Activities Committee six years later labeled SCHW a communist front. HUAC was notoriously unfair, unbalanced and ideologically driven, but in the hysterical Red Scare days its attention was fatal to do-gooders like SCHW. Its board didn't want to overthrow the government of the United States. They wanted to overthrow Jim Crow. In the 1930s and '40s, the two acts were perceived as one and the same. Such temerity was suicidal.

The vehemence with which the anti-New Dealers went after the naïve, well-intentioned SCHW is a case study about right-wing power and liberal weakness. Charles DeBardeleben and his attorney, Jim Simpson, saw in CIO support of SCHW the threat of union wages in the DeBardeleben coal mines. They also were socially offended by the audacity of Negroes casually exchanging views publicly with whites. DeBardeleben wrote SCHW's first president, Dr. Graham, his disgust at allowing whites to "mingle and associate with Negroes." The next barrage from right-wing cannon was fired through its propaganda organ, *Alabama: The Newsmagazine of the Deep South*. Diane McWhorter wrote that the magazine "invented" six hundred "dyed-in-the-wool" communists among SCHW's "long-haired men and short-haired women . . ."

A twenty-first century Republican officeholder gave this light-hearted definition of the two wings of his party, "We have our conservatives, and then we have our Nazis." In DeBardeleben's case, the latter was close to the literal truth. His office building was headquarters of the Southern branch of the extremist Constitutional Educational League. Within weeks of the 1938 SCHW meeting, the League gave a banquet in New York for the American Nazi leader, Major General George VanHorn Moseley, who advocated, among other breath-taking proposals, the sterilization of all Jewish immigrants to the United States.

The fires of right-wing economic self-interest and cultural hatred burn with a fury and persistence that is lacking in liberalism. Harboring subversive ideologies didn't bring the Lamar Society low. As far as I know, there weren't any Communist Party members on our board. Nobody cared to hunt for commies in the 1970s, anyway, Joe McCarthy was gone and the Red Scare of the 1950s had long since passed. Neither was the Society a threat to any economic self-interest.

At the end of the day, progressive voices in the South fell silent because liberals do not burn the fuel—fear and hatred—that keeps the right wing taut, suspicious, alert, and strong.

12

Smoke

Social movements—and their enemies—do not respect the neat cat-
egories of historians. The force powering the civil rights movement
carried right through 1970, as if it didn't realize that the Old South
had died and was laid to rest alongside legal segregation that year. Neither
had the Snopses run out of venom.

The regional spear-point of the movement, the Southern Christian
Leadership Conference (SCLC), was to remain a force nationally and in
small towns such as Anniston until it ran out of Bull Connors to bait.
Eventually, SCLC's moral force would wither, its economic and political
agenda no more inspiring than that of a union or chamber of commerce.
It would become largely irrelevant. In its latter stages, as a family business
with plump Martin King III at its head and an aging, dignified Coretta
King as Queen Mother, SCLC would be reduced to trivial complaints,
searching for something to awaken outrage. Not finding anything to fire
much passion, the living embodiment of a force that routed the armies of
legal oppression became . . . boring, merely boring.

A similar fate would befall the Snopeses. Deprived of support from
friendly police forces, even in places like Birmingham, increasingly isolated
by a resigned conformity to changed mores in the South, the KKK and
NSRP were relegated to a scorned fringe of society. A local Klan weakly
pleaded for "publicity" from one of our papers, the *Jacksonville News*. The
Invisible Order was firmly refused on the grounds it wasn't a charitable or
civic group along the lines of the Kiwanis, Lions, Elks, etc.

The 1970s had been a favorite decade for those of us who yearned to
see the best of Dixie on the march. Those years also brought into our family's lives a new, delightful and enriching creation, the birth of the Alabama

Shakespeare Festival, which ripened into a nationally admired repertory theater under Josephine's leadership and the artistic direction of Martin Platt.

ONE SOLEMN NOTE UNDERCUT the decade's satisfactions, the decline and death of my mother. After Dad died in 1964, Mother lived on for another thirteen years, the first half of which were full. She inherited Dad's title of chairman and publisher of the *Anniston Star*, a role she undertook more as a queen regent than chief executive. Hers was a presence in the *Star*'s lunchroom that was welcomed and enjoyed by employees regardless of rank: an approachable sovereign. She was also deeply involved in research and writing of her book, *The Old Main*. This was a loving task, a family memoir and a tribute to the high culture of St. Olaf College in Northfield, Minnesota, which her father helped found and stabilize financially. Family and college were intertwined through kin who went there as students or who taught there as deans and professors, including an early president. The culture she describes in the book was of puritanical Lutheran morality and deep learning. Classical Greek was so prevalent on St. Olaf Avenue where she grew up that the first time she encountered the word "milestones" she pronounced it as if it were a Greek word, "mi-LIS-tonese." The book was finished in 1969; by 1971, at seventy-three, she decided to quit active involvement in the paper and made me publisher.

She and Dad had led active lives, meeting interesting people at editors and publishers conventions in major American cities, in Europe and Latin America. Mother used to tell the story of the bold answer she gave a speaker at one of those conventions. She had not heard him being introduced and thus did not know who he was when he spoke to her later; "What did you think of my speech," he asked. "Well, I don't know but you surely murdered the King's English," she tartly replied. The speaker, charmed by her honesty, engaged her in further conversation. Only later did she learn he was the department store mogul Marshall Field.

Mother and Dad's home life had been full, too. As the Depression loosened its grip, anxious talk of selling the house and living over the paper's downstairs offices and printing plant ceased. There were presidents, governors, and senators to elect and scold, praise, or instruct on the editorial page. There was civic work as state governor of Rotary and chairman of the Chamber's Military Affairs Committee, which among other duties included a Christmas-morning cocktail hour at home for officers from Ft. McClellan.

Mother was a star of the Little Theater, which she founded in 1927, and played the female lead in *End of the Dance* by University of Alabama creative writing professor Hudson Strode, which was the 1929 winner of a national competition in New York. Her stunning interpretation in the title role of the caged tiger, *Hedda Gabler*, so affected the audience that a widely known, scandalously liberal (for Montgomery) character, Virginia Durr, decades later told me with wonder in her voice of Mother's performance. She learned to smoke for that role, a small vice but, in the end, a fatal one.

For a small-town couple, their life had been a multi-faceted ball turning in the light but the light began to fade in the early 60s. In fact, life had been in slow motion since Dad's illness began to drain his vitality and curiosity. Her final six years were not good ones. There were no exciting trips, old friends had died off, and the civilization she had come to know in the South was itself dying all around her. Standards were falling, or so it seemed to her. The paper wasn't what it used to be—too liberal. Mother and my sister Elise viewed my winning a prized Nieman Fellowship not as an honor but as desertion of my brother-in-law, Elise's husband Phil Sanguinetti, who had been recruited away from a career with Monsanto to be an officer at the paper. Phil became an intelligent, careful, and popular operating president of the company, a likable conservative who nicely balanced my more liberal instincts, and a mediating presence when family tensions threatened an actual breach. Mother continued to smoke; long lonely days and an extended cocktail hour affected her health. Though she did not find much enjoyment in life, she did have an old trouper's interest in the development of the Alabama Shakespeare Festival under Josie's leadership. In July 1977 she fell ill and was hospitalized. When we visited her at Regional Medical Center, she wanted to talk with Josie about the Festival's sixth season, which included *Hamlet* and *Rosencrantz and Guildenstern Are Dead*. The audience increased by 52 percent that year, but Mother was not among them.

On Wednesday evening, July 20, I sat by her bedside and thought that her struggle against emphysema wasn't as hard. Her breathing didn't seem quite so labored. After small talk, her face took on a serious expression and she asked, "Is there something you want to ask me?" The finality of the question surprised and unsettled me. I couldn't think of anything to say. "Well, no, I don't think so," I mumbled. She then told me a strange childhood story. She recalled being one of the elementary school children invited to perform at a graduation ceremony for the college: one played the violin, another sang, a third recited poetry, and then it was her turn. She did a dance. "I represented smoke," she explained, a writhing, sensuous performance, which urbane audiences would call modern dance. Her wholly innocent movements were seen in the context of morality framed by a succession of deeply conservative Lutheran sermons against drinking and dancing in a severely repressed, sex-segregated society. It was shocking! Dark thoughts of a child being possessed by the Devil hovered. The child, her mother, the family was disgraced. When she finished her sad story, she did not draw any conclusions; she did not speak of life-lessons learned or offer any signposts I might follow. She just told the story, and that was that. I felt immediate sympathy for the brave, imaginative little girl and anger toward a cold, narrow, unforgiving morality. I left for home that night pondering the meaning of such a surprising story.

In the morning Elise called to tell Josie and me that Mother had died in the night.

The dance makes ironic bookends in her life. She performed a dance the night she met Dad, and her last story was about a dance of disgrace. But what did it mean? Why did she tell a deathbed story of a creative child's free expression being subdued by a closed-minded, disapproving society? Surely the experience found a vehicle in her memorable portrayal of Hedda. In the Ibsen play there was a war of smoke and fire against a suffocating society. But what did the childhood memory mean offstage? Did she have an unhappy life? Did her breeding in the world of the mind, of intellectual curiosity, surrounded by music, especially the great St. Olaf choir in which she had sung, did those influences make her feel confined in the small-town South? Would she have found greater fulfillment in the arts, as an actress, dancer, or director? The mystery is shrouded . . . by smoke.

A BITTER PERSONAL DISAPPOINTMENT was Anniston's lapse of civic, economic, and political imagination, which resulted in the loss of its cultural
crown jewel and prime tourist attraction, the Shakespeare Festival. That
was a loss whose pain will not go away. This should have been Josephine's
story, told in her own voice. As chairman and executive producer, she was
central to its thirteen seasons here. She could tell the story so much better:
How an amateurish *Hamlet*, performed in the hot, airless auditorium of an
abandoned high school, became a soundly professional—often riveting—
repertory company that gained national prominence, and then was lost.
She doesn't talk about it. It is a numb spot in her emotional memory—a
vital, living, all-absorbing, deeply loved thing that left her, but not without
first hurting her.

It was a preposterous idea. The Little Theater's new director, Martin
Platt, one year out of Carnegie Tech in 1971, was proposing to establish a
Shakespeare Festival in our little city. The market was wide open, he argued,
since the Bard's works at the time were performed nowhere between Dallas
and Washington, D.C. So Martin began the hunt for actors who would work
for virtually nothing, and next year a little band of volunteers, including
Josephine, scurried to mount the first production, *Hamlet*. The prop she
contributed was a shovel for the graveyard scene, "Alas, poor Yorick . . ."
Alas, poor shovel. She never saw it again.

But four years later, Martin Platt's 1976 production of *King Lear* made
Christopher Plummer's later performance in the title role at Lincoln Center a deadly bore by comparison. Plummer dragged the body of his dead
daughter, Cordelia, onto the stage as if she were a sack of oats, and howled
in grief over what appeared to be a crumpled bag. In Platt's production a
talented but unknown actor, the late Charles Antalosky, came onstage with
the limp body of Cordelia in his arms. He did not stop in midstage to do
the "howl" scene; he kept coming and coming until he reached the lip of
the thrust stage and laid his lifeless daughter down almost in the laps of
the audience, but so gently, as if she were a flower that would bruise. Then
he howled, and howled again, drew a deep, deep breath as if the last howl
would split the heavens . . . all that came out was a strangled sob.

The audience sprang to its feet, among them the Southern correspondent for the *New York Times*, Roy Reed. In his story for the *Times*, noting the presence of the Talladega 500 NASCAR track a few miles down I-20, the piece began, "William Shakespeare is gaining on Richard Petty in Alabama." Shakespeare was also exorcising the ghost of H. L. Mencken, who had called the South "the Sahara of the Bozart." With playful vengeance, I paid my respects to Mencken's ghost with an Op-Ed piece in the September 7, 1976, *Washington Post*, "The Cultural Yeasting of the South," in which I noted that in the new New South which was emerging in the 1960s and the 1970s, there was a wave of development of theater, opera, and other fine arts forms across the region. In the essay, I urged Southern businessmen and state governments to develop new habits of generous support for the arts because "the quality of life is advanced more by appropriations to the arts than to state sovereignty commissions" [see full article in the Appendix].

IN MY OWN BACK yard, my exhortations to Southern business leaders played out in an unexpected fashion with Anniston's own Alabama Shakespeare Festival Theater. Despite growing national attention, we had a hard time raising the kind of money it took to keep a professional theater afloat. Driving back from a disappointing fund-raising trip to Tuscaloosa, the thought occurred and I said to Josephine: "You know why this is so hard? We are the first generation of an establishment of philanthropy devoted to the arts in the Deep South." We were artistic entrepreneurs in a region that hadn't had time or money for the arts. The South's economic takeoff speed wasn't reached until the 1960s, and CEOs of that generation had little experience with the arts (for the ladies, they thought) and had not yet realized that endowing the arts conveys prestige as it had on captains of industry and finance for generation after generation in the northeast.

Then Juliette Doster, a leading member of the fledgling Shakespeare board (and of the Ladies Guild, costumers and social sewing club combined), conceived a gold-plated fund-raising possibility. The wealthy international builder Winton "Red" Blount of Montgomery was having an affair with the beautiful and very feminine wife of U.S. District Court Judge Robert Varner. Carolyn and Red were headed for the altar through the divorce court when Juliette hit on the idea that Carolyn would be a good board member. She had come to plays in Anniston, and she might reel in Red, with his deep pockets. (Ironically, Red had been sent a mail solicitation, but the letter to the former Nixon postmaster general was returned "addressee unknown.") Carolyn got his interest all right, but it was more covetous than supportive. Red wanted to please his beautiful, doting new wife, but he had a larger vision: he imagined on the rolling farmland behind his house a vast park with a lake that would mirror a fabulous professional theater and an art museum.

In 1982, as the ASF's expenses approached the $1 million mark, it was already too late. The city's business and political leadership did not have the imagination to hold onto its defining cultural asset. The Festival board had bowed to Red's offer to move the operation to Montgomery in exchange for writing off the deficit, which was pocket change for him. When a majority of the board caved in and accepted his offer, Josephine took it in good grace. She said new T-shirts should carry the slogan, "Better Red than dead." Red laughed and said he'd wear it at the Montgomery Country Club.

In the negotiation that led to the deal, though, he was insulting. Red was a misogynist; not that he hated women, he just thought they were not to be taken seriously. Josephine, the chairman and executive producer of the Festival, was not invited to be part of the negotiation. She was left outside the conference to be entertained by Carolyn while Red "negotiated" with male board members. Josephine was philosophical, knowing that the Blount empire and its vassals could do more for the Festival than Anniston. Red did invite her on a flying tour of the best theaters on the North American continent, maybe as a peace offering but more likely as a resource in a field about which he knew little, architecture of the arts. He underestimated the cost (well over $20 million) of the beautiful theater his architect son, Tom, envisioned. As Josie put it, "Red gave Tom an unlimited budget, and he exceeded it."

The handsome, graceful structure is mirrored in the lake at the center of the park, which includes an art museum and a life-sized sculpture of Red. For his obituary editorial in 2002, I wrote, "Red Blount is one of those rare individuals whose contributions and ego were the same size."

13

Rabbit Sausage

Nowhere were the struggles to negotiate new cultural ways in the South easy—or over. In 1971, as George Wallace began his third term as governor, Mother ceded her role as publisher to me. The passing of the torch was in an unceremonious meeting in her office, Dad's old office, in what is now our former site across the railroad tracks on West 10th Street. What lay immediately ahead for the new, thirty-five-year-old publisher and his city were a few nights of firebombs and gunfire that threatened to career into a miniature Watts riot.

I didn't see red flags signaling: Danger Ahead. I doubt any of the first-rank community leaders could have anticipated a week in the early fall of 1971 when the city was literally on the razor's edge. A fog of complacency had crept over most of the city in the fall of 1971. There were no more Klan marches or white man's rallies; the bus burning and nightrider murder were history, and we had a functioning biracial committee. The Human Relations Council could see warning signs ahead but service on the council had been passed down to the second- and third-rank leadership. The Great Validators paid little heed to its jeremiads.

As a new leader of our generation's New South movement—through the Lamar Society—I had focused my interest far beyond the city limits or even the state line. I was thus looking away when at home the irresistible civil rights movement met the sturdy resistance of Wellborn High School, a previously all-white institution cherished by residents of the neighborhood that skirted the western borders of Anniston. Here were two cultures, two sets of hair-trigger sensitivities whom a maliciously mischievous god on Mount Olympus would conspire to bring into confrontation: a mortal cockfight for the amusement of the gods.

The movement's righteous anger had a cutting edge in many black students' rejection of cherished school rituals such as standing for the "Alma Mater." Students with Wellborn roots found abrasive the new students' insistent demands for instant acceptance as cheerleaders, class officers, and equal-standing participation in other extra-curricular activities, and that black students would be disciplined only when whites are disciplined—in equal numbers and severity. Many of the black students also were fired with the passion of the exemplary teenagers who had faced dogs and fire hoses at Kelly Ingram Park in Birmingham.

The Wellborn community was and is a tight-knit neighborhood of universally neat homes whose hard-working, church-and-Friday-night-football-going families earned hourly wages or middle income salaries. The beating heart of the community was and is Wellborn High, the Panthers. Men of the community had built the library with their own hands when the county school board lacked funds for the project. To be a trustee of the school was to achieve the Wellborn equivalent of knighthood. The principal was an important man in the community. Howard Waldrep, ironically nicknamed "Mouse," was not just big—he was a mountain of a man, a mass of friendliness and good will, normally, and passionate about *his* school. He shared with the community one major failing. He had a chip on his shoulder. For all the bonded virtue of a sense of community, and Wellborn surely had that, the neighborhood almost made a fetish of being insulted. It was touchy, quick to take offense. When the paper loosely referred to someone from the area as a "Westsider"—an error often made by new reporters—a Wellborn patriot, whom I liked, on our advertising staff would confront me, fire in her eyes: "We are *not* the West side [by implication, the "colored" section]; we are the Wellborn community." Its loyalty and testy pride were made all the more explosive by its tradition of playing "Dixie" and waving the Confederate battle flag at football games. The mingling of loyalty and prejudice was exhibited later when black athletes made Wellborn a feared competitor. One Wellborn parent remembers the Friday night when a black cornerback picked up a fumble inside Wellborn's five-yard line. He had reached the fifty-yard line with pursuers close behind, when a large white man stood up in the stands and shouted fan loyalty in the language of his rearing, "Run, Nigger, run!"

It is not hard to understand that the community would resent the sudden arrival of 190 new students, strangers, who weren't from Wellborn, didn't know its traditions and icons, pushing their way behind federal court orders into "our" school. It was lighting a match in a gunpowder factory. A story told at a Lamar Society conference in Jackson, Mississippi, summed up Wellborn's feelings. J. C. Red, former president of the Jackson school board, described the reaction to court orders integrating schools in the Mississippi capital:

"The board was like that little boy whose Momma was trying to give him a dose of Castor Oil.

"'Now, son, you've got to take this.'

"'No'm,' replied the boy.

"'Now, son, you have to take it. It'll make you feel better.'

"'No'm,' said the boy.

"Finally, with threats of dire punishments, she got it down him. But he was still rebellious. 'All right, Momma, I swallowed it, but I ain't gonna *do* nothin'!'"

Like all vestiges of the old civilization, Wellborn had to *do* something: admit dozens of black students. The new situation was strange, feelings were strained on both sides, but efforts were expended to keep the lid on. At one point, Mouse's wife, Mary, sat her gym class down on the polished floor of the basketball court. Sitting cross-legged, she looked into the eyes of the circle of students around her and said, "Now, we've just got to get right in our hearts." She was also protective of her husband, proud of the way "he stood up to them" and hurt by "these reporters for the *Star* that Mr. Ayers brought down from the North [who] made us look awful. It's hard for people not from around here to understand what all we were going through."

In fact, the *Star*'s beat reporter on that story, Mike Sherman, was an Alabamian (who later became an editor in Montgomery); another reporter covering the story, Frank Denton, was a graduate of New York's Columbia University but also a Texan.

Looking back years later, Mary was sensitive to the casual humiliation of separate water fountains at places such as Sears: "for that to be allowed to happen was just not right." But as she remembered those days, "tension was building up and they [black students] were acting up and being ugly to the white kids. It wasn't all the black kids, just the ones who listened to [the civil rights leaders]. The other black kids were embarrassed." Inevitably, tensions would boil over. The trigger was the expulsion of a black student. His punishment ratcheted up black student grievances, pushed Mouse's temper to its threshold, and became part of the stage-managed process of a formal civil rights demonstration. That in turn would light the fuse on a citywide explosion. It all started by an incident of a sort that in years ahead would go unnoticed.

A STUDENT NAMED HARVEY Garrett intervened in a scuffle between two white and two black students. All five were sent to the principal's office, where equal justice was applied to four of them: a biracial paddling for two and a biracial suspension for the other two. Garrett was suspended also but Mary Waldrep defended him, having witnessed the boy's innocence. There are conflicting memories of what happened next. Either Mouse pointed a finger at Garrett and inquired why one of the black students involved would implicate him or the principal advanced on the frightened boy, making a threatening gesture. Both agree that the young man slapped Mouse's finger away, at which point Mouse did or didn't say, "Why, you black s.o.b.," and the two were restrained by witnesses to the scene. Young Garrett was out—O.U.T.

All sides agree that the Calhoun County School Board then met and approved the suspension for "violent misconduct." When Garrett had not returned to class by Tuesday, October 26, a crowd of fifty to sixty students appeared at the principal's office to ask why he wasn't in school. When Mouse told the crowd that the matter was in the hands of the board, they refused to return to class and instead began roaming the halls, creating a disturbance. A white mother was startled when her seventeen-year-old daughter called. "Mom, come get me," the frightened girl said. "They're rioting. They are running through the halls with sticks and clubs and tearing up everything. Oh, Mom, it's awful." The protesters broke into the band room, damaging a trumpet owned by a white student, and shattering the glass on the trophy case before being stopped and ejected. A snap roll call identified seventy-two absent students, all black, who were summarily suspended; classes were dismissed early.

The frightened white girl's mother later wrote the *Star* with a note of regret that she had been wrong to teach acceptance and tolerance to her children. She said that only civil behavior by blacks could renew her belief that "a black is different from a white only as a brunette is different from a blonde." A black woman saw the disturbance as a situation of "justice against injustice." In her letter to the paper exhibiting uncommon shrewdness for a sideline observer, she defined the issue as the City Council versus the Civil Service Board, the Human Relations Council versus the police department and now students versus the Board of Education. If both races would follow Jesus, she concluded, the city would know "there isn't time to say who is to blame. There is time to preserve peace and harmony."

Wednesday morning a large crowd of black parents and roughly half the black student body assembled outside the school with something less than peace and harmony on its mind. The demonstration was led by a twenty-eight-year-old minister, the Reverend John Nettles. He had been called to Mount Olive Baptist Church four years earlier and had quickly assumed a leadership role co-equal with Nimrod Reynolds. In a speech many years later, Nettles told his localized version of the popular light-hearted civil rights era anecdote about a black minister or leader being called to a tough town: "They wanted me to come to Anniston, and I got on my knees and prayed and asked the Lord to go to Anniston with me. The Lord spoke and said, 'I'll go as far as Atlanta with you, but in Anniston you're on your own.'" Also, in the fullness of time, revealing how bitter grievances can be healed in a small town, Nettles revisited Wellborn and was greeted warmly by Mouse Waldrep. Mouse noted a medallion around John's neck, and said, "I've always wanted to have a medallion like that." Nettles smiled, took off the decoration and hung it around the principal's neck. Mary, recalling those tense days, remembers Nettles laughing, "I was young. I didn't know what I was doing."

But in the anxiety of that moment, both sides were apprehensive as they experienced their first civil rights confrontation. To those inside the school, the demonstrators had a menacing air. "I was teaching physical education at the time," Mary recalled thirty-two years later, "and I brought students in the gym and locked the doors so the white students could be safe." Police and sheriff's deputies arrived and gave the crowd twenty minutes to disperse. When they didn't, 136 were arrested, including Reverend Nettles, and were transported on three buses to city and county jails.

Thursday morning some one hundred black students and parents staged a sit-in at the county school board offices. Superintendent Charles Boozer, who had one of the more "interesting" jobs of the era, agreed to meet—for the first time—with representatives of the parents. Boozer, board attorney H. R. "Pat" Burnham, Nettles, and Reynolds met privately to discuss a list of grievances including: unfair suspension of black students, the readmission of Garrett, amnesty for students involved in the Tuesday fracas, an end to playing "Dixie" and displaying the Confederate flag, participation in extracurricular activities, and the firing of the principal.

A regularly scheduled board meeting Thursday night took testimony from Waldrep and Garrett before a crowd that overflowed the courtroom and spilled into the courthouse lobby. When the board announced it would determine Garrett's status at a later date, blacks left but white parents remained. A supporter of Mouse Waldrep told the crowd, "If he is persecuted in this thing that's come up, we as parents will have failed him." Loud cheers greeted him and each of a succession of speakers, all of whom spoke in support of the principal.

Late Friday, the board decided to expel Garrett for the year, a decision almost forgotten in the tumultuous days ahead. Just after 8 p.m., while John Nettles was working in the study of his church on South Christine Avenue, the phone rang in the living room of the residence next door. Mrs. Nettles picked up her four-year-old daughter, entered the room, sat at the telephone table and picked up the receiver. "Hello," said Mrs. Nettles. At that moment, a fusillade of bullets riddled the house, two striking either side of the chair where she and her daughter were sitting. Bullet holes were found in the front door and on the posts framing it, in the front bedroom windows and the picture window in the living room.

"I think they meant to hit somebody. I think they were out to kill me," an agitated Nettles told the *Star*. "This might encourage more violence;

violence by blacks. I think it probably will," though he said he did not condone violence.

On that Saturday, when Josephine and I made the two-minute drive to the Nettles' house, we saw a cordon of armed black volunteers surrounding it. Inside, there was a funereal air. There was the same Roman feast that accompanies Southern funerals. The living room was crowded and people talked in hushed voices. A stranger would have thought someone had died. We gave our condolences to John and Mrs. Nettles, offered to help in any way we could, and left. I guess we must have been recognized as friendly or harmless, because the armed guards weren't otherwise allowing vehicles driven by whites to enter the block. The night before, a white taxi driver had been ordered to turn away; as he sped off, he threw a beer can hitting one of the guards. A shot was fired but the driver wasn't injured. Through the night Friday, sporadic gunfire could be heard in South and West Anniston's black neighborhoods. Two hours after the attack on the Nettles residence, two *Star* photographers saw three young black men throw firebombs at a West Anniston building supply store. The fire department responded to four other fire-bombings during the night and early morning. As a gray light dawned over the city, officials were relieved that there had been no serious injuries or property damage. They looked toward Saturday night with apprehension. It was Halloween.

Urgent meetings were held during the day. City Manager William Kell called together black leaders to request they use their influence to quell further violence. At a "mass meeting" at 17th Street Baptist Church, Reynolds's church, Nettles addressed the crowd along with a representative of the U.S. Justice Department's Community Relations Service (CRS), Johnny Ford (soon to become the first black mayor of Tuskegee, Alabama). Ford and local black leaders met again with Kell and city councilmen, after which Nettles joined city officials "requesting blacks to get off the streets with their guns." The city experienced the quietest Halloween in memory, but it was only the calm at the eye of the storm. Troubles began Sunday shortly after 8 p.m. with six fire-bombings and several shootings reported. Plumes of smoke rose a hundred feet from flaming autos set ablaze at Totherow's Auto Sales and a gasoline-filled soda-bottle bomb destroyed a storage area at the rear of Wakefield's Noble Street store, causing smoke damage throughout the retail shop. Minor damage was reported at Kelly Supply, Day's TV, Medlin's Service Station and LeRoy's Pic'n'Pay.

The crowd at 17th Street Baptist Church that evening was told by Chester Weeks, county NAACP president, that fire bombs had been reported in the city and that Nettles "cannot move. We think we should keep him where he'll be safe." Complicating matters further, the entire third shift of the police department staged a sit-in. It was the second strike in a week protesting actions of City Manager William Kell. The officers disputed his judgment that riot gear, shotguns, and nightsticks were provocative; the officers insisted on being fully armed for patrol in black areas. The Sunday sit-down protested the suspension of officer Charles Dansby until an investigation could be made of a complaint that he had used excessive force against a black co-ed at Wellborn. The striking officers demanded that the charges be dropped, Dansby be reinstated, and that they be allowed full riot gear. Officers had shown disdain for Kell when they altered his signature on a police dayroom blackboard to read, "By order of City Nager." They further displayed contempt for city leaders by ignoring Mayor Clyde Pippin's personal appeal to resume duty. The officers sat on the police department steps as the mayor pleaded with them to help control the violence. They feigned boredom, some with chins in hands, others staring past the ranking civil authority.

Faced with an escalating threat of chaos, Pippin agreed to the police demands, but then called in a force of fifty to seventy-five state troopers who arrived early Monday morning to cordon off a thirty-nine block area of South Anniston. The blockade was to prevent armed blacks from leaving the area and nonresidents from entering. City officers went back to work shortly after a sniper shattered a plate glass window at the Downtowner Motel. Minutes later, the shooter fired on police and newsmen who had gathered at the scene. Police returned fire. They also fired shots to prevent a firebombing of Beshears Auto Sales, but there were no reports of injury by gunfire.

Meanwhile, Nettles was escorted to the mass meeting. He told a cheering audience that city officials and police weren't concerned about the shots fired at his family; they only wanted "to keep blacks in their place." "Hell, man," he continued, "black folks ain't scared no more," evoking cheers. He counseled nonviolence but promised, "Tomorrow will be Black Monday," a march of one thousand from South Anniston to the courthouse to deliver "an ultimatum. We're gonna tell that [county school] board what black people want and what they're gonna get."

By morning, Nettles had thought better of the "ultimatum march," agreeing in a meeting with the city council, Kell, and a representative of the Justice Department's CRS division that it would inflame an already overheated atmosphere. The council also brought steadying leadership to city police with the appointment of businessman Gerald Powell as assistant administrator for police affairs. He had been appointed by Governor Albert Brewer as interim sheriff in the summer of 1970 after the death of veteran Sheriff Roy Snead Sr. Powell knew many of the Anniston police officers from his years as a former federal alcohol and tobacco tax agent. He shared some of the local officers' beliefs that "misguided judges" and the U.S. Supreme Court made their jobs harder. Powell's no-nonsense demeanor and the physique of an all-pro linebacker gave him added authority as head of the city's law enforcement. He reluctantly accepted the $1-a-year post only after being assured he had the 100 percent support of the city council. He promised "equal, fair, and impartial enforcement of the law on a professional basis. We're going to make it work."

UNFOUNDED RUMORS ON SUNDAY night of an interracial rape—the mythic, centuries-old white fear—alarmed me. I felt that heightened state of alertness that comes with danger, and the thought of that rumor racing like wildfire among an anxious, edgy public was truly scary. The tension lighted a dormant memory that could be helpful. I recalled that rumor-control was one of the recommendations of the Kerner Commission, the body chaired by Illinois Governor Otto Kerner that had investigated the causes of the 1960s urban riots. I drove over to the old, yellow-brick City Hall and met with City Manager Bill Kell in his vest-pocket office. Bill readily agreed to the rumor control plan and Gerald thought it worth a try. Kell called Southern Bell and the company hooked up a Rumor Control phone number on a priority basis. The *Star* publicized the number and the first night forty to fifty calls were received; Powell judged the special line a success.

As calm began to return to the city, the special line fell into disuse—the fate of all emergency measures, until the next crisis. The beleaguered county school superintendent, Charles Boozer, and his chairman, Gerald Acker, moved to resolve the warring grievance petitions from black and white Wellborn parents by forming biracial committees and holding "get-acquainted" meetings. The fragile stability achieved by the end of the week coincided with the long-scheduled football game between traditional rivals Wellborn and Anniston that Friday night. For such heated rivals, in such a racially combustible atmosphere, to be shut up together in a stadium didn't seem wise. The game was cancelled—an extreme measure in the South.

Easing tensions allowed the resumption of regular police patrols and the state troopers departed. One former state trooper remained, a reassuring one. Gerald Powell had asked respected Major Bill Jones, former chief of the investigative division of the state police, to come to Anniston as a consultant. On November 7, at a called Saturday morning meeting of the city council, Jones was named police administrator, allowing Powell to return to his work as an executive at Dixie Clay. With racial stress receding and the first professional head in place over a mutinous police department, city leaders exhaled for the first time in weeks. We all began to analyze the week's events, asking ourselves and each other: What if some crazed redneck, his courage cresting on a foam of beer suds, had actually shot and killed Reverend Nettles? Would a seditious police department have had the cool professionalism to deal with simultaneous explosions in South and West Anniston?

Turning that question over in my mind, a scene from an early 1950s summer mentally replayed itself. It spoke volumes about the degree of professionalism and respect for civil liberties of cops in that era. I was a teenaged cub reporter during vacation. I thought it would be exciting to ride with the police at night. Seated in the backseat of a patrol car driving for aimless, uneventful hours, my excitement dulled until we parked at a house in west Anniston . . . *Something's about to happen*, I thought. I followed the two officers as they entered the house—without knocking—and went straight into the bedroom. A lone figure in the bed had been asleep. I don't recall what the officers said to the older woman in the rumpled bed but they knew her. They addressed her by her first name. We were there only a couple of minutes but I was intensely uncomfortable. *This isn't right,* I thought but reasoned, without conviction, *They are the police, authority figures. I guess it's okay, but it doesn't feel right.* Back in the squad car, I squelched my doubts about the incident, but it haunts me to this day.

When I replayed that scene against the backdrop of recent events my answer was: We could be in trouble. If one of Kenneth Adams's boys crawled out of his hole, guns blazing, he'd touch off the mother of all riots. I had confidence in the professionalism of Major Jones and Gerald Powell, but not in their rank and file officers. Later we traced the contemptuous independence of city police to a banal source, local politics. But at that moment in mid-November 1971, we were in trouble and something had to be done.

Thinking the Kerner Commission report might have some ideas I looked at it again. The report's summary wasn't helpful. It blamed urban riots on "white racism," and said the nation was "moving toward two societies, one black, one white, separate—and unequal." If white racism was the cause, what do you do about that? Wholesale arrest of whites on suspicion of prejudice? The body of the report, however, spoke eloquently about the woeful lack of preparation for any city to deal with a crisis in a timely, judicious, and effective manner. Neighborhood leaders did not know and trust city officials—and vice versa. So when a triggering incident occurred, or a false rumor spread, neither side knew what to do, who to call with an early warning that could contain the situation before its internal dynamics whipped it into a firestorm.

The self-evident solution was putting all those elements together in some organized way—an organization that didn't exist. The first, obvious step would be to bring carefully selected black and white leaders together often enough so they could get to know each other and develop trust—even friendship. But who would be the puzzle master to assemble all the parts? At that time one of the major real estate developers, the late Hoyt Howell Sr., had demonstrated sound, patient, genial leadership. He had "convening authority." Leading citizens would come to a meeting he called and give him a respectful hearing.

My friend and broadcast competitor Tom Potts and I talked it over and agreed that Hoyt was the man to point us in the right direction. (His son, Chip, would one day become mayor.) One evening shortly after the nights of tension, we met in his unpretentious real estate office. I brought a draft of a speech outlining the hybrid organization that would marry community leaders, black and white, with city officials. What the draft hoped to do was to weave different tempers, interests, races, religions, and castes into the miracle of community. That is, the simple act of calling someone you know, and who knows you, whenever a problem arises. We discussed the concept at some length and decided to call a group of proven white leaders to a meeting at the Downtowner Motel where Hoyt could outline a crisis-management plan, get feedback, and engage the interest of the city's leading bankers, merchants and professionals.

The city leaders knew the meeting was related to the racial crisis, and were looking for leadership. The rows of civic soldiers were attentive as Hoyt rose and walked to the podium. He had reworked my draft into his own words, but began with my quote from Alexis de Tocqueville. He said,

> Someone whose name I can't even pronounce visited America in 1835 . . . and said the following:
>
> These Americans are the most peculiar people in the world. In a local community in their country a citizen may conceive of some need, which is not being met. What does he do? He goes across the street and discusses it with a neighbor. Then what happens? A committee comes into existence and then the committee begins functioning on behalf of that need. You won't believe this, but it's true. All of this is done without reference to any bureaucracy. All of this is done by the private citizens on their own initiative.

A renewed sense of community could spring from such a new, ad hoc committee, Hoyt said.

> I believe that a new sense of purposeful unity will produce a new will to action, and through this sense of unity in participation will come a new

and broader representative group—fresh from the people and responsive to the people—which can initiate the needed action . . . Our goal should be to do something about any problem that comes up in this community. If we do nothing but listen to the problem, hopefully a member of the group would be in a position to solve or . . . call it to the attention of the agency that has the power to solve the problem.

That meant a new body composed of elected and appointed officials as well as civic and civil rights leaders from every section of the city. He went on to say that the ad hoc group could do the following:

Provide a means for broad citizen participation in the democratic process leading to decisions and action on community concerns.

Provide a forum for discussion of issues in the public domain and an information framework for continuing civic education.

Achieve consensus on community goals or on issues affecting the total community.

Initiate needed community action through information and inspired desire.

Hoyt's speech crystallized the urgency we all felt. And so in the next few days, a steering committee headed by Hoyt drafted a proposed structure and governance. Student leaders thought the committee should have a name, which fit its purpose . . . keeping things cool. They suggested it be christened COUL, for Committee of Unified Leadership. A larger, broadly representative plenary group was invited to a meeting at the YMCA Friday afternoon, November 19. On the recommendation of the steering committee, the body elected by acclamation Tom Potts as chairman and John Nettles as vice chairman. The salaried director selected was Carl Riffe, owner of a court reporting business who lived on the West side and had children in neighborhood schools.

Two weeks from the nights of anxiety and violence, the leadership of both races agreed on the composition of a crisis-management committee. COUL was in business, and every Tuesday morning for the next few years, the chairman of the executive committee would open the closed meeting by asking a biracial audience of officials and civic leaders, "Is there a crisis problem?"

THERE WAS AN AIR of edgy caution as two sets of leaders came together as strangers. Whites in their dealings with each other had established well-worn rituals of civic and political action: consultation, discussion, debate, and especially persistence, which often—not always—led to action. Such prescribed patterns worked well in the interplay of chambers of commerce but did not prepare white leadership to deal with suspicious and impatient black leaders, who had developed their own theories about the behavior of the other race. Blacks did not bring with them a climate of trust. Their experience convinced them that the elaborate processes of the Chamber of Commerce were duplicitous delaying tactics. By their very nature, chambers of commerce committees were better at postponing than acting. They are like merry-go-rounds, each year a cadre of civic soldiers gets on and an equal number get off, and around they go, the new riders unaware of or disinterested in the agenda of the previous board. Blacks had found success by a different process. If negotiation failed to achieve results, direct action might, and often did. The two systems did not mesh well, but black leaders did have a deeper understanding of the white man's culture and politics than vice versa. James Tinsley, who would become a dominant spirit of COUL, had listened and learned as an "invisible" tailor at Wakefield's clothing store on Noble Street. "We knew the white man's politics," said Mr. Tinsley, "We had to."

Mr. Tinsley has been gone now for many years, but when he died at ninety-six he left an empty place in the soul of our city. I never thought of calling James A. Tinsley Sr. "James" or "Jim," only Mr. Tinsley—out of respect. He called me, many years his junior, "Mr. Ayers"—a formality born of a different time. Mr. Tinsley was our "Honorary Mayor," liked and respected by black and white alike. No ingratiating, step-and-fetch-it Uncle Tom, he was unbending in his principles, but he also was a gentleman. He could suppress his own ego to make others feel comfortable. Though always a gentle man, Mr. Tinsley had seen troubles. He came to Anniston with his parents in 1911 seeking foundry work, and to escape sharecropping. Mr. Tinsley explained that pastoral practice this way: "They called it share-cropping, but the Big Man didn't do much sharing."

In 1923, with a degree in tailoring from Tuskegee Institute, Mr. Tinsley took up his trade on the economic margin assigned to "colored" people. For the next forty years he bore stoically the humiliations his race suffered. He endured with the calm patience of deep faith, of a Bible-reading, Bible-believing Christian. His forbearance was a lubricant between the strangers who came together in COUL. Time and again, he made us laugh with self-recognition as when whites were congratulating themselves about a lone black city councilman and school board member.

Beginning with his ritual preamble, "I want you to know I say this with love," he rolled out one of his famous parables: "You white folks' idea of equality puts me in mind of the fellow up in South Carolina who made so much rabbit sausage, he shipped it everywhere from Virginia to east Texas. Someone got suspicious and asked, 'What do you put in there with the rabbit meat to make sausage?' He answered, 'A little horse meat.' 'How much?' 'Fifty-fifty. Every time I put in a whole rabbit, I put in a whole horse.'

Mr. Tinsley could command the attention of the most dogmatic segregationist or Afro-centrist by suppressing his ego and turning upon them the power of his unyielding love. His diplomacy was so natural, so politically savvy, and value-based that, had he been born in a different era, I can easily imagine Mr. Tinsley as Secretary of State—perhaps in a Colin Powell administration.

One of the thorniest issues COUL had to confront was the police department. Membership on the Law Enforcement Committee by Mr. Tinsley and Gerald Powell gave it added influence. The committee learned from then-State Representative Hugh Merrill a prosaic explanation for the defiant behavior of the rank-and-file police officers. They were so out of control that a cop could physically assault the city manager, as one did, without fear of punishment. That was possible because the police department nominated members of the Civil Service Board, whom Merrill duly appointed. "It has always been a police department appointment," he explained. "No one has complained before." With the judicial arm of city government in its pocket, a gun and a billy club on its hip, the police force was the small-town equivalent of a military junta.

By the time the dogwoods had bloomed and faded, through changes in the Civil Service Board and the leadership of Major Jones, the department had become prouder and more professional. Jones had done a complete overhaul by the time he retired in 1973. He had established a training officer and a community relations bureau, and sent officers to the FBI Academy and to nearby Jacksonville State University's police academy. His intervention stopped the practice of fixing traffic tickets, and more importantly, the losing or reducing of criminal charges against friends. In a letter to Carl Riffe on April 30, 1972, Powell noted the climate created by COUL, "It is quite evident to me that no amount of law enforcement, coercion or arbitration could have prevented a disastrous confrontation without the influence that COUL has exerted."

Despite those hard-won changes, the inevitable morning came when a young black member of the executive committee made an accusation of police brutality. Two sets of egos collided in the center of the table. Before verbal blows could be launched, Mr. Tinsley set two rhetorical rabbits on the table to draw poison from the air.

His parable began with the ritual, "Now I want you all to know, I say this with love, but you white folks never been black and seen the poo-lice coming. It puts me in mind of the time the dogs declared a moratorium on chasin' rabbits. For three months all the dogs agreed they wouldn't chase any rabbits. Well, one day a couple of rabbits was sittin' by the side of the road, just visitin', when over the hill come a pack of mean-lookin' dogs, a-runnin' and a-hollerin'. One rabbit turns to the other and says, 'I think we better be movin' out through the woods.' But the second rabbit says, 'Naw, brother, we don't have nuthin' to worry about; you know about the moratorium.' Then, the first rabbit says, 'Yeah, I know about the moratorium but from the looks of them dogs, they don't.'" Everyone laughed, and a tense moment passed. Mr. Tinsley had gently guided white listeners outside themselves so they could see the police as blacks did.

COUL continued to meet through 1972 and 1973 with a calming effect. There were other successes. Tom Potts and I were assigned to address the

Wellborn High situation. Our objective was to win acceptance for a black assistant principal who could help Mouse by presenting a more comfortable and familiar face for black students, whose discipline would be voluntarily accepted. In the process of suggesting a personable black educator, William Hutchins, for the post, Tom and I deepened our understanding of the tenacious loyalty Wellborn people had for their community and their school.

By 1974, it didn't seem obligatory to attend COUL meetings, and it began to fade as an important civic force. In a sense, it had succeeded. We all knew each other. The miracle of community was closer to realization. "I think so," recalled Carl Riffe thirty years later. "We were at the point where we all felt comfortable with each other, where we were all on a first-name basis."

Of course, we had not resolved all or most of the endemic issues that lie between the races. There would be other bruises and abrasions suffered by two races occupying the same space, burdened with their separate histories and levels of trust, demanding respect, and competing for their share of the American Dream. The gulf had not closed, but leaders of both communities knew and liked people who lived "on the other side"—and tragedy had been averted. God had changed his mind again. Anniston did not become Selma; it was, as Nick Katzenbach wrote me from across the millennium divide, "a bright spot" in those tense days.

14

A Fateful Meeting

Our civilization had been dying for nearly two decades without anyone really noticing, but the 1970s finished it. The passing is marked for me, of course, by the panel of 1970 governors in Atlanta, but also by an inconsequential hometown scene. The Johnston Junior High School "midget" football team was practicing on the wide lawn which fronted on Leighton Avenue. Driving by, I saw little black boys and white boys playing together, shoulder pads preposterously large. It hit me: That unremarkable scene would have been impossible five years earlier!

Change. What was the South doing about it? What was it doing to the South? It all depends on what kind of change you are talking about. Racial politics in its more blatant forms began to be practiced with a wink. In gubernatorial elections since the 1970s, Republican candidates have eschewed naked racism, using a more polite, encrypted form: phrases such as "I didn't leave the Democratic Party, it left me [when it integrated]" and "bloc voting" and "special interest groups." Our racism had become ever so refined, practically as polite as the Yankee variety.

Language and views that used to be commonplace in the 1940s and 1950s, words like "mongrelization," used even among the genteel, Eastern-educated such as former Alabama governor Frank Dixon, had become shocking in the 1970s. This alteration in what the public found acceptable occurred despite the fact that these same people had, generation after generation, heard from pulpits and political platforms that integration would unleash pandemic interracial rape, followed by the disappearance of the white race.

Evolving attitudes may have affected even the most hard-bitten. Asa Earl Carter was born in Anniston in 1925, served in the Navy in World War II, attended the University of Colorado, and returned home to take up a career as a professional racist, hosting a rightwing radio show in Birmingham and founding the north Alabama chapter of the White Citizens' Council and an independent KKK group. A rabid anti-Semite as well as a violence-prone white supremacist, he was also a gifted writer and is credited as one of the authors of Wallace's infamous 1963 "Segregation Forever" inaugural address. He was his old fiery self in 1970 running to the right of Wallace in the Democratic gubernatorial primary, getting only 15,000 votes. He threw his support to Wallace in the runoff against Albert Brewer, whom he called "the number one white nigger." His votes were enough to put Wallace over the top and block Alabama's last best chance in the twentieth century to join the ranks of the New South.

Perhaps Asa sensed that changing attitudes in the region made his peculiar skills an irrelevant art form, leaving him a beached white whale. He is long dead and the reason he shed one identity for a more respectable one as a mainstream author remains a mystery. The evolution of Asa Carter, however, was to have a dramatic effect on a similarly volatile friend, a member of Calhoun County's legislative delegation, State Representative Ray Burgess. Ray was a big, muscular, outgoing man of sunny charm that concealed internal rage. I once explained to him how his economic views fit the populist movement of the turn of the century. A look of wonder and regret came over his face when he said, almost sighed, "God. I wish I had an education." Upon learning a year or so later that his wife had shot him dead during one of his rages, I thought, "How sad. What a waste."

Before his violent end, Ray was to have a moment of epiphany among the dwindling legions of the Snopeses. This is the story as Ray told friends:

Asa Carter had been invited to give the keynote address at a convention of racists in Jackson, Mississippi. Asa didn't want to give the speech himself but he wrote it and asked Ray if he would do it. When Ray read the speech, emotive words exploding from the page, he knew he was in possession of dynamite. He worked on the speech, hard, and gave it with all the fire he had. He had those ole boys virtually standing on their chairs, whooping, whistling, and cheering. He was a star!

On the plane returning home, he turned to Asa and said, "Ace, I don't understand you. If I could write a speech like that, I wouldn't let anybody give it but me."

Asa answered, "Ray, to really give a speech like that . . . you've got to believe that shit."

Had Carter abandoned the central tenets of his white supremacist faith or did he just shrewdly calculate that his audience was moving on and he'd better take up a new line of work? Regardless, Asa Carter disappeared, denying to the end his racist past, and the novelist Bedford Forrest Carter was born. By 1972 he was in Sweetwater, Texas, using the local library to work on his first novel, *Gone To Texas*, published in 1975. The film version, *The Outlaw Josey Wales,* starring Clint Eastwood, is still showing on cable. His next work, *The Education of Little Tree* (1976) was sold as a memoir based on his life as an orphan raised by Cherokee grandparents. The book was a sleeper bestseller. But, like his speech-making buddy Ray Burgess, he would meet a violent end. The furies within doomed both men to igno-minious deaths. Asa died in Abilene, Texas, on June 7, 1979, choking on food—strangulation complicated by clotted blood from a fistfight. He is buried near Anniston.

As JIMMY CARTER (NO kin to Asa) once said: "The civil rights movement freed the white people of the South and, incidentally, the black people, too." By the time Governor Carter made that admission, the last and most significant conversion had taken place, that of George C. Wallace. Perhaps it was the assassination attempt in Maryland in May 1972 that precipitated the change in George Wallace. He had felt the breath of mortality on his face, palpably close. The power of that presence has a way of making views that once were thought to be important seem trivial.

At any rate, as Wallace began to recover he was seen to move symboli-cally, to do things he had never done before: crowning a black homecoming queen at the University of Alabama where, a decade before, he had stood in the door to bar two black students from entering; attending a black mayors' caucus; exchanging public pleasantries with Ted Kennedy at a July Fourth celebration. For me, a consistent Wallace foe, the opportunity to see person-ally how much my old enemy had changed came when the editorial board was interviewing candidates for statewide office during the 1974 primaries. During previous campaigns, his visits to the *Star* were with the printers and pressmen in the back, where the votes were. He knew he'd carry the building without bothering with the newsroom and editorial page which he figured, rightly, he'd already lost. But this year was different.

Governor Wallace was wheeled into my office on a Thursday afternoon, March 28. The conversation began awkwardly. The gulf that had lain between us was a presence in the room. An opportunity to clear the air came through Neal Pierce's series of books, *The Deep South States of America*. Neal had quoted me at some length on what George Wallace represented beyond racism. I marked the pages and handed the book to the governor. When he finished reading, he looked at me warmly and said, "Hell, Bran-dit, we aren't too far apart." His answer gave me the chance to ask a question, which on "Meet the Press" wouldn't be asked in the same way.

"We never have been too far apart, George," I said. "You have always said you were standing up for the little man, and we have, too. I inherited my newspaper principles from Dad. He always said, 'It is the duty of a newspaper to become the attorney for the most defenseless among its subscribers.' Our policy, and Dad's before me, has been to champion the cause of the little man. But, George, it didn't take walking-around sense to know who the real 'little man' was in Alabama and the South and the nation: it has always been the black man. So, we tried to give him a voice, to stand up for him, because he was the nation's number one underdog. But you never did, George. Why?"

The only answer Governor Wallace gave was to look at his useless legs for a moment that seemed to go on and on. There were no quick, slicing debater's points; no sly evasions or overlong explanations; no attempts to hide an ancient wrong under a constitutional camouflage. There was no deceit; neither were there any confessions or apologies. That was not his way. There was only a very long silence. I believe I saw in Wallace's face, and in his wordless answer, an acknowledgment that perhaps his victories had been won at too great a cost and a wish that, some of it at least, had been different. But, ever the politician, he wasn't above exploiting his condition. After the meeting, I walked out to his car with him, his powerful arms propelling the wheelchair. When we got to the car, he took my right hand in his left, looked up at me and said, "I hope you can endorse me this time, Brandt, it will help my morale." What do you say to a paraplegic's plea—a man who once stood for everything hateful about the South, a man who was changing but whose unforgivable demagoguery had retarded the development of our state, a man whom you had no thought of supporting? "I'll promise you one thing, " I said. "We won't say anything to hurt your feelings."

The old George Wallace wit resurfaced in an autographed picture taken at that meeting, a picture of the two of us looking at each other as if we were boxers who had just touched gloves in the center of the ring. On it, he wrote: "No big problems we can't settle. That is, if you see it my way." That was an echo of the feisty George Wallace on his hind legs in 1966 aiming darts at liberals, the federal government, the mighty and pompous. I went to his rally outside Anniston's twin city of Oxford, because I never felt I'd experienced a campaign until I'd been cussed personally, and he didn't disappoint me. "And where wuz the librul edituh of the *Anniston Star* when they was raisin' yo' utility rates? You know where he wuz (pause) he wuz out at that country club, drinkin' tea . . . with his finger stuck up in the air!" He then demonstrated a pinky salute, to the delight of the crowd. In my office, at that fateful meeting eight years later, I got him back. "You told a lie about me, George," I said reminding him of the rally. "Awww, that was just politics," he said smiling the conspiratorial smile that said both of us know the game, which I did, but I wanted to sting him. "You know damn well, that wasn't tea I was drinking." He took it back—an honor he accorded few politicians and no journalists.

George Wallace's journey from an older to a newer vision of the South covered a distance of only one city block. In January 1963, he stood on the Capitol steps where Jefferson Davis was inaugurated and proclaimed: "Segregation forever!" In October 1974, he sat in his wheelchair where Martin Luther King Jr., had preached and welcomed an audience of blacks to the Dexter Avenue Baptist Church, a stone's throw from the Capitol. From the cradle of the Confederacy to the cradle of the civil rights movement: A breathtaking conceptual swoop? Perhaps. But in a region where past and future crowd each other, trying simultaneously to occupy the same space, it doesn't seem such a remarkable distance.

My feelings about this man George Corley Wallace were conflicted. Like the South itself, he was Manichean: instincts were marbled through him of varying intensity from white to light gray to dungeon dark. It was hard to dislike him personally because he so very much wanted you to like him. He was funny; his wit was sharp and pointed enough to prick the balloon of pomposity. His gut-level populist feeling for working-class whites appealed to me. God knows the working stiffs didn't get much sympathetic understanding from the educated, good-government elites who scorned them as "rednecks," North and South. During Wallace's end days, when his hearing shut down and he was captive in a silent cocoon of pain, I felt deeply for him and blame myself for not going to see him. He would have liked that. But drawing the bright, unforgiving line of judgment, he was bad for my state, my region, and my country. He deserves the condemnation of history.

Like the governor, State Representative Chris McNair is a symbol of continuity and change. In 1975, he was one of nearly one hundred black legislators elected in the South; he served as chairman of the Jefferson County (Birmingham) delegation, which was two-to-one white. But like the governor, McNair knows that no one gets to ride the glory train free. He has paid his dues. His daughter Denise would have celebrated her twenty-fifth birthday during the nation's bicentennial year if she hadn't been attending Sunday school at Birmingham's Sixteenth Street Baptist Church in September 1963 when the KKK-planted dynamite exploded.

The death of a child is an injury that never heals. It hurts Chris McNair every day but, incredibly, he isn't bitter: "If a man is forever lamenting yesterday, he doesn't give himself time to do anything about today, or plan for the future. In 1963 we were dickering about integration. Today I'm down here in the rotunda of the State Capitol and the problem now is to do something about education, period, what our whole society is based on.

"If I'm a Christian, I've got to believe in the possibility of redemption," says McNair. "I'm not in love with the George Wallace who stood in the schoolhouse door, but if he's still in power and talking differently, I'm not fighting him; I'm moving with it. What we demonstrated for in the sixties was to get inside. It's a different era but, basically, I don't think I'm any different from where I was all the time."

Tragically, McNair himself is in need of redemption after being imprisoned in 2011 for stealing in his capacity as a Jefferson County commissioner—a shattering disappointment to thousands who had been warmed by his friendship and who admired him as a trailblazer of the New South. His fall sharply reminds us that man is capable of nobility and low crimes, that the formerly oppressed, when tempted by new fame, power, and riches can behave distressingly like the old oppressors.

Chris McNair is imprisoned by the present, but the past, the relentless hound of memory, pursues him at a distance. "The past is never dead," said Faulkner in *Requiem for a Nun*. "It's not even past." He didn't mean to say that the South would never experience change. What he was saying is that Southerners have collected an attic-full of historical instincts; they are not going to throw them away just because the South has changed from a rigidly segregated society to a relatively free one, or because its people have moved from the farm and small town to the big city.

THERE WAS A LOT of moving and changing going on as the civil rights storms passed into history. Southerners were sure they wanted to move past racial politics, but as they turned off the farm-to-market roads onto the fuming rapids of steel that ring the metropolis, there were second thoughts about the effects of uncontrolled growth. Ever since Henry Grady, Southerners have been hankering after the twin sentinels of Yankee material progress: cities and factories. Urbanization and industrialization meant the South could slice off a bigger chunk of the Gross National Product, enhancing regional prosperity and leading to better lives for individual Southerners.

But there were some second thoughts . . .

God knows, Southerners can't be blamed for wanting a little more of the mass being produced and consumed in other parts of the country. A black co-ed, class of 1975, confirmed the rank of the gods of city and industry in the mind of the South. She understood the virtues of Southern life well enough to articulate them clearly, but there was one thing she would leave the South for, even if it meant living in a worn-out industrial city. "For a good-paying job," she smiled, "Sure!"

She was young, rural, black; she wanted to feel some pavement under her feet. She would go to the city, but what was she willing to pay as a toll for that journey? After she furnished her apartment with her own things, put a little money aside and, more importantly, accumulated a past and memories of her own, she might remember that there are other things she needs.

These issues sparked a verbal wrestling match between the poet, James Dickey, and me at a 1977 Auburn University conference on the impact of technology. The event began with a film that portrayed Haleyville as a poor, forlorn county seat of Winston County in northwest Alabama. The town had recently shown some signs of prosperity with the arrival of textile mills and a mobile home manufacturing plant.

Dickey hated what he saw in the film. "The industrialization of some little old place called Haleyville, Alabama, is part of a leveling process to reduce the South to being like any other place in the country. We are going to lose our music. We are going to lose our cookery. If we don't say 'No!' to this thing, if we keep on with mobile homes, we are going to lose all that. We are going to lose everything that makes us unique. And we are all going to end up in that great Rexall's in the sky."

In response, I tipped my hat to the value of an agrarian heritage and a unique history that packed two thousand years of experience into two hundred, but . . . "Poverty was one such experience. Some of us—I for one—[and Dickey, too] have been exempt from poverty . . . But I never had the feeling that I could sit up there and look through an academic picture window at some poor son of a gun scratching in a field of red clay that's deader than hell, where nothing will grow, while his hernia's hurting him, and say, 'Oh, isn't that lovely and picturesque, the romantic yeomanry!' I don't feel any sense of romanticism about a man like that, dying early and living a pretty desolate life without much material comfort and without much self-respect."

Dickey was a presence full of booze and poetry, out there in the dark—beyond the mechanical, orange mercury vapor daylight of his native Atlanta at night—raging at the growth, which ruined his Buckhead community and drove him out. He had been born the son of a successful lawyer, grew up in the wealthy Buckhead suburb, and was educated at Vanderbilt, home of the Agrarians, poetic defenders of the inviolable land and the lily white

South. Dickey, a fabulously entertaining and talented old fraud, answered me with an invented childhood. "I remember my early days in the country and I felt that I had been expelled from the lost paradise, that I had traveled eastward from Eden."

I should have said, "Aw shit, Jim." But instead I argued that Holiday Inns and bank buildings with revolving restaurants and plastic food will not eradicate our regional heritage. "Some of (those buildings) are horrible, and all of them look alike, but I can't believe that the weight of those structures is going to press out of us two hundred years of cultural memory."

At lunch, Dr. Kenneth Boulding, an author confident enough to undertake such works as *The Meaning of the Twentieth Century*, turned toward Dickey at the head table. His British accent and stutter transformed words into boulders bouncing down toward a frozen victim below: "As for you, Mr. Duh, duh, duh Dickey, your agrarian romanticism makes me want to vuh, vuh, vuh, *vomit*!"

Dickey is gone now, but maybe Dr. Boulding didn't get the last word. The ghost of the wonderful old fake, full of booze and poetry, may visit that black girl in her apartment to warn that there is something more permanent than pavement under her feet. That apparition, the ghost of a South yet to come, may speak to her from his film *Deliverance*.

"The reason we're going up this river is because it's gonna be gone. You're never gonna get to see it, if we don't see it right now. That's why we're going. It's gonna be gone! Every day they pump a little bit more of that air conditioning into Atlanta. They're gonna rape this country. They're gonna rape this whole landscape."

15

The Day Sisyphus Lost His Job

There was a "New South" once, but it is gone now, too. It ended years ago, after Jimmy Carter's presidency, before Bill Clinton decided he could be President. Measured by the clock of history, that New South was a brief shining moment that could not possibly last. But when Jimmy Carter and the other apostles of the New South arrived, it was the day Sisyphus lost his job. The Southern Sisyphus had grunted behind the rock of poverty, pellagra, and prejudice since it was put here at Appomattox; its weight all the more deadly because of an attitude of scorn which we were quick to sniff—out of defensive pride and wounded self-respect. The rock was the way Southerners defined themselves, and other Americans.

In Anniston, there was a good deal of talk about that symbol of scorn in Gene Sparks's Courthouse Cafe and Jimmy Turner's Courthouse Barber Shop during the presidential primaries of 1976. A typical conversation went: "If 'they' take the nomination away from Carter, they'll never let us live it down. It'll be another hundred years before any Southerner has a chance."

Carter's nomination and subsequent election meant the rock had finally, truly been lifted—or so we thought. The nation had elected a president from the Georgia black belt. It was a Hallelujah moment.

For the most part, the celebration was victimless. I can imagine similar feelings of validation in South Boston when John F. Kennedy became the first Catholic president. Irish Catholics are Celtic cousins of the Scotch-Irish South and the Irish, like Southerners, are no strangers to defeat and scorn—or to elation at the triumph of "one of our own."

But you can't keep even a good party going forever.

Eventually, the people of the South began to regard Carter as they might someone we used to know in the neighborhood but who moved away years ago. This sentiment measured a turn of a few more degrees away from passionate parochialism, toward a sense of us as a distinctive part of the whole, away from defining ourselves in terms of an Old South, New South, or James C. Cobb's "No South," toward a feeling of being Southern Americans. But that would not last; in time we would return to our natural home, the parochial South, living in a kind of voluntary apartheid.

As the days of Carter's presidency lengthened, we forgot he was a Southerner. Public perception of him in the cafes, barber shops and other universities of common wisdom at home in Anniston were little different from the opinion of him held by my friends who lived in, say, the working-class Chicago neighborhood of Marquette Park.

He wasn't president of the Confederacy. He was president of the United States. Jimmy Carter is a complex man of simple tastes and well-organized intelligence, wonderfully equipped to be a tenacious diplomat where the highest political skill is a steel-trap memory for detail and patience—talents he used to brilliant effect at Camp David in making peace between Israel's Menachim Begin and Egypt's Anwar Sadat, a feat still unrivaled in the first decade of the twenty-first century. But when he was mired in endless postponements and compromises with Congress on energy policy, when he addressed the nation in the tedious, wooden words of policy, Southerners, like other Americans, were unmoved.

The civil rights movement was on its way into the history books, along with the Old South, even before Carter's inauguration. There were no images on our television screens to remind Southerners of our apartness from the American value system. Southern blacks, like their Northern brothers and sisters, were no longer in the grips of a moral struggle, but were becoming a classic interest group with their own agenda for the economic and political future. North and South, Americans yearned for the same thing out of the bitter experience of a depressing decade, during which we learned that our cities can be scary places, that the strength of our arms and ideals can be frustrated, and that our leaders can be crooks and liars. Pandora's box erupted in three explosions: urban black rebellions, Vietnam and Watergate.

In his campaign Carter sounded as if he understood the spiritual distress of the nation. His self-confidence seemed rooted in something steady enough to survive tomorrow morning's headlines: values from the South Georgia soil his family had worked for generations, words that had the integrity of earth, sweat and the Bible. While his competitors in the Democratic primaries buzzed on like worker-bees about issues and politics, he made a favorable contrast because he was speaking to the spirit of the country. His was a litany of simple words: duty, faith, honor, love, truth. "I will not lie to you," he said.

Then the message stopped, the promise dulled. He lost his tongue in the general election, and for most of the first 1,000 days of his presidency, he droned on about programs and policy, not knowing until too late that the nation wanted definition, to hear about purpose. "I'm still waiting for President Carter to tell me what his goals are, what his ideas and programs mean to me and the country," said Anniston's Jimmy Turner, summarizing the sentiment from my "University of Common Wisdom," the Courthouse barbershop.

THE SOUTHERN FEELING OF ecstasy had already gone flat by October 1977 when Jody Powell arranged for me to visit the White House and to be the first editor to interview President Carter. The press secretary and I were chatting with our backs to the smaller room where the president does his non-ceremonial work. I did not know the president had entered the room until I heard his greeting, "Hello, Brandt." When I turned, he stuck out his hand and asked, "How's the South?" It was an offhand remark, as if he were inquiring about some place he had visited once or twice during the campaign. We talked a good bit that afternoon about a subject he and his senior staff had been discussing, symbolism: how to project to the country by action or a single phrase the hope his presidency promised. We could not have known then that the failure to make that connection would be a major reason he was limited to a single term.

For the Carter presidency and for the changed but no longer just-reborn South, the question had become: What does Sisyphus do when he loses his job? What vision would replace the discarded mythologies of the past: the subtropical Camelot of the Old South, with graces for the few and grits for the crew, and the 1970s version of the integrated, urbanized "New" South?

This is a troubling question of values and policy. The South has always hankered after the twin gods of Yankee materialism: cities and factories. And, God knows, Southerners can't be blamed for wanting a little more of the national output for so long produced and consumed elsewhere. It meant that the South would cease to be a capital-deficit region sometime in the 1980s. For most people that meant fixing up the house, sending the kids to college, and buying a camper, although it also meant a growing establishment of philanthropy devoted to the arts: theaters, symphonies, civic ballets, museums.

These are good things, but there is a kind of uncritical and unintended mimicry to the post-New South South. The same random economic forces which built the ghettos of the older industrial cities went to work here. The "Chickenbone Special" was now a short-line railroad. It no longer hauled poor blacks and whites from the stymied, choiceless life of the rural South to swell the ghettos of DEE-troit. It now ran from south Georgia to Atlanta, where the city produced its own urban ghettos, refugee camps for its own stateless Palestinians. Atlanta's former mayor, the late Maynard Jackson, could look at the South Bronx and see what the future would be for large numbers of his citizens.

The Agrarians who once clustered around Vanderbilt University had tried to warn us in their 1930 manifesto, *I'll Take My Stand,* what would happen if young Southerners succumbed to the lure of the industrial idea. "They must be persuaded to look very critically at the advantages of becoming a 'new South,' which will be only an undistinguished replica of the usual industrial community."

To those of us who had sought a South with a larger vision, an end to years of being hostage to the retarding mythologies of the past, the greatest disappointment was the failed promise of Carter's presidency and the failure of the New South dreams that accompanied his election. It was such a grand dream, too big to be fleshed in reality. We had thought the entry of blacks into the political system would purify politics by removing race as an issue. That we would create an enlightened electorate by good schools for all. That we would build cities that were gleaming citadels of high culture.

That was not to be: the entry of the black man into the political process instead led to a white Republican South that in its loyalties and prejudices was no better than the white Democratic system it replaced. The new GOP majority busied itself with scaring Hispanic workers with draconic immigration legislation and narrowing of the franchise to the disadvantage of blacks and the poor. Schools were mostly resegregated with resulting social consequences. Cities were built but they came equipped with urban ghettoes and rush-hour quagmires.

The Southern Sisyphus had found new employment by building its own skyscrapers and malls while ignoring the scolding of the Agrarians. The Agrarians grossly exaggerated the virtues of the Old South, but they did ask the right question: growth for whom, growth for what? One of their number, Allen Tate, died in February 1979. He was a Southern poet, a voice crying in the wilderness of skyscrapers in downtown Atlanta. His death was a single leaf falling into the fuming flood of rush-hour steel and exhaust inching along the interstates and beltways ringing the city. In the void left by the end of the "New South" celebration, Southern city-dwellers could hear again Tate and his Agrarians asking what good is it to "receive the illusion of having power over nature, and lose the sense of nature as something mysterious and contingent?"

Three days after Tate died, CBS telecast *Gone With the Wind*, and the Old South perished again in the flames of Atlanta. That same evening in the "New" Atlanta, blacks and whites dined together in a revolving restaurant at the top of the Peachtree Plaza Hotel, a seventy-story finger stuck impudently toward heaven. The integrated diners slowly revolved, looking down on blacks and whites dining together in an earlier but smaller Atlanta hotel marvel, the Hyatt Regency, similarly turning in place. In the artificial-orange, mercury-vapor daylight of the canyon far below a solitary voice, wary of muggers lurking in the shadows, asked: "Is this all there is to it?"

MY GRANDFATHER, DR. T. W. Ayers, was a boy during the Civil War. He used to tell the story of General Sherman's officers using the family's north Georgia farm as an ersatz motel during his travels through the state, where he demonstrated remarkable carelessness with matches. Grandfather would amuse the family by remarking that the source of any residual resentment he felt toward "Yankees" was that his pet chickens became dinner for some of Sherman's officers and NCOs and his staff. They repaid my great-grandparents' hospitality by not burning their house.

The decades that followed brought injuries that have not yet completely healed, including being looked upon and spoken about as an inferior culture. The pain was so old that it became almost a friend, a point of reference that Southerners used to define their relationship with each other and to the rest of the nation. It had become almost a physical presence, a door shut at Appomattox that kept us in the comfortable, familiar, safe, albeit threadbare rooms within—secure against the uncertainties outside. We leaned against it for support. Then, on the morning of November 3, 1976, it was yanked open. We lurched outside blinking, disoriented but happy. What did it portend for the nation? What was the state of my own feelings about having a Southern president?

To understand the average Southerner's feelings (and perhaps even more the Southern intellectual's) about a Southern president, it was necessary first to understand what made the South different. It wasn't only the Civil War, although that was an un-American experience—knowing that defeat is possible. But we'd had more than a century to get over that.

Neither was it a feeling for the land and a sense of small-town community. That was part of it, too, but is not unique to the South. There were and are plenty of friendly small-town Midwesterners with an affinity for the land and each other. But America never thought to look at the entire Middle Western region with amused condescension. New England never heard the nation, with terrible consistency, speak of its people with sarcasm—heavy words, spoken lightly, cheaply, but so damaging to the spirit. No other region has been regarded derisively as "backward" or had lived so easily with a moral evil, as if it were normal, the way things are. Whether we were black or white, there were words for us and none beckoned us to partnership in the national enterprise, or uplifted our soul. We listened to the same radio programs and laughed at our own foibles because there was an element of truth in the caricatures of *Amos 'n' Andy* and in the red-necked Lum and Abner's world, the Jot 'Em Down Store.

The old injury, our constant companion, drew us together in a kind of corporate communion, more instinctive than verbal, from east Texas to

Virginia. We didn't have to say anything; we knew each other and knew we were different from those on the outside.

There was a time during the Roosevelt years when rich and poor, North and South, shared the same Depression and the same war. FDR liked us. He told us stories and was even known to sample the explosive liquid brought him in fruit jars by county politicians in Warm Springs, Georgia (not far from Plains). But the old ache came back with a vengeance during the civil rights movement of the 1950s and 1960s, when the courage of Southern blacks made Southern whites struggle with their consciences. Social revolution at the cutting edge of change is not a normal environment that encourages calm reflection and cool behavior. What made matters worse for white Southerners was the attitude conveyed to us in our own living rooms by television. It seemed that the original sin of prejudice had just been discovered and isolated, like some exotic virus that flourishes only in subtropical climates.

Most Southern whites, who never committed nor considered committing any atrocities, who were trying to adjust to the new ways, got fed up with the adjectives applied to them. Their anger had roots in unacknowledged shame, soul deep—their own impotence when face-to-face with dehumanizing wrong. Good people were handcuffed by cultural cowardice. How that happens was described from the personal experience of a decent man, a juror who had no deep feelings of racial animosity. Yet he voted to acquit two white Mississippi half-brothers of the savage murder of a fourteen-year-old black child, Emmett Till. The juror said that to do the right thing and convict the brothers he would have had to scale a four-level test of moral courage—a summit he could not attempt. He would have to believe that the bedrock of his civilization should be changed, that it was possible to do so, and finally, he would have to believe that he personally could do something to alter the old ways for the better. Southerners torn by helplessness in the face of evil, burdened by such a load of cultural history, had not been conditioned to expect good news.

THEN, WITH CARTER'S ELECTION, when Sisyphus's rock was finally lifted, there was some jubilation, some hallelujahing, and some echoes from the

Amen corners. In one corner Eli Evans, the expatriate North Carolinian and foundation executive, whooped at friends across New York traffic, "Free at last," he shouted. "Free at last. Thank God Almighty; we're free at last."

Joy burns out at the moment of ecstasy, but in the days and weeks after that brief spasm of elation, a quieter sensation spread warmly through the soul of the region—a sense of confirmation, validation. It was like the awareness of some rural Mississippi boy reviewing his freshman year at Harvard, no longer terrified by the place, knowing he can compete, and beginning to think about the responsibilities that would come with his attainments.

That sensation was evident when Southern governors, legislators, businessmen, and scholars gathered at Boca Raton, Florida, in December 1976, for serious talk about the future of the nation's and the region's economy. That good and decent man, then-Florida Governor Reubin Askew, set the tone: It is no longer necessary to starve the imagination by feeding it the retarding myths of the past. Though it was not a time for recalling old wounds, I couldn't resist a light jab at "Secretary of Everything" Elliot Richardson, then doing a tour as Secretary of Commerce. The New Englander spoke enviously of the "Sunbelt South"— almost as if he was commander of a defeated army. "We must be magnanimous, gentlemen," I remarked to my tablemates at the luncheon, "tell the secretary that the men may keep their horses; they will need them for the spring plowing." The remark leapt like St. Elmo's fire from table to table, until it reached Elliot, who received it with a dour Yankee expression. Years later he remembered the remark, still unsmiling.

We wondered then where to find the language of détente with our separated brothers in the Northeast and Midwest. From its great oral tradition, we thought at the time, the South might find the words to use like a poultice to drain poisonous tension from debate, to suspend hostilities by telling a story that creates simultaneous laughter and understanding. But mockery at someone else's expense is hard to resist. President Carter put it this way in his memoir:

> Southerners had some messages to send to the world . . . The most important was that we in the South were ready for reconciliation, to be

accepted as equals, to rejoin the mainstream of American political life . . .
Before we arrived in Washington, some of the society-page writers were
deploring the prospective dearth of social grace in the White House and
predicting four years of nothing but hillbilly music, and ignorant Bible-
toting Southerners trying to reimpose Prohibition in the capital city. The
local cartoonists had a field day characterizing us as barefoot country hicks
with straw sticking out of our ears, clad in overalls, and unfamiliar with
the proper use of indoor plumbing.

Growing up in Plains, Jimmy Carter had been shaped by experience
beyond the satirists' understanding, by attending so many baptisms, weddings, and funerals in the same place, among people whose families had
known each other for generations (his family has lived on the same land
since 1830). He learned in that tiny Georgia village—with fewer people
than in a big-city apartment building—the importance of self-respect.

He acknowledged the prevailing courage and pride of blacks even before
he hung the portrait of Martin Luther King Jr. in the Georgia statehouse.
Some say that ceremonial act was cynical, political. Surely he was not unaware that the gesture would be noted with approval in a national political
campaign, a race he had already decided to run, but he did not celebrate
the black man at the expense of those who are rural and white. He spoke
about that while flying back from the 1976 convention:

> It's not right to stigmatize people—"All of you are wrong. You shouldn't
> have done what you did. I'm better than you are." The point I'm making is
> that the South, including Georgia, has moved forward primarily because
> it hasn't been put into the position of having to renounce itself. You've
> got to give people credit for the progress they make and the changes in
> attitudes. It would be easy to sit around and say, "Look at those terrible
> people in Georgia who don't want to bus their kids to school." But that
> doesn't do any good.

The politics of self-respect acknowledges that neither sorry folks nor
good folks come in just one color. Carter knew that, but his plain, hard,

disciplined upbringing did not allow for the flowering of parables that would make a warm, understanding connection between president and people.

JIMMY CARTER'S PRESIDENCY THUS brought liberal Southerners to the heights of elation, and then down, down, down to disappointment and depression. The jubilation we had felt on his election had turned to fatalism by mid-May of 1979 when his approval ratings were in the 30s. National morale was in a nosedive. Inflation was rising and gas lines were lengthening while Congress and the White House dithered. Troubled by the downward spiral of his presidency and by the president's inability to get in touch with popular expectations, I went to the White House to talk with members of the senior staff, whose anxiety level was as high or higher than mine. If there was value to the message I brought the president's aides, it was that it came not from a divided staff locked into the elegant prison of the White House, but was a fresh, outside perspective.

My first appointment was with Carter pollster Pat Caddell. I told him what he seemed already to know, "The people are down on the country and themselves, and they don't see any leadership from the White House. What the hell is wrong with you folks?" Caddell agreed with my somber assessment, a view held more widely among the staff. As writer Robert Schlesinger has disclosed, at the time of my visit in May communications director Gerald Rafshoon and domestic adviser Stuart Eizenstat were working on tough memos to the chief. "You're going to have to start looking, talking, and acting like more of a leader if you're to be successful—even if it's artificial," advised Rafshoon; advice Carter's unbending honesty would reject. At a critical moment in June, Eizenstat wrote a strong memo citing a 55 percent increase in gas prices and a threatened strike by gas station owners, and concluding, "It is perhaps sufficient to say that nothing which has occurred in the administration to date . . . [has] added so much water to our ship. Nothing else has so frustrated, confused, angered the American people—or so targeted their distress at you personally." Eizenstat is a cool, analytical thinker, not given to giddiness or depression. His memo from the precipice of the abyss was a measure of how dark the mood was on Pennsylvania Avenue when I arrived.

Caddell said that his polls agreed with my assessment of public opinion and surprised me by suggesting, "You need to talk to Rosalynn." The staff knew that she was more attuned to the temper of public opinion than the president, and that she was more able than they to persuade her husband to take corrective action.

(Many years later, after the Nobel Peace Prize, during a break from hammering on a Habitat for Humanity house in Anniston, the former president confirmed that his wife had a better ear than he: "She's a better politician. She likes it more.") A politician who dislikes politics? As Robert Schlesinger makes clear in his exhaustively researched book on presidential speech writers, *White House Ghosts*, Jimmy Carter had maybe the most talented speechwriting corps of modern presidencies—Jim Fallows, later of the *Atlantic*, and Rick Hertzberg of the *New Yorker*—but he did not care for the art and considered the process an unhappy chore instead of a leadership tool. He did not have FDR's gift of metaphor and rhetorical magic to explain, for example, support for England in World War II in language as homey as a garden hose. Rick Hertzberg, put it this way: "There must be a vocabulary of common feeling between leader and led—a vocabulary based to some degree on what people are thinking. But it must go far beyond merely telling people what they want to hear. It must embody the people's inchoate yearnings and combine them with the president's own vision of where he wants to take the country.")

During my next appointment, a call came through in Gerald Rafshoon's office in the ornate Old Executive Office building. Gerry put down the phone and said, "Rosalynn wants to see you." He helped me navigate the underground passage to the White House and escorted me to the ground-floor Map Room near the southwest corner of the residence. Rosalynn was already there, slight and pretty, wearing her soft, searching, tentative expression, as if she expected to be startled or hurt. Hers is a femininity that makes her seem more fragile than she actually is. After brief pleasantries, we sat in straight chairs, hers facing the series of maps Franklin Delano Roosevelt used to trace the progress of World War II. She asked why I had come and I'm afraid I gave a little patriotic homily, concluding: "Rosalynn, we look to the President and you as head of the American family. When the family is hurt or afraid or down on itself, as it is now, we look to you to sit us down around the kitchen table and remind us who we are. Tell us what we have to do."

Her response stunned me: "Brandy, what can we do? Jimmy doesn't know."

Those two, simple sentences ripped the bottom out of my belief, admittedly naive for a forty-year-old, that the center of national life, the Oval Office, is occupied by superior beings—and that the center always holds. Some have argued that the twin agonies of Richard Nixon and Lyndon Johnson had already demystified the presidency, but I still believed in the power that emanates from the Great Seal because . . . I guess because I wanted to. I hoped that my expression did not betray the shock I felt. Recovering, I replied, "Rosalynn, you need to host a series of dinner parties, inviting people who have authority to speak about the condition of the country, and who're not afraid to tell the President—with the bark off." She nodded assent and concluded the conversation, "Go make a list."

I did, immediately. In the Old Executive Office Building, I found a bright young communications staff assistant, Linda Peek, and dictated a list of names to her for Rosalynn's dinners. The list included CBS newsman Charles Kurault, whose "On the Road" series probed the strengths and oddities of the country down to the village level, and Daniel Yankelovich, president of one of the most respected opinion polling companies, who also chairs the non-profit Public Agenda Foundation. When Pat Caddell saw the list, he brusquely erased Yankelovich's name, "There will be only one polling organization in this White House." Something about the baneful white skunk-stripe snaking through Caddell's thick black hair, his greedy territoriality and amoral brilliance cast him as a misfit among the nice-guy Georgians—more interested in his own career than in the fate of the president.

Back in my room at the Madison Hotel, a bit lightheaded from the events of the day, I pondered a day spent far above the normal precincts traveled by a small-town publisher. That sense of mysterious expectation grew when President Carter greeted me next day at a meeting in the East Room with, "I understand you're coming to supper."

MY BRIEF TIME IN the White House did not turn out to be a life-altering experience. There would be a domestic summit at Camp David in early July along the lines I had suggested to Rosalynn. Meanwhile, worldwide oil shortages caused in part by the Iranian revolution deepened public anger and longing for leadership. As if he had overheard that Map Room conversation with the First Lady, chief speechwriter Bernie Aaronson summed up public hankering for absent leadership: "We want to go back to the old days in America, the most powerful nation on earth, when, by God, we won't have to be kicked around and we won't have to worry about Japanese goods underselling us and we won't have to worry about OPEC oil . . . There's a hunger for somebody to say, 'All these changes haven't taken place.' But I think that's the wrong kind of leadership because the fact is that those changes HAVE taken place and the country has to deal with them. But, what you're saying is that somebody's got to lay that out and bring the country along with him, right?"

While the Carters were at a seven-nation economic summit in Japan, the situation at home was spiraling down to crisis levels. Eizenstat finished his stinging memo on June 28. The family arrived back on July 2 to receive a staff warning not to give a previously scheduled nationwide address on energy unless the president could reveal a transformative policy initiative. The president canceled the speech, put off a planned vacation trip to Hawaii, and retreated with Rosalynn to Camp David from July 3 to 12 where a stream of guests from politics and the professions was invited to consult with the president about the state of the nation. As I had hoped, they gave it to him "with the bark off." He later wrote in his memoir, "They told me that I seemed bogged down in the details of administration, and the public was disillusioned in having to face intractable problems like energy shortages and growing inflation . . . The consensus was that the public . . . doubted my capacity to follow through with a strong enough thrust to succeed."

On the final day of the summit Press Secretary Jody Powell invited me to the concluding luncheon at Camp David. Marine Two, the vice president's helicopter, flew us, a small group of senior journalists, to the Maryland mountaintop retreat. From the landing pad, it was a short walk to the main house, Poplar Lodge. In the living room Jimmy and Rosalynn Carter welcomed their guests with friendly informality, as if they were old friends dropping by for Sunday brunch. She wore a simple, belted white dress with blue piping and he had on a blue blazer with silver buttons, trousers with a light blue pattern, and white dress shirt open at the collar. The president and I went down the buffet line together and so we were seated together at the lunch. Small talk is not one of his talents or mine, so neither of us could recite what was said. But I did inquire half-seriously whether the button he was fingering was the one used to blow up the world. He replied, "No, it's to call the waiter." The luncheon guests were some of the "faces" of American journalism such as Walter Cronkite, all drawn there by the drama of the canceled nationwide address on energy, followed by the mysterious mountaintop meetings.

After lunch he spoke about the challenge of his presidency: rallying the American spirit and confidence, and reasserting American leadership in energy, not just as an economic issue but one that affects the security of the industrialized world.

ON SUNDAY EVENING, JULY 15, Carter spoke to the nation about what he had learned from his mountaintop vigil. It was the most riveting speech of his presidency. He did not speak as he had in the past with an engineer's logically ordered lists but directly to the American spirit.

> The threat is nearly invisible in ordinary ways. It is a crisis of confidence. It is a crisis that strikes at the very heart and soul and spirit of our national will. We can see this crisis in the growing doubt about the meaning of our own lives and in the loss of a unity of purpose for our nation . . .
>
> Energy will be the immediate test of our ability to unite this nation, and it can also be the standard around which we rally. On the battlefield of energy we can win for our nation a new confidence, and we can seize control again of our common destiny.

Rehearsed with Stu Eizenstat as a demanding critic, the president delivered the speech with unaccustomed feeling and force. The president thought it was his best speech; I did, too, and evidently the public agreed. His opinion polls shot up 11 percent. At Jim Turner's barbershop, a patron enthused, "Did you hear the president last night? Man, he really told it like it is." Two days later, when Carter let five cabinet members go, including Health Education and Welfare Secretary Joe Califano, a popular Washington establishment figure, the national press reported the cabinet realignment as a "massacre." No secondary shock wave reached Noble Street; no stricken-faced merchants or customers rushed onto the street with shouts of "[Secretary of Transportation] Brock Adams is falling! Brock Adams is falling!"

Sadly, after the summit and cabinet changes, there were no dramatic, morale-building initiatives launched from the White House. The next thing we heard from the president was that the first family was taking a cruise down the Mississippi. The national doctor's diagnosis was not followed by any treatment for the national ailment. The doctor was out—on a riverboat. An anonymous speechwriter summed up the problem, "There was a real aversion to planning for effect. There's no news management. No follow-through. Look at energy . . . we put out an energy program and then there's no following through for months." The ringing words of Carter's best speech—"On the battlefield of energy we can . . . seize control again of our common destiny"—were erased by the cabinet reshuffle and a lack of follow-through. Even one great speech is not enough to turn around a continent-sized nation.

I went back to Washington in the early fall but nobody was interested then in talking to an outsider about presidential action to fill the growing vacuum. I was invited to lunch with Jimmy and Rosalynn in the upstairs family dining room, an awkward meal where I tried to engage the president in ways to dramatically connect with the people, Rosalynn said little, looked slightly alarmed, and Amy read a book. In the absence of subsequent vigorous presidential initiatives, the best speech of his presidency morphed into the so-called "malaise speech," a gloomy shorthand for his term; and the cabinet reshuffle, instead of being portrayed as refreshing the team, cast doubt on his leadership. The vacuum magnified every national and international problem.

Why was Jimmy Carter, a man of such high intelligence, personal integrity and moral purity unable or unwilling to dominate the news, thus dooming his presidency to failure? Maybe it was the spare strictness of his upbringing in rural Plains, Georgia, where he was eleven before the family abandoned the outdoor privy for an indoor facility jury-rigged by his father to a windmill. Hard, unmechanized farm labor on weekdays and the bare wood plainness of his Southern Baptist faith on Sundays, they toughen a man, teach him the values of earth, sweat, and the Bible. Carter's years as a young naval officer, a disciple of Admiral Hyman Rickover, were also a period of stern mental discipline: the unforgiving perfection of nuclear physics. In those early shaping experiences may be found clues to a president strongly disinclined to the artifices of presidential leadership. The man and the office were a poor, or, as it turned out, an impossible fit.

On November 4, Iranian students stormed our embassy in Tehran, and as the crisis lengthened, the president seemed immobilized in the final, frustrating months of his term. Though the polls remained close, Ronald Reagan so dominated the debate that Jody Powell told me my informal barbershop poll duplicated almost exactly their internal polls. Josephine and I, knowing how bad the results would be, fled to England. On election night, we were in Stratford-upon-Avon, where we saw *Henry V*, had dinner and repaired to our room to watch the BBC color most of the nation red in Reagan's decisive victory.

Those who felt as I did viewed the inevitable collapse of Carter's administration as a tragedy. He had been a powerful symbol of the desires of men like my grandfather, my father and me, who yearned for the South to be rejoined with the nation. Beginning with my great-grandfather, Southerners experienced the violent separation of Civil War, and subsequent generations accustomed ourselves to being viewed disdainfully by other Americans, even while we struggled to free ourselves from the bog of a third-world culture and economy.

Our nation after Jimmy Carter was more complete than it had been just a few decades ago. To be born in any of thousands of small Southern towns no longer meant the door was closed at birth. The door was open to natives of every region. A boy born in Hope, Arkansas, could compete for and win the presidency.

End of the story? Of course not. Then, where were we as the new day dawned? We had put a Yankee polish on our prejudices. Now that the

Republican Party's distinction as "the Colored Party" had been discarded, we were Republicans. After a fifty-year evolution, the GOP was now the respectable white party. It would take a completely goofy Republican to lose a statewide election and an unusually talented Democrat to win one. We had raised from the cotton fields new cities where the arts flourish and capital is abundant. And, deliberately shunning the humane models of Savannah and Charleston, we had made the capital of the New South, Atlanta, a carbon copy of the capital of the New West, Los Angeles. Both are about as distinctive as an airport.

But we have not become indistinguishable duplicates of a national personality. We may have more Sons of Confederate Veterans chapters than the Confederacy had under arms. We have more *hell-far-and-brimstone* evangelists on radio and TV per capita, and in a hundred different ways we refuse to dissolve into a national melting pot, because we drag around a long vestigial tail called . . . history.

If Carter's presidency ended in defeat, well, that's not a new experience for us in the South. His departure from Washington to take up a much-admired former presidency of global good works also corresponded with the fading of the glow that had illuminated the few years that we called the New South.

A Matter of Soul

That solitary voice rising among the downtown skyscrapers of the "new" Atlanta asked, "Is this all there is to it?" Has the weight of all those capital structures pressed the life, squeezed everything that was unique and interesting out of the city? Sadly, yes, though there was a brave insurgency in midtown bent on humanizing the investor-created towers with a little of the graceful living of a small town. It failed. Then there is Charleston where downtown residents dining late at one of the city's splendid restaurants after attending the Spoletto Festival would say, yes, there is something more to a richer, more tolerant post-New South South.

That lonely voice might also ask, "Why aren't there more Charlestons?"

An equally interesting challenge is posed by Robert Roark who, in his book about the Mau Mau rebellion, quotes an African proverb that goes roughly, "If you must change the old ways be sure to replace them with something of value." The Old South is gone but does that mean all of the old ways with their signs, songs, ensigns, badges, and totems must be changed or repressed? There usually is a price to be paid for cultural repression.

It is an article of faith among Southern people that there are some things they are unwilling to change. It is a matter of soul. Southerners of both races and all ages aren't willing to give up their distinctiveness of food, speech, custom, and tradition, in self, in "our kind of folks," and in the place where we live. White Southerners of a certain age aren't willing to say there is no longer any reason for pride in the bravery of the Lost Cause. You no longer hear appeals to "our way of life" as an excuse for segregation any more, but still Southerners are touchy about matters of the spirit, and that isn't a statement only about black people. There is black soul and there is white soul, too, just as there is mountain soul and Delta soul.

How do you define Southern soul? Since Quentin Compson went to Harvard, there has been a search to find and unearth the mind of the South in all its tangled filigree. Maybe it will help to listen to a few Southern voices, talking and singing. First is reporter Roy Reed, the Arkansas boy who has seen Harvard and Washington and covered half the South for the *New York Times*. Reed, before retiring to his country house at Hog Eye, Arkansas, made a talk to Mississippi reporters and editors:

> One night last week, I was out with a bunch of men in a Louisiana marsh catching alligators. I was sitting in that boat with six or eight alligators hog-tied and piled up around my feet, and it occurred to me—this was a Southern experience. There is no place I know of north of the Mason-Dixon line where a man can hunt alligators. I've heard those stories about the sewers of New York City being full of alligators, but I don't believe it, because if it was true, my friends from Breaux Bridge and Lafayette would be up there right now poaching them "long green boogers," and selling their hides. The fact is, this part of the country is still physically different from the north, and no amount of air conditioning is going to change that. In the long sweep of things, what are a handful of air-conditioned skyscrapers on Canal Street compared to a thousand miles of bayous that are air conditioned by a million live oak trees?

How do you describe the South? One way is to make a list. Reed's list includes:

> . . . the sugar cane workers of Louisiana and Florida, the gut pullers and gizzard splitters who work in the poultry plants, the peculiar hill people of the Ozarks and the Blue Ridge Mountains, and the honkytonkers who walk along the edge of violence every Saturday night in two or three thousand little towns like Wiggins, Tylertown and Poplarville. It includes those thousands of certifiably insane racecar drivers, on and off the official tracks. I also include on my list a lot of trivial stuff that only a Southerner would even recognize, much less appreciate, things like fried okra and purple hull peas; Coca-Cola used as a chaser for whiskey; Merle

Haggard perceived as a superb musician and not just a kinky fad who is good for a few laughs at a Washington cocktail party.

Despite the list, Reed the veteran reporter knows intellectually that old Dixie is a goner. He has read the books and articles that say so, even written some himself. And yet, his gut may have the truer vision:

> I'm sure it's silly to fret over these things. The prophets are right—if old Dixie is not dead, it at least has one foot in the grave, and it's just a matter of time now. But I have a small comic vision of what's going to happen when they finally hold the funeral. The graveside music will turn out to be "Precious Memories" and "Shall We Gather at the River"— and the only people there who will know the words will be the loved ones from Arkansas and Mississippi.

EVEN THE YOUNG EXECUTIVES whose community center is the country club know the words. It is Saturday night on Sunset Drive in the late 1970s; the house is new but the money old. Inside, the twin guitars are manned by textile and advertising executives. The advertising man, son of a former Republican congressman, strums with his partner and recites the Hank Williams song, "The Funeral," about a black child's death. In Williams's lyrics, in the patois of the Southern black church, the preacher cautions mourners not to question the Almighty and explains the mystery of God's plan:

> *He didn't give you that baby . . .*
> *He jus' think you need some sunshine*
> *So he lent him for awhile.*
> *And he let you keep and love it,*
> *'Til your hearts was bigger grown*
> *And them silver tears you're shedding now*
> *Is just int'rest on the loan.*

It was an odd scene, one that couldn't be recreated in Newton or Pasadena: young men and women of privilege moved by a verse written by the poet of blue-collar whites about the funeral of a black child. It was a transcendent moment when the "perfectly irrational" sense of being Southern erased divisions of politics, race, and class—a moment ruined by a rude surprise. I asked the textile executive if he knew "Blowin' in the Wind." Feigning deafness for a long minute, he finally answered curtly, "I don't play communist songs." It was a shot across the bow, warning of the culture wars that would come—kindled in part by whites who felt their culture had been put down by the "superior" classes.

GEORGE WALLACE. HIS ANTI-GOVERNMENT racism was the ideological cornerstone of the modern Republican Party, a political culture that is more cultural than political, as much about resentments as issues. It was a party that appealed to Southern whites, not only because it *was* whiter but because it said: "We like you, your values are our values, and we can't stand those liberal elites looking down on us." The refined conservatism of most Republicans of even a generation ago would be hard pressed to fully behold and comprehend what their party has become. So the search must go on . . .

Turn again to the late C. Vann Woodward, the indispensable historian and interpreter of the South, who taught that other sections of the United States have been exempt from the burdens of history. The South's experience has been far closer to the common lot of man:

> For Southern history, unlike American, includes large components of frustration, failure and defeat. It includes not only an overwhelming military defeat but long decades of defeat in the provinces of economic, social and political life.

Others confirm the Yale scholar's insight. A transplanted executive, who in many ways has never really left home, has a one-sentence answer for New Yorkers who ask what it is like to be a Southerner: "It's like being Jewish." Both have a clannish affinity for their own, and each experienced a hard history of separation and scorn.

Defeat in war, moral complacency, poverty, protein deficiency, and pellagra are truly un-American experiences. But there is another factor beyond Woodward's litany of Southern distinctiveness that is perhaps as important as the others. It helps explain Southern clannishness: the deep suspicion of critical or exotic ideas and people, which Southerners are quick to label "outside agitators."

Southerners are defensive because the South is the only region of the United States that has suffered the scorn of other Americans, heavy words meant to crush the spirit. Black and white, the people of the South have been called lazy, no-'count, shiftless. There have been names for us all: niggers, jigaboos, rednecks, lint-heads, white trash, crackers, hillbillies, and hicks. As a group, Southerners have suffered blows to our sense of personal worth that is a necessity more important than material comfort. Self-respect has very little to do with a new car or an indoor toilet; it has to do with the way Southerners take what fate has dealt them and how they are regarded by friends and neighbors.

Black and white, Southerners have always been more like each other and more different from "other" Americans; but it is this human necessity, self-respect, which has been the catch-22 in their relations with each other and in the South's relations with the rest of the nation. Until recently, white Southerners couldn't find words to champion the cause of "the little man" without ignoring or damaging the self-respect of the black man. And, in the great centers for export of moral concern, the talent was lacking to champion the cause of the black man without demeaning the average white Southerner.

For a region which values courtesy out of respect for the feelings of others and because it makes human contact pleasant, we are shamed—or ought to be—by the words our white citizens spoke so casually about our black citizens. North and South we are aware—or ought to be—of our sinful disregard for the self-respect of black Americans. But what about the sensitivity of the white Chapel Hill taxi driver? He is the paradox which white Southern elites could not explain but that George Wallace could. To me, riding in his cab to the airport one day in the late 1970s, he was no abstraction. He was a mass of unhurried good will, a good ole boy. Passenger and driver got a quick fix on each other, as Southerners tend to do, and were communicating free and easy until George Wallace's name entered the conversation. A perplexed look came over the driver's face when my antipathy for Wallace became apparent. "Explain something to me," he said. "How come you educated people are always raising up the nigger but looking down on folks like me? I've done every kind of nigger work there is: chopped cotton, washed dishes, scrubbed bathrooms. Why are 'they' always taking up for the nigger and don't give folks like me no respect?"

I was not stung by his repetition of the n-word because it was evident from the nature of our conversation that he used the word not to demean a race but as a cultural and social divider between those who had gotten a better deal from changes in the old way and his belief that the old way had not been replaced by something of greater value to him and his class. The driver chuckled agreement when I suggested that sorry folks don't come in just one color. "And, second," I continued, "you never had as much of your self-respect peeled off you as the black folks did. When you put on your Sunday-go-to-meetin' clothes, that was your passport; you were as good as anybody with a little change in your pockets. You went anywhere you damned well pleased: to the movies, hotels, motels, restaurants, and nobody told you to go around to the back—unless he wanted trouble."

It would have been too much to expect the cab driver to be blinded by the light of a new reality, to go through a Saul-like conversion behind the wheel on the way to Raleigh-Durham airport. He nodded gravely, indicating he would think about it. From the friendly farewell he gave his passenger, I thought he really might think about it and come to some new understanding about blacks, his own kind of folks, and the "educated people."

He would have had to get over some cherished resentments, however, because he and the people like him have long been accustomed to thinking they have gotten the short end of the stick, and with some justice. This is what George Wallace understood so well—the bruised self-respect of many average white Southerners—and evoked powerfully. It is what beyond racism made Wallace, not so much a universal political leader, but an ethnic spokesman. He had soul-knowledge of a people who believe they had earned some respect, too, because they have been the first to fight and the majority to die in the nation's wars, and, like blacks, they have planted our fields, built cities with their own hands, and been among the first to gauge hard times with supper-table reality.

Attitudes are changing; the populist demagogues are all Republicans now. And even cussing illegal immigrants and sneering at homosexuals doesn't get the blood boiling like in the old days. In part, working-class Southern whites now vote Republican because they think it's the only way they can protest the bum deal they believe they got. We have a political culture of fighting mad resignation. Republicans aren't as much fun, either. Old Lester had his last "phooey" in the Georgia primaries of 1974, getting only 40 percent of the vote. But does that mean that 40 percent of the Georgia electorate are haters? Isn't it just as plausible to believe that many Georgians saw in Lester Maddox something of themselves, and liked what they saw? He (like them) didn't have much of an education; he clowned around some but didn't do any harm with his harmonica-playing and backward bicycle riding. He was friendly and courteous to everyone he met, white and "colored" alike, and he had given his life to Christ.

The Maddox and Wallace people—now Republicans—liked to think of themselves as good people and asked little more than anyone else, human respect. They are puzzled and hurt when educated people refer to them as "crackers" or "rednecks," but they'd never admit it. And, for the life of them, they can't understand why they can't sing their song, "Dixie." It is uniquely their song; it awakens a whole cluster of native memories of home and hometown, of families and friends and high school football games, it is cultural adrenalin. It brings them to their feet. Even though their grand-children couldn't care less.

"Dixie" is a symbol of a place and of the things that happened to a people along the way. The mingling of native pride and tragedy speak to me about the story of my land. It is a merry tune, but it does not make me want to stand and shout. I prefer the symphonic arrangement with melancholy cellos that tell of tragedy. To others who harmlessly enjoy the symbols of the Confederacy, the song means simply: "We are Southerners, a little bit different, and happy to be what we are." To most, the flag and the song are no more aggressive in intent than the high school colors and fight song. The flag spotted in Egypt's Valley of the Kings would draw white Southerners in the tour group to it, knowing that they'd find kindred folk. That ensign belongs to only one tribe; it says we are a singular people, our story is unique. It is an unfortunate fact that the same flag displayed at home has taken on toxic meaning because of its misuse by the Klan and racist cops.

Blacks, of course, do not understand the innocent belief that those symbols are for everyone. Growing up in Selma, for instance, they saw the Confederate flag as a specially designed license plate on the front of police cars. The symbol was like somebody else's religion, which excluded all non-believers. It is a mystery of the soul that can be fully understood only by living for generations in the skin of another creed. That cannot be done, so each perceives the other in the false half-light of incomplete understanding.

WHATEVER IT IS THAT history has made of Southerners, it is a sense of community that preserves them and must itself be preserved. Community, which values the personal over the abstract, can develop only in places that are made to fit a humane scale. Because modern cities are built for profit rather than people, there is much to fear from those Yankee inventions, cities and factories, which most Southerners have longed for since Henry Grady's time, and the Agrarians dreaded and opposed. The birth of a city does not automatically mean the death of civility, as citizens of historic Savannah and Charleston will confirm. And community can be stifling in some small towns whose enforced conformity narrows the vision and dulls the wits.

But the virtues of neighborliness, community, and courtesy are better nurtured in a small town than they are among the army of strangers in many modern metropolises. Can the softer virtues of a more agrarian South be used to shape its great cities—the Atlantas and Nashvilles, Birminghams and Columbias—on a more humane scale? It was tried once, in Atlanta.

In May 1975 with crime rising, whites continuing to dribble out of the central city with their taxes, and the city's first black mayor, Maynard Jackson, having a hard time getting his administration organized, there was a growing fear in the minds of city leaders that their city might, after all, become Newark South.

But the beginnings of urban anxiety didn't penetrate the space between 10th and 14th streets on Peachtree. There, a new urban idea was taking shape out of the oldest instincts of the agrarian South—a small town right in the heart of "big town." Colony Square was to be twelve acres of urbane small-town living. The population would be about the size of a small Georgia or Alabama town, if you counted the people who'd work in the twin office towers, the Fairmont-Colony Square Hotel, the retail shops (fifty were planned), and the residents of the apartments, condominiums, and planned townhouses. While only some small-town residents can walk to work, every resident of Colony Square would be able to do so—and shop at Rich's, pick up a loaf of bread, or mail a letter on the walk home by the all-weather skating rink or past the Japanese gardens.

It was to be living proof that the nontransferable cultural values of the city could be had without sacrificing the convenience of small-town living. A Colony Square couple, of any color, could browse at the High Museum of Art across the street; attend the ballet, symphony, or theater also across the street or at the Woodruff Arts Center; and then come back to their little town for a gourmet meal with live entertainment and wine, or for a beer and ham sandwich. It could have been a model for livable urban development (its 1974 value was $100 million). But it was not to be. The development sank in a real estate depression in the late 1970s.

I consider the late Jim Cushman, the developer of Colony Square, a tragic hero of the urban South. Cushman was a small-town boy himself and described Colony Square as "my struggle to regain in the midst of a big city that which I lost when I left a small town in South Carolina" [Chester, pop. 7,000]. Bankers need marketing studies to confirm what Cushman knew instinctively, that "millions of people living in big cities want to return to the basic small-town values: friendliness and warmth, personal identity, simple convenience and accessibility."

Unfortunately, the bankers won.

THE FACE OF CONTEMPORARY Atlanta is changing because many executives and professionals tired of creeping in rush hour traffic are coming home, looking for condominiums closer to work and entertainment. Younger businessmen decided that the crabgrass stampede to the suburbs wasn't worth the price and stayed put. Upper-income blacks, many in the entertainment industry, returning to the South say they feel a warmth and welcome in the new affluent Atlanta that is understandable and true. But the houses of new-rich whites and black celebrities seemed more ostentatious than welcoming on a recent, rather odd-ball trip to the city . . .

Spring had come early on a cool rainy Saturday, unleashing a bombardment of dogwoods, cherry trees, and tulips—a perfect potpourri of newborn colors. Even the rain was welcome in this parched city. The natural world was in resplendent order, but on a quiet, upper-income street there was a discordant, incongruous thing—a tour bus, which was being filled by casually dressed native Atlantans of a certain age.

A friend of ours, a former managing partner of a top firm, Bradley Hale, with roots and a country house in the Alabama Black Belt, had gathered some of his close Atlanta friends for a pre-April 1st tour. The mission: observing some of the preposterous mansions (mini, mac and major) that have sprouted all over town. After some debate, Josephine and I decided that the sheer kookiness of Bradley's invitation was too good to miss, and so we went.

With a sense of dubious adventure, we arrived at the side door of their house, were quickly shooed out the front door and down to the bus. When I entered, maybe a third of the seats were filled with expectant faces curious about the non-Atlanta stranger. I announced who I was, an "auslander" from Alabama, and said, "I don't know if you're thinking the same thing I am, but I'm thinking this may be the tackiest thing I've ever done." Apparently several had the same thought because the remark was greeted with laughter. As the bus filled, connections were made with a college friend, a hometown expatriate and—as people do who belong to the same rung in life—we discovered shared interests with women in the seats in front of us. It was a congenial group as we set out . . . to what? To sneer at what someone called the "new nouveau riche?"

My senses dulled after about forty-five minutes of confronting live-in fortresses such as the one on Tuxedo Road, a pseudo French chateaux with seven bedrooms, ten baths, three half baths, pool, four-car garage, exercise room, family room, library office, and recreation room, for only $19 million. On West Paces Ferry loomed another French castle with six bedrooms, seven baths, four half baths, heated pool, four-car garage, bonus room (whatever that is), family room, office/library, and a second kitchen. It can be had for $20 million. A block down from the $19 million job on Tuxedo Road is a columned manse that offers a lot of extras: five bedrooms and nine—count 'em—bathrooms and three half baths, second kitchen, four-car garage, bonus room, computer, family and great room, ballroom, catering kitchen, four-stop elevator, complete with lobbies, movie theater, wellness center, oval dining room and second-floor sitting room with terrace overlooking the pool. This one is a bargain at $12.5 million.

We stopped at one, which an architect on board knew intimately. He disclosed these stunning facts: the driveway is marble, as are the floors, walls, and stairways. I wondered if the owner had realized, "My God, I have built my own mausoleum, and I am in it—alive!"

As we drove on past one multi-million-dollar house after another, only once or twice did we see signs of life, a car driving through gates to park somewhere in the rear, smoke curling from its chimney. That house came alive for me, I could imagine a husband entering from the attached garage, catching the scent of a wood fire and calling out to his wife who might be reading by the fire. But that was the exception. Most of the houses were lifeless: no lights were visible, their windows dead eyes staring back at us. As the tour went on and on, a growing sorrow crept into my consciousness. I thought of sad, lonely people in vast echoing rooms, and my mind turned to thoughts of two great houses that have been a part of our lives.

An Italianate house on a bluff near Louisville once shone with the charm, intellect, and wit of the city's media baron, Barry Bingham Sr. and his beautiful, smart, tart-tongued wife, Mary. Barry Senior's media connections, wartime service in London and postwar role as Marshall Plan administrator in France made his Kentucky Derby parties brilliant affairs. The house was full of laughter, high-level conversation, parties, dancing and guests. It was a tradition carried on by his son Barry Junior and his wife, Edie, until the younger Barry died. The great hall and the spacious drawing rooms, once filled with radiant people and sparkling conversation, are now dark empty echo chambers.

It was a house big enough for the luminous lives lived there, but no one knows what the future may hold for it.

There is another house we often visit, which stands on the grounds of an earlier sixteenth century dwelling in Oxfordshire, England built by Sir Henry Lee, who served Henry VIII. He later gave a famous entertainment for King Henry's daughter, Elizabeth I. It is said the "Virgin Queen" stayed longer than expected, at great expense to Sir Henry. As his successors grew in title and wealth, so did the house, becoming one of England's great Georgian country houses in the eighteenth century. Ditchley House has forty bedrooms, filled then by the Earl's guests for balls, hunts, and royal visits. It was built to the scale of its use. A famous visitor most weekends during World War II was Winston Churchill. There are no balls or hunts anymore but the rooms are still almost continuously in use as a conference center supported by the British government.

Great houses are born, filled with life for a term; then some decline and die. In Atlanta it seems, some enormous houses are built to impressive size but remain lifeless, sterile.

On Sunday after the fun and interesting weekend with Bradley and Anne, both of whom are now gone, we drove home and, turning on to our driveway found the wisteria had bloomed. We were happy to be back home at our one-kitchen house in the country, Booger Hollow.

ONE MEASURE OF THE Southerner's attachment to "soul" is our fear of losing it, however each of us defines it. There has never been a shortage of pallbearers ready to cart off the mortal red clay of Dixie in a pine box. Every generation has produced its professional mourners who prematurely announced the death of Dixie. In 1930, the Agrarians predicted that if the South allowed cities and factories to breach the Mason-Dixon Line it would be the death of the region. "So it is gone now, whatever it was we had, . . ." wrote Harry Ashmore in *An Epitaph for Dixie* in the late fifties. And there is John Egerton, the reporter of sad countenance and sweet nature, who in 1974 proclaimed "the Americanization of Dixie" in his book of that title. Over the past several decades, Hodding Carter III has given any number of funeral homilies for the lost South. James Dickey was a vivid symbol of the breed. Dickey and his brand of soul brothers loved the South and despaired of the changes they believed were ruining it, have ruined it. But in spite of them, and in large measure because of them, Dixie refuses to die.

It is one of the enduring ironies of the South that the death of Dixie has been proclaimed at least as often as the arrival of the New South. In fact, the birth of a New South is just another way of saying the South is dead. Neither has happened although many have said they could see it. The old lady was right when she scolded the speaker who bad just given a New South oration: "Young man, you speak as if the South is just beginning."

Yet, the questions persist. Will urbanization and industrialization turn Southerners into die-cast Americans? Surely the combined weight of Holiday Inns, new bank buildings, and filling stations will press out of Southerners the last drop of cultural memory. Doesn't the end of racial politics, the emergence of cities, and better paychecks mean that the Southerner is doomed? No. As long as there are children of both races born into families with a sense of being Southern, Dixie won't die.

Yet there is an active conspiracy to suppress any visible sign that there is or was a place called Dixie, and I have been part of it. For most of my adult life, I have cringed at the site of the Confederate flag because of its abuse by a minority of thugs. The conspiracy has been advanced by northern culture-shapers, the national Democratic Party and liberals, North and South. I no longer wish to have my feelings manipulated by the memory of racist cops and the KKK whom we left behind in the dung heap of history long ago. I consider it ridiculous that the Democratic Party every four years concedes enough electoral votes for victory because the party is spooked by Confederate ghosts. It turns out there is a cost to cultural suppression, the price is continuing to feed the most fevered right wing of the Republican Party: cultural revenge bought by a white majority voting against its own interests.

History has made Southerners what they are: a history of loving and hating, of atrocities committed and borne, of enduring without hope, of finally catching hope and prevailing. No region or nation has an exemption from original sin. The history of all people is mottled with success and failure, sin and redemption. White Southerners have rightly been called to account for their sins but they should not be asked to live on a diet of shame for eternity. No people should be asked to repress their culture forever. With a little self-confidence and becoming humility, all Southerners should resist homogenization.

There should be no pureed, neutered Southerner stepping out of the discarded skin of his old creed. Like his dog, which sheds the useless winter coat in summer but remains a dog, the Southerner will be talking about different things in a different way—even if he is in a meeting held in a revolving restaurant on top of the new bank building.

17

Please Go Away

In the mirror of other nations there have been familar transformations like the death of the Old South and emergence of a different society—seemingly static societies suddenly disappearing to be replaced by unrecognizable new civilizations. China, the medieval country Grandfather served as a medical missionary, vaulting into the twenty-first century; Russia's "classless" communism transformed into a consumer society on its way back to the iron rule of its isolated past; South Africa, where once I relived my segregated past, turned upside down, leaving white veterans of the struggle a brigade of has-beens, disconsolate and frustrated.

My own interest in exploring foreign cultures was bred by Dad, who was fond of saying, "He who fails to take heed of troubles far away will soon find troubles near at hand." How many times had Dad uttered that homily from his armchair at the north end of the dining room table? Enough times to influence his son. His and Mother's travels in Europe and Latin America, exotic expeditions at that time for people from our little town, also inspired my wanderlust. Until the 1970s, my foreign travel had been limited to a 1956 Mediterranean cruise as a paid guest of the U.S. Navy, memorable moments of which were a fine paella in Valencia and a disappointing interview with a prostitute in Golfe Juan. A 1975 invitation from the Young Americans Political Association, however, launched a series of foreign sorties that over time yielded unexpected discoveries, among which were the absence of communist ideology in Communist China, and a touchy defensiveness in Russia that echoed familiar traits of the American South.

Nations with a hard history such as China and Russia and South Africa are more interesting, which may explain why I felt an affinity for Soviet Russia and the transition years of Gorbachev and Yeltsin, empathy I did not feel with the material success of the Putin era which followed. Both Russia and China in their latter market-obsessed incarnations seem to have created a new ideology, "Market Dictatorship," a form of fascism that allows free markets to flourish but suppresses democracy and free expression, especially by the media. Russia, with its exaltation of nation and native religion, bred a form of nationalism that is fed by deeply suppressed insecurity.

Ahhh, Russia, so abused by history, so poor in spirit, so rich in oil, so desirous of strutting on the world scene to spread awe and fear in all directions. Josephine and I have been there more times than we can remember. When you learn the history of a people, develop lifelong friendships, view their art treasures, recall adventures and fun times there, a beyond-tourism feeling for the country seeps into your unconscious. On one of Josephine's last trips to Moscow to visit a godchild, the self-assured New Rich displaying themselves on the old city's streets filled her with "a stab of gloom." We both find this new version of old Russia depressing. For me, the glitz of self-conscious new wealth does not alloy with the base metal of my memories.

My firsthand introduction to then Soviet Russia in November 1975 was during the second phase of the Cold War, during the Nixon/Kissinger- organized "détente" under the plodding leadership of Leonid Brezhnev. I was awed by its size and especially impressed by the grit of young Communist shock troops in Ust Illimsk who built a huge power dam and a city out of the Siberian tundra. But I was put off by the unnatural language of the "New Soviet Man" as spoken by our party-supplied guides, who seemed to have had neither mothers nor memory, for which all human history began in 1917 with the arrival of the Spaceship Lenin from the Planet Marx. When I think of that Russia a single melancholy note, like that of a Russian Orthodox bass, hovers over the experience. It speaks of a people who had been attacked from all sides for centuries from the Middle East, Sweden, France, and of their incomprehensible suffering in World War II—more than 23 million dead, more civilians than soldiers, 1.2 million in Leningrad alone.

On that first trip, and each subsequent visit to the memorial to the dead of Leningrad, the most eloquent exhibit—a permanent picture in my mind—is a scrap of stale bread, a vivid reminder that most of the city's losses were from starvation. In every chapter of the Russian story the people have looked up to a czar, some more brutal than others, whether

Christian or Communist, and they bore their lives with a sense of fatality, expecting and accepting punishment because that has always been the way with Father Russia, the only father they had known. Returning home just before Thanksgiving on that first visit, my feelings for the people of the Soviet Union were not enmity or fear; instead I was filled with profound sorrow. I understood Russia in the way Southerners instinctively understand history: to experience the destruction of war on one's own soil, to know defeat, privation, isolation and, worst of all, the scorn of luckier peoples. Connecting with Russia's harder history gave me clues to its soul as made visible on that first trip by encounters with two very different women.

A muscular young female Russian journalist thought I said we were afraid of Russia. Her smile was that of someone who had physically beaten a bigger, richer more admired opponent, a smile that betrayed sadistic pleasure. When I corrected, "No, we are afraid *for* you, and the knock of the secret police on your door." Her face fell from triumph to despair in an instant. At an embassy party, when I told a pretty young writer for *Soviet Life* that I thought we, Russia and the American South, were connected by isolation and scorn, she answered angrily, "Yes, people speak of us as if we aren't even human beings." I could have hugged her; hers was the first natural human reaction I encountered on that trip.

I wished a better life for Russians and on visits in the early 1980s, I was cheered by my newspaper colleagues' less-guarded, non-ideological private conversation. They were beginning to speak openly of the Afghanistan war as "our Vietnam." After 1985 when a new generation represented by Mikhail Gorbachev came to power with policies of openness and economic reform, Russia was changing before our eyes: journalists were free to explore anything, including the nation's true past, daring paintings were shown, good restaurants appeared. But the reforms didn't work. The contradictions of socialism, the strains of maintaining an empire, and swollen arms budgets were too much. Gorbachev destroyed the Communist Party, and as a direct consequence the Soviet Union fell like a house of cards. He, not Reagan, ended the cold war. But Gorbachev could not raise a democratic, modern, and stable nation in its place. He was rewarded with the contempt of his people and of the hard, czar-like new leaders such as Vladimir Putin.

My friend Vitaly Korotich was editor of the magazine *Ogonyek*, which was wildly popular during the early Gorbachev years, especially for revealing to Russians true pictures of their own past. In our living room one evening, he compressed Soviet history to poetic math, "If every one of Stalin's victims were given one minute to speak, it would take seventy years." He also discovered how the dead hand of comfortable routine was undermining the reforms of perestroika. He laboriously assembled a team of experts to show the manager of a state tank manufacturing industry how he could transform the plant to manufacture a money-making product. When repeated calls over time revealed no action on the refitting plan, Vitaly went to see the manager again. At the end of what would be their last conversation, the manager pleaded, "Look, Vitaly, we make tanks; we know how to make tanks, we like to make tanks. Leave us alone."

The Russia that Putin inherited was a vast paraplegic, struggling pitifully to make its gigantic arms and legs function. Bitterness was bone-deep among a shrunken military and the general population. An editor of a prestigious journal of the time was on a panel with some high-ranking officers and felt their hostility toward him, "They were like wounded animals who could not discover the source of their pain." Putin evidently thought he had found the source of the pain in meddling journalists, and in the demeaning policies of the U.S. and Western Europe, so he played on the historic insecurities of his people—a George Wallace in his time and place. When hard, cold-eyed men like Putin seize the government, the first to feel the steel bridle of censorship are the seekers of truth. Poor Russia, for years ahead the truth will be what the State says it is, just like the old days.

CHINA, SINCE MY EARLIEST childhood, had always been a real place to me. Dad had lived there and would amuse the family—and hilariously break up newspaper conventions—by singing "Sweet Adeline" in Mandarin. Grandfather had been a medical missionary there forever and wore medals from a Chinese president in his portrait on the living room wall. Visiting Grandfather in his Atlanta retirement home, I got an early sense of how emperors conducted themselves. Dr. Thomas Wilburn Ayers was a short, slight man, but he had presence as he reigned from an overstuffed chair much like the ones later favored by Mao Zedong. Behind him were a Chinese tapestry and a tall, sky blue vase with a white magnolia blossom. I can't imagine him kneeling on the living room floor, shooting marbles with grandchildren. At dinner—the noon meal in those days—the plates were Chinese. Similar, more colorful plates adorned the large Welsh dresser at home, which I faced from my place at the dinner table. They were old, very old, maybe as old as Jesus and the disciples or so it seemed to me the way the grownups talked about them.

We inherited two of Grandfather's large vases, which Josephine displays in protected glass niches in our two-story, oval dining room. I call them "The Mandarin's Revenge," after the story of how they came into Grandfather's possession. Early in his mission work, so the story went, he was called to the house of the mandarin, a figure of great authority and learning, a proud man, steeped in the Chinese classics, the most important official in the area of Shantung Province where Grandfather lived. His son had fallen ill and none of the ancient remedies healed the boy. So in desperation this great man stooped to summon Yang kwei-tzu, the foreign devil man. Grandfather treated the boy, he got well, and the mandarin invited the foreign doctor back. The learned official made a graceful speech, "Nothing can repay you for the life of a son, but anything this humble house has is yours." Grandfather, not having been briefed by the Asia desk of the State Department, armed only with Christian compassion and Southern courtesy, replied, "Oh, I couldn't accept anything. I did it to help the boy and for the glory of God." He left certain that by his cultural lights he had done the right thing, not knowing that he had humiliated the most important man in the region by refusing his gratitude. A few days later a retinue appeared outside the mission residence, at the end of which two coolies carried large matching blue and white vases with wide mouths. A minor figure of the mandarin's household presented the vases, repeating the governor's graceful words but putting a sting in the tail of the speech, "These vases were made by Chinese artists before your little country was discovered." So there! We've regretted that Grandfather didn't offend any other mandarins.

Uncles and aunts who had lived in China, a house full of Chinese arti-facts, talk at dinner about the evil Dowager Empress, the Christian commandant Chiang Kai-shek and his beautiful American-educated wife; all of this made China real to me, though it was for so long inaccessible behind the red curtain of what we called communism. It remained distant until the curtain was parted by historic visits to Beijing by Henry Kissinger and Richard Nixon. Then, in 1977, President Carter brought Deng Xiaoping to Atlanta as part of normalizing relations with China for the first time since 1948. There I shook the small soft hand of a tiny, insignificant-looking man in a Mao jacket who had merely crafted political hinges that would swing a giant nation from medieval to modern times in just a few years.

Looks deceive.

Soon after having met Deng, we were visited by a group from Radio Peking. They were a delegation of rubes, crude enough to have made their way up the ladder during the ideological violence of the Cultural Revolution. I took them to my cultural listening post, Jimmy Turner's Courthouse Barbershop, where they cackled at a colleague committing the capitalist indulgence of a shoeshine. Their guide and interpreter was a lovely, articulate, educated woman, who noticed the Chinese porcelain plates and gave graceful dining instructions in Chinese to her baffled delegation. I don't know how we impressed the rube red broadcasters, maybe it was the visit to the proletarian barbershop, but soon after they had departed, we received an invitation from Xinhua, the New China News Agency, to visit China. Of course, Josephine and I wanted to go and I asked if it was possible to visit Grandfather's old mission station, which didn't seem to be a problem.

When we arrived at Beijing's dusty old air terminal our bags were the last ones on the belt, a cause of some anxiety but which also gave us an opportunity to collect evidence of the rapid commercialization of an ancient culture: it seemed that every other item on the baggage belt was a Japanese TV set. A large poster behind us advertised a French restaurant, Maxim's. Hotels in the 1980s were still college-dorm modern. First-class accommodations on the overnight train from the capital to the coastal city of Yantai (formerly Chefoo) weren't much better: four open bunks, shared with two Chinese, one of whom was sick. Josephine spent the first night of her life in her clothes, which attracted quickly growing crowds of gawking Chinese women when she stepped out to get a breath of air at the few stops we made. She was the only woman those rural Chinese women had seen dressed entirely in Saint Laurent, and the only woman on the train in a skirt.

Arriving in Yantai with our party handler from Xinhua, we were picked up by a van for the drive on poor roads to Grandfather's small county, a trip that took us three hours but by ox cart had taken grandfather three days. Our arrival at the official guesthouse was a celebrity moment, more an example of Xinhua's authority than our fame. Greeting us was the county manager, the mayor and a television crew, which recorded Josephine tripping as she exited the van and almost falling into the camera.

It was an eventful, moving, and revealing visit, which I summarized in the *Star* [see appendix], describing what we saw and experienced in the small town where my grandfather spent twenty-five years of his life beginning in 1901. I had always been amazed that he seemed relatively untouched by the momentous events he witnessed there. What little I knew of his China life came from a small book he had written and from rare dinner table conversation. Visiting Hwangshien 56 years after he left, I hoped to find clues to what he had been like before he became the remote, imperial figure that he seemed to his grandson. Happily, a few old citizens of the town did help bridge the gap.

WE LEFT WONDERING WHETHER China would ever curl inward again, flagellating itself with a renewed Cultural Revolution to purify its communist ideology or will it continue to modernize and welcome contact with the industrial democracies? Another way of asking one of the major questions I went there to answer is: how "red" do you paint Red China? Reporting and vacation trips, a dozen or so basic books, and conversations with a few China specialists in and out of that vast and ancient land hardly qualify me as an expert. But all the evidence gives me confidence to say that China will follow the road it is on now for a long time to come: toward an autocratic, free-market, gigantic version of Singapore.

Harrison Salisbury, the late, great correspondent and Op-ed Page initiator for the *New York Times*, spent the bulk of his career studying Russia and China. On completing a 7,400-mile journey retracing Mao Zedong's Long March, he talked with all of China's senior leaders and offered this mildly startling assessment of China's commitment to communist ideology. "I am yet to meet a Chinese who knows very much about Marxism," he told me. I heard only one rather light-hearted reference to Marxist philosophy in the entire two weeks of our first trip there.

My last conversation before leaving Beijing on that trip was with Li Shenzi, reputed to be one of the politburo's chief advisors on U.S. affairs. He answered my questions about the governing philosophy of the nation with a broad smile. "China is not a very ideological society," he said. On that last morning the Communist Party newspaper, *People's Daily*, in a front-page editorial declared obsolete much of the thoughts of communism's founding fathers. "One cannot expect the works of Marx and Lenin, written in their time, to solve today's problems."

In conversations with peasants and students at the astounding treasures in the Forbidden City and the Temple of Heaven, and talks with people on overnight trains, in cities out in the countryside where few westerners go, I never heard a discussion of the finer points of Marxism. I sensed that the deepest feeling of China's citizens has nothing to do with party ideology and everything to do with simple patriotism. Ask anyone out in the country who is at or near retirement age why he or she joined the Party as a young adult in the 1930s and early '40s and they will tell you, "To fight the Japanese." Mao did; Chiang accumulated weapons to eliminate Mao.

The proud practicality of China is summed up in an often-quoted saying of Deng Xiaoping, "It does not matter if the cat is black or white if it catches mice." In Huanxian in the 1980s the cats of free enterprise were beginning to catch mice. Peasants were in their fields at night, not as forced labor for a collective, but to earn money for a TV, washing machine, or motorbike. Some numbers tell the story. The per capita income for Huanxian in 1978, when Deng first introduced western-style market incentives to Chinese agriculture, was $386 a year. The year we visited it had risen to $1,256. The new prosperity was evident in a building boom a visitor could see from the road, in the cornucopia of goods at the county trade fair, and in the 100 percent increase in appropriations to a county high school. Huanxian is in Shandong Province, one of the nation's poorest. They had never—never in 2,000 years—had it so good. At the time I concluded that any hard-line party ideologist who yearned for the purity and clarity of the old Maoist days and sought to turn China inward, away from global ideas and influence, would have his work cut out for him.

How 'red' do you color China? Think of it this way: China was a unified nation with a bureaucracy reaching down to the county level two hundred years before Christ was born, when America was an unknown, virtually unpopulated wilderness, and my European ancestors were crude barbarians. Other outsiders, the Mongols and the Manchurians, have attempted to remake China in their image but, instead, became Chinese.

The thirty-five years of communist ideology on this ancient subcontinent is the thinnest of veneers compared to the seventy years of Soviet rule in Russia. Thinner still is China's experience with pure democracy; are there any historians who would claim Chiang Kai-shek's regime was democratic? But by 1976, when Deng Xiaoping's leadership was formalized, there were millions of Chinese, many well-educated in China or the West, who remembered the workings of commerce and trade, a memory that seven decades of real communism had erased from Russians' minds.

China is unique. It does not fit any American-made label of a "red" country or "blue" country. What then do you color China? Neither "red" nor "red, white, and blue." Color China the brown of its loess mountains, the silver of its rice patties from the air, the green of its grain fields, and yellow, the imperial color and the color of its great river.

Color China Chinese.

CHINA, RUSSIA, AND SOUTH Africa, they all call out to me because, in one way or another, they have had a hard history as has the American South. As each has turned on the lathe of history, national characteristics have been shaped: Russia, touchy, defensive, and suspicious; China, proud, self-confident, but obsessed with order; and South Africa, whose legal revolution is too recent for a biracial national character to have formed.

When we were last in Cape Town and suburban Johannesburg (crime was bad downtown, we were told) friends there were discovering what we have found to be a truth in the American South: When the formerly oppressed attain positions of wealth and power, their past suffering does not providentially stamp nobility into their character. Instead, they behave distressingly like the people they replaced, or joined. Nelson Mandelas are as rare as George Washingtons. Black officeholders are just as capable of abuse, demagoguery, and fraud as were their former masters. And why shouldn't they be—they have learned at the hands of the experts.

Around Helen Suzman's table in the winter (their spring) of 2005, there was fierce criticism of President Tabo Mbeki for his tolerance of the monstrous misrule of Robert Mugabe in neighboring Zimbabwe. There was contempt in their voices for a formerly liberal white editor of the *Cape Times* who, as a Mbeki spokesman, explained the president's diffidence about Mugabe's grotesque rule as the bonding of "a revolutionary brother."

Helen herself was feeling neglected, banished from the arena and not temperamentally ready to let a new generation have a go at making a better society of what, in her view, was a blatantly imperfect one. Her fame and the physical totems of a rich and consequential life seemed to give her little satisfaction. There was no evidence of it on the walls of her study (twenty-seven honorary degrees not displayed, nor even a picture of Queen Elizabeth II installing her as an honorary Dame of the British Empire). Helen was constitutionally unable to retire into the glow of a life well-lived. Her mindset was: There is work to do. Mbeiki is a fool. The prisons are overcrowded. And on and on . . .

That was the picture of Helen stored in my head when the BBC announced her unexpected death in January 2009. The impact of the bulletin caused a sudden intake of breath, followed by the hollow realization that I will never see that fabulous spear-point of a woman again. The cause of death was not announced but I would guess she died of frustration, raging at the stupidities of a South African government which she had helped create but at ninety-one no longer had the power to affect. That's how she was that last morning in her study, impatient with folly and sad that her day had passed.

We parted with the shared realization that only veterans of the human rights struggle know what the war was really like, and what it was all about.

Afterword

A third generation has been born since the economic and social quakes which tore down and remade the South in the last half of the twentieth century. How has life changed for the people living in the new cities and small towns of that reborn South, and what does the socio-political exclamation point of a black president portend for the region? First, an intimate look at small-town life, partly framed by a conflict between, on the one hand, hometown values as popularized by television's "Walton Family," and, on the other, the assault on the economic basis of small towns as led by that other "Walton Family," the Wal-Mart effect. And then a wider focus, looking at culture and politics in the region and some of the notable personalities and events encountered on our journey.

As the moral dynamism of the civil right movement dissipated, its leaders dying off or becoming old and sick, and the new economy's great banks merged into giant national institutions, there was an implosion of leadership in Anniston and small towns like it throughout the South. Simultaneously a combination of the digital revolution and the fruits of unregulated private greed—the Great Recession—staggered newspapers, in a sense, journalism itself.

Pushing the rewind button on fifty years in journalism triggers a replay of technologies leading to . . . what? For me it all began in the sweaty back shop of the "old" *Star* building, across from the courthouse. My first job was pouring lead "pigs" for the linotype machines—the behemoths of old hot-type newspapers, 2,645 pounds of steel, nearly seven feet high, with arms moving like praying mantises. Each keystroke by an operator typing on an oversized keyboard squirted drops of molten lead into tiny forms, which became first lines then whole pages of lead type, which were then cast in lead plates for the press.

In time, perforated tapes came into use, which allowed one operator to run the entire array of linotypes. Then came photo-offset printing, which consigned the hot-metal behemoths to a scrapyard of extinct technologies, and finally desktop computers, which allowed reporters and editors to do all the work that once was done in a loud, bustling back shop filled with craftsmen and characters.

New laborsaving technology and the lift of a rising Southern economy from the 1960s on meant that the *Star* and newspapers everywhere in the region were making money. But the family paper—at the end of World War II the dominant form of ownership—was doomed, too. The disappearance of family newspapers, now fewer than 250 out of roughly 1,500 dailies, is part of a vast depersonalization of twenty-first century society. Where ownership became dispersed among large families, the few family members actually working at a paper were often pressured to sell so the other heirs could cash out their share of the family asset. Crippling federal inheritance taxes made it next to impossible to pass the paper on to another family member. Too many family publishers simply threw up their hands and sold to media conglomerates or to private investment firms. Years ago one such investment firm, with an excess profit it didn't want to pay out in taxes, made a cash offer of $50 million for our company. We said thanks, but no thanks.

When a family member is no longer head of the local newspaper, the intensity of the paper's commitment to its community pales and withers. Investment banks and great corporations don't care about local communities and their institutions. Earlier I described these relationships in these terms: "The human dynamic of the relationship between a family and an entire community is unusual: close and caring, but sometimes jarring and painful . . . It is precisely that sensitivity that gives a family newspaper its unique personality. It is more caring. It scolds, supports, consoles and chides. It hurts and is hurt, and it loves—like any slightly dysfunctional family."

In cities the size of Anniston or smaller, if its newspapers and its banks are insignificant links at the end of long, long corporate chains, they infect the community with a sickening ennui. Anything that saps the energy of caring, committed local leadership is the enemy of community vitality. What does Wells Fargo care if local businesses close for lack of a patient, friendly financial adviser? Who cares if local civic enterprises founder and starve for lack of leadership and funding? Wal-Mart and other big box stores aren't gathering places that nurture community.

What does community vitality mean to the Wall Street titans of the new Gilded Age? The original period of great concentrated wealth, the time of the Vanderbilts, Rockefellers, Mellons, Carnegies, and Morgans, was one of "conspicuous consumption of conspicuous leisure," as Thorstein Veblen put it. But the economic giants of his time pumped up the industrial muscle of the adolescent nation such that its output was greater than that of Britain, France and Germany together. By comparison what did the no-name titans of twenty-first century Wall Street create to match the railroads, mines and steel mills of the early Gilded Age? They gave us bundled derivatives and a heart-stopping recession.

When Anniston had its big three local banks, First National, Commercial National, and Anniston National, their presidents were generals of the civic army and their boards of directors were the field grade officers of those brigades. If the general spoke something happened. If all three spoke in unison, the whole civic army was on the march to victory. They are all gone, swallowed in the movement of giant banking conglomerates. Their local presidents are mere managers, and nobody knows or particularly cares who is on their local boards. Whole bank buildings became ghostly silent, lobbies empty where once friends greeted friends.

Another kind of implosion affected the black community in cities like Anniston. The passing of local civil rights leaders left a vacuum without a leading personality or structure to fill it. Civil rights organizations such as the SCLC were single-issue advocacy groups. When their agenda was largely adopted, they had little to do. Protest movements without anything important to protest are hollow vehicles. They were never designed to be professional organizations to school successive generations in leadership protocols; so, in the absence of a leading personality or structure, the vacuum was filled with a cacophony of gossip, backbiting, demagoguery, resentment, and suspicion.

There were clashes in the past between white civic leaders and local black leaders, usually preachers, but when they spoke something happened. When they made an agreement, it stuck. The transformative effect of President Obama—from a vocal, confrontational leadership to a more unifying, coalition-building leadership style—had not reached my hometown or towns like it during the president's first term.

The conditions faced by newspapers in the early 2000s led some informed people to doubt that community newspapers could survive. The drought of advertising in the Great Recession caused even community newspapers to shrink, shedding editors and reporters and other staff, struggling to keep up payments for building loans to uncaring giants, and puzzling over how best to use new technology to interest newly wired readers and gain revenue.

Which brings us back to the beginning question raised by the latest turn of the technological kaleidoscope: it is leading to . . . what? Readers will not rely on our print or digital editions as their only source of national or international news; there are online sites to satisfy those interests. But our web pages can be the town square or back porch where neighbors can drop by and pass the time of day about local affairs or cordially argue with each other. Until somebody repeals human nature there is only one platform where 4-H Club ribbon-winners can be seen by parents and friends; where the United Daughters of the Confederacy can display their outrageous hats, ample bosoms, and good works; where classmates, parents, neighbors, whole towns can share the exultation of their high school team winning a state championship; homeowners can learn if crime has touched their neighborhood, whether the local schools are achieving or falling behind and learn what the city council is up to. Community papers, whether delivered on paper or dots on a screen, have always been accountable because their owners and employees go to the same church or grocery or movie or restaurant as their readers. Their owners and managers are accessible, their numbers are in the phone book, and because they are accessible, they are believable.

As long as there are mothers to cry at their daughters' weddings, as long as there are fathers to swell with pride at their sons' exploits on the football field, as long as people fear crime, are suspicious of local politicians, cheer for the economic boost of a new industry or mourn the death of a beloved citizen, as long as people want to share with others, there will be a need for someone to connect them.

So, no, newspapers aren't dying. Regardless of whether the paper is delivered on paper or on line, human nature is a constant force drawing us to a center. Call it the town square or the back porch, newspapers will continue to invite readers . . . "Y'all Come."

And so where was the Deep South after the great and terrible events of the "movement" dimmed in our memory, after the New South epiphany faded into the Reagan '80s, the Clinton '90s, and across the millennial bridge to George W. Bush and Barack Obama? A new black middle class had emerged in the South; in fact we all lived better in the cities and shopping malls of the new economy. And yes, black and white, we did get along with heightened civic sensitivity. But what had we built with the skyscrapers and multi-lane highways? What was its moral core?

Morally, millions of white Southerners would have to confess they recoil at the idea of being governed by a black man. However, partially in their defense, the average white in the Deep South had not heard or felt an invitation to Barack Obama's e-pluribus-unum national oneness.

"We" used to be the Solid Democratic South, an impenetrable phalanx arrayed to stop the black man from entering. "We" are now the Solid (White) Republican South, arrayed with similar intent, lessened effect, and excused with heightened deceit.

America stunned the world by electing the first black president of the United States, a gifted speaker who merged his vision with the unspoken yearnings of a majority. He swept the country with an almost three to one electoral margin, but in the crescent of Deep South states from South Carolina to Texas, he lost decisively. Forty years had intervened between the fading afterglow of the New South and the election of Obama. What did they purport for the South and the nation?

A summary of those decades would have to begin with the mystery of Ronald Reagan. By 1980, Fate had rained such a punishing flurry of blows on our innocent nation that we were ready for a man on a horse, a handsome Warren Harding figure to restore a word Harding himself invented, "normalcy." The nation's battered condition—two decades of civil revolution, urban rebellion, Vietnam, Watergate, and the Iranian hostage crisis—was the perfect setting for a supremely confident actor. His sunny conservatism and mellifluous voice soothed a troubled nation with the promise of a restoration, the comforting thought that the old verities abideth still. Thus did Ronald Reagan's personality dominate not just a decade but a generation, yet leave a riddle without an answer:

Can a galvanizing national consensus, a new governing philosophy be built from a celebration of wealth and the proposition that government is the enemy—what nation has pretended to greatness by declaring its own government the enemy? If all the virtues of the new faith were distilled into two tenets, they would be a celebration of unregulated wealth and "family values."

The main precept of the former was: government is bad; pursuit of private wealth is good. Wealth corrupts the poor, but ennobles the rich. Its ultimate expression came in the frightening recession of 2008–09.

The other tenet of the new faith, the ethereal phrase, "family values," means different things to different people. Instead of creating a galvanizing new governing philosophy, the blinkered opponents in the culture war fell on each other with a vengeance, which resulted in an angry, polarized stalemate during the first decade of the twenty-first century.

FOR ME, THE 1980s was a doleful decade. The bright promise of a New South had dulled into the monotonous construction of a one-party Republican South that looked very much like the old segregationist Democratic majority. The country was newly alert to the possibility that whites might be the victims of discrimination, as played out in the *Bakke* affirmative action backlash of the early 1980s, and which has reemerged in new so-called reverse discrimination cases in 2012. Still, it is hard to claim the *Bakke* case as a great victory for human rights.

Yet I had to admit that the nation that Ronald Reagan bequeathed to George H. W. Bush was a calmer, more confident one. Bush I was a decent, experienced, worldly man but in comparison to the outsized Reagan he seemed diminished as a personality and communicator. His bold declaration of conservatism, "Read my lips, no new taxes," was courageously and responsibly reversed. In doing so, he revealed an inner struggle between conflicting loyalties: to his natural father, Prescott Bush, the Eastern Establishment moderate, internationalist U.S. Senator from Connecticut, and to his political father, the conservative Western populist, Reagan. Bush I was, in a sense, a man without a country, perpetually choosing between a fedora and a Stetson. An economic slump set up the elder Bush to be knocked off by another sunny, outsized, brilliant and articulate political phenomenon, the man from Hope, Arkansas.

JOSEPHINE AND I FIRST met Bill Clinton, then the baby-faced attorney general of Arkansas, while visiting our friend Dale Bumpers, then the Arkansas governor. We were impressed and kept up with Clinton, expecting already that he would run for president someday. I learned that the day had come when, on a flight from Washington to Atlanta, two friends from New South days, former Governors Bill Winter of Mississippi and Dick Riley of South Carolina, came aboard followed by then-Governor of Arkansas Bill Clinton. He confirmed his intentions on that flight.

After his election in 1992, it was satisfying to know that I had made a suggestion that became, and still is, part of the White House policy structure. Bill had campaigned promising that, due to a post-Soviet world, he would create what I called an "Economic Security Council" with equal access to the president as the National Security Council. A similar body but with a less threatening name, the National Economic Council, was recommended by a big-name Carnegie Commission, which included my friend Ted Sorensen. (Ted, who died in 2010, had been the closest non-family advisor to John F. Kennedy.) When I next saw Ted I kidded him about his commission being late coming up with my idea. He replied, "That idea has a thousand fathers." I asked the president to referee our good-natured joust and in a hand-written note he said, "On the chronology/paternity matter between you and Ted Sorensen, you are right about the chronology and closer on paternity. *I had long felt we needed an NEC.*"

In personality, talent, temperament, and strict fidelity to marriage vows, Clinton was a latter-day Franklin D. Roosevelt. Both men exhibited a genial forbearance in the face of vicious criticism that, in Clinton's case, sank to the level of a political lynching with his impeachment by the Republican House. Of course, Clinton is forever doomed to be ranked among the good, but not great presidents. Unlike Roosevelt, he was not tested by gargantuan challenges like the Great Depression and World War II.

Clinton managed merely to leave a country that was at peace, prosperous as never before, and universally admired, even by those who resented its cocky strength. He left office more popular than Ronald Reagan, with a legacy much larger than a stain on a blue dress. Therein lies a longer tale, of a night in the Lincoln suite and a nightcap with the president.

Josephine and I were, of course, elated by Clinton's election and happy to see casual friends as new renters of the house at 1600 Pennsylvania Avenue. We stayed in touch and Bill and I kept up regular correspondence during the mean times for him and Hillary, which I hope lifted their spirits in a small way. Hillary always said to let her know when we planned to be in Washington.

The White House was quiet and virtually empty the night of February. 12, 1998. It was Lincoln's Birthday, a day not widely celebrated there, so it was just Josephine, our daughter Margaret, and me alone with the First Family.

After dinner we were in the historic Solarium, which the Clintons used as a family room because of its sunny isolation from the formal rooms on the family floor. A homey gallery of pictures of friends and family line either side of the ramp leading up to the parlor. There was only one world leader among the gallery, Yitzhak Rabin, a memorial to and evidence of a close, quality friendship.

The subject that night with the Clintons was, dare I say, wonkish: What to do for working-class victims of globalism? We talked through the issue, but nobody knew how to relieve the unintended consequences of a problem spread across the entire planet. Hillary showed her own fascination with problem-solving and left the room in search of an administration policy document. Returning with a two-inch-thick book, she rifled quickly through the book and declared, "Yes, here it is on page 100." There were laid out a few pages of policy palliatives.

Later, pleading the effects of a winter cold, she left and the president took our family on a tour of the mansion, most of which was familiar to me from prior visits as an occasional "outside adviser" during the Carter years. It was then that the ghost in the house made its presence known. This was three weeks after Monica Lewinsky had become a household word. Standing in front of his desk in the Oval Office, the president swept his hand in a wide arc encompassing the tall windows looking out into the Rose Garden and said, "Imagine having sex in this office, with all these windows."

On a totally different subject, he pointed out a specific pane of one window right behind his desk, which had special meaning for the president. On some evenings late at night he would come down to his darkened office and, seated, look out where the U.S. Signal Corps told him he would be eye-level with the author of the Declaration of Independence, Thomas Jefferson, a blue light illuminating his marble figure in the monument across the river.

Entering the inner sanctum of the president's private space, the intimate dining room and the cramped working office, Margaret and Josephine exchanged a wordless glance that said, "It was here." It was, as Special Counsel Kenneth Starr's investigators confirmed with pornographic curiosity and made public in lurid detail. Already the national press corps was proclaiming Clinton's presidency finished, though the commentators were puzzled by the public's insouciant attitude to the scandal. The public already had a pretty good idea that Clinton's charm glowed with special warmth in the presence of pretty women, as it did in the presence of Josephine, whom he understandably much preferred to me.

The public, which is willing to believe almost anything about politicians, seemed able to forgive a dalliance here and there as long as the office holder was doing a good job, and they thought Clinton was. The economy was roaring, debt was evaporating; he'd reformed welfare as he said he would, and we were at peace. But like most men, the president flinched from the pain; the cold angry separation that he knew would be coming if Hillary and Chelsea knew the truth.

He was in denial.

A moral choice of heavy consequence haunted him that February night. And like the Vietnam draft, he chose at first to avoid facing the music. His denials finally crumbled under Starr's assault that began as an investigation of a failed land deal but which pursued every sniff of potential scandal with the relentlessness of Inspector Javert in *Les Miserables*. When tapes and DNA evidence proved that the president and the intern had engaged in oral sex, he had to make his shame-faced confession to his family, the nation, and the world.

The Starr report was sufficiently detailed to arouse the sexual curiosity of any repressed old man. It was salacious. In addition, a ferociously partisan Congressman, Tom DeLay of Texas, encouraged other members to view raw, uncorroborated accusations that had been rejected by the thoroughly detailed staff.

Bill Clinton was stripped naked before the whole world. Month after month as articles of impeachment were drafted and debated, his morals, his honesty, his sexual preferences, even the size and shape of his male member became subjects of conversation. The Senate—a year to the day after our evening together—acquitted him, and his poll numbers rebounded. His post-presidency role as drum major to billionaires fighting hunger and poverty in the world demonstrate further dimensions of a many-sided character.

All of that was still in the future when the three of us, and "Buddy," the family's friendly Labrador Retriever, concluded the tour in the president's comfortable and inviting private office on the family floor. He wanted to talk; rather he wanted to vent. He was controlled but angry and frustrated. Until well past midnight, he verbally struggled against what he knew was coming: the paralyzing onslaught of depositions, press conferences, and endless consultations with staff and attorneys. He was Gulliver, pinioned by a thousand threads tied by little men for no great purpose, keeping him from giving himself fully to the work of the presidency. I was mesmerized. Josephine, with a woman's sixth sense, said she saw frequent flashes of guilt.

Finally, a call came through that he had to take. Josephine and I slipped out and went back to the Lincoln suite. We looked at each other, unable to articulate in a word our feelings. I spoke first, "God, I'd give anything for a big shot of brandy." At that point, there was a knock on the door; it was the president, come to say goodnight. "Mr. President," I said, "I know these rooms have been occupied by Winston Churchill many times. If he needed a little something to top off the night, how would he go about it in this house?"

The president grinned and waved, "Come on." So the first among world leaders led a little delegation of a small-town newspaper publisher, the publisher's daughter, and the First Dog, later followed by Josephine, into the First Kitchen. In his search for just the right "topper," the president opened a pantry and spied what he wanted on a top shelf, way in the back. He pushed over a three-step ladder, mounted it and reached for a teak-colored box. I was below him, arms raised, hoping he wouldn't fall, writing mental headlines: "PRESIDENT AND PUBLISHER INJURED IN DRUNKEN FALL." Safely back on the floor, to my relief, he removed from the box a bottle of hundred-year-old Irish whisky, a gift from Irish Prime Minister Berte Ahern. The president opened the sealed bottle and poured a little shot for himself, and a more ample one for me. We toasted each other, and with great anticipation, I lifted the whisky to my lips, and . . . it was *awful!*

Beautiful whisky, gone bad. It was an apt metaphor for Bill Clinton's presidency in the balance of the impeachment year.

THOUGH LACKING A POPULAR vote majority, Bush II entered the Oval Office more comfortable in the mantle of Ronald Reagan than his father had ever been. George *fils* was a sure-nuf Texas Reagan conservative. He had the country and the world with him in the searing tragedy of 9/11, and when he defeated the Taliban protectors of al Qaida, perpetrators of the attack. Yet within two years, he invaded Iraq, the wrong country, for the wrong reason, and thus inflamed Arabic hatred throughout the world.

The wars, the bungling of the New Orleans disaster, debt stretching out to infinity, social engineering to comfort the up-trodden, and policies that led to a frightening economic collapse, all combined to make Bush the second most unpopular president in history. As viewed by a nation staring over the brink into a deep Depression, the Reagan "philosophy" of feeding the fat cats and of "family values" looked small, weak, wrong. The conservative movement conceived by William F. Buckley, launched by Goldwater, ratified by Nixon, and deified by Reagan collapsed into the Great Recession under the cheerful, jaunty ineptitude of George W. Bush and the grim belligerence of Dick Cheney. Conventional religious morality as part of Buckley's fusion ideology was eroded by scandal and by separation of important religious universities such as Baylor and Samford from the increasingly politicized Southern Baptist Convention.

The Reagan mantle was in tatters, lashed by economic storms as Bush and Treasury Secretary Henry Paulson frantically fought to keep mega banks from crashing even as they graciously—gratefully—vacated the White House for the first African American president.

OBAMA WON A SIGNIFICANT victory but achieving a post-racial realignment of American culture and politics is a more daunting task that requires an affirmative Southern Strategy. It will be an unfinished puzzle until the missing piece is put in place: the tier of states on a scale comparable to Western Europe from South Carolina to Texas.

The premise of these thoughts—the hope of a lifetime—is that the Deep South can be persuaded to come out of its voluntary apartheid of the mind by an affirmative appeal—a "Nixon in China" strategy, if you will.

Let's face it; Obama and the South are strangers to one another. Strangers have to meet before they get to know each other. The first rule of politics is: Show Up.

A second premise is that, if Obama wishes to unify the Deep South with the nation, he will have to understand the cultural sensitivities, the virtual sacraments of the region. The South is different. It is different because it is the only region to have been defined by a series of un-American experiences: defeat in a war fought on its own land, long periods of economic discrimination and poverty, the disappearance of one civilization and the sudden eruption of another, and worst of all—the unbearable difference— the scorn of more fortunate Americans, their media and their politicians.

A people who have lived through a hard history tend to be clannish, defensive and, for some, deeply resentful. These feelings, for a large minority of white Southerners, are soul deep; their touchstones are symbols of suppressed anger and open pride: a flag and a song, the Confederate battle flag and "Dixie." Those who would demean or suppress cultural sacraments inherit bitterness that will not go away. The Republican Party has exploited the feelings evoked by those symbols since 1964. When Johnson's omnibus civil rights act was passed, he won a national landslide but Goldwater carried Alabama whites by 77 percent and Deep South whites by 71 percent. The strongest segregationist wing of the Democratic Party bolted en masse and became the core of the solid GOP South. They have had Southern Strategies aimed at the white Southern majority with a message of welcome: we like you, and, subtly now, we don't like the (black) Democratic Party.

That was two generations ago. Attitudes have changed about race. Obama carries with him the aura of the Great Seal. Times are more favorable for a "Nixon in China" effort by Obama to make it at least thinkable for national Democrats to compete for the Deep South. If, if . . . he can disarm the cultural land mines embedded in Deep South white culture.

Inevitably, Southerners would wonder how he would treat such explosive symbols as the Confederate flag. He could wrap those symbols in the one-nation theme of his first campaign by saying, in effect:

I am reminded again that we are one undivided America, that the honored dead at Gettysburg wore blue and gray; they fought under different flags that deserve honor and respect but are equal inheritors of one America, indivisible, because in their fighting and in their dying they made a nation out of a scattering of states.

It is good that people set aside quiet, peaceful places to remind us that even in defeat, there was nobility of character and the men who fought under such leaders represent universal values of courage, honor and loyalty. Cultural symbols speak to people of important events that happened to them along the way; they deserve respect—and must never be dishonored by being used as symbols of hate.

Such a statement would have lightning effect. Critics would say he is endorsing a Ku Klux Klan symbol, which he would wave off by asserting the vast majority of people in the South oppose the Klan and the way it cheapens a cherished symbol. In the South, it would convey respect for a people and culture as well as a surprising understanding of that culture. With the curtain of alienation swept away, Southerners would be more willing to hear what a Democratic president has to say on the serious policy agenda for the nation. The development of a genuine two-party system in the South would enable the parties to divide on real issues, discounting emotive fringe topics such as same-sex marriage, and contribute to a more serious national dialogue.

As the second decade of the new century began, there were stirrings among several former Southern governors and U.S. Senators as well as other regional leaders that there should be a nonracial Democratic Southern Strategy that could create a normal two-party division in the South, and elevate the national dialogue. In early 2012, Democratic chairmen and professional organizers from throughout the region met in an Atlanta summit to debate how best to revive the party in the South. Out of that meeting grew an outline of a strategy that borrowed, for instance, from how the party had made inroads into the formerly solid Republican West. The Blue South Project is a vehicle—steered by senior former governors and senators and pushed by younger leaders—that can carry out a step-by-step, multi-year strategy to recreate a two-party system in the South. Once again, in the white-hair phase of my life, I find myself as a founding officer of yet another attempt to unite South and nation. Many progressive impulses in the South have shown promise only to fizzle, yet the crypt has not been sealed. Hope keeps the urge tenaciously alive.

Contemplating the real possibility of such a thing, and casting my thoughts way, way back over the road that has brought us here, I feel the oncoming rush of sentiments so deep and calmly satisfying that I can say, "Lord, I am ready now that my people and the nation are truly one, but just a minute, Lord, let me enjoy the sensation for a while before you take me."

So, the journey ends with the hope of a lifetime still unfulfilled, but certain in a belief that the Deep South is the key to a truly unified nation.

Appendix

This Citation for Alumnus of the Year was presented to the author in 1998 by the Wooster School:

Whereas: Harry Brandt Ayers . . .

Of Anniston, Alabama, entered the Third Form at Wooster School in September, 1949, and actively participated in the life of the school by waiting on tables, washing dishes, cleaning toilets (eventually becoming Head Setter-Up), baby-sitting the Verdery kids, struggling with French and math, challenging and being challenged by Schwartz, Grover, and the Wooster rule book;

And Whereas he was affectionately known as "The Colonel" and the school's leading Confederate, the only member of his class from the South;

And Whereas during his sports career at Wooster he earned five varsity letters, two in football, a lifelong obsession nurtured early by Coach, and three in tennis, the team he captained his senior year;

And Whereas he displayed great comic ability in the 1953 production of "Woosteria Paree," stopping the show with his hillbilly number "Don't Be Ugly to Someone Who Loves You";

And Whereas at graduation he captured the Donald Cameron Slater prize for work on the student newspaper and yearbook, thus upstaging the owner and publisher of Alabama's leading independent newspaper, the *Anniston Star*, none other than his father, Harry Mel Ayers, who delivered the commencement address;

And Whereas he graduated from the University of Alabama, pursued a career in journalism, and with his wife, Josie, returned to Anniston to take the helm of the *Star* from his father and mother eventually becoming the chairman and publisher, distinguishing himself in the journalistic field with his courageous and provocative stands, instructing his readers on the importance of conscience, conviction, civility, citizenship, courtesy, and particularly, the civil rights of all individuals;

And Whereas his voice has been heard far beyond Alabama in the *Herald Tribune*, the *Washington Post*, the *New York Times*, and on National Public Radio;

And Whereas he has generously given of his time, expertise, and moral leadership to the Twentieth Century Fund, Talladega College, The National News council, The Board of Foreign Scholarship, and many other worthy institutions and causes;

And Whereas he found at Wooster an extended family which cultivated his intellect, his spirit, and his sense of independence, and for all the years since, he has with his wife Josie and daughter Margaret, warmly embraced the school as part of his family;

And Whereas he wonderfully celebrates Wooster's values of Hard Work, Intellectual Excellence, Religion, and Simplicity in his very life and work, as everyone from The University of Common Wisdom, better known as The Courthouse Barber Shop, to the movers and shapers of our national institutions will clearly confirm;

Therefore Be It Resolved that the Twenty-third Annual Alumni Award of the Wooster Alumni Council is hereby presented to Harry Brandt Ayers, of the Great Class of 1953.

2.

This article by Grover Hall Jr. appeared in the Montgomery Advertiser *on May 16, 1963, two days after the event.*

WASHINGTON — So President Kennedy and a considerable deputation of Alabama newspapermen sat together at lunch in the White House to discuss Birmingham and all that embodies.

Considering the President's combative relationship with Alabama, which included a snub of the Crimson Tide in the Orange Bowl, and considering the combative relationship of the newspapermen generally with the Bros. Kennedy, a striking thing occurred.

That was, before and after the lunch, a large element and perhaps a majority of the newspapermen aggressively sought President Kennedy's autograph on the luncheon menu, for, they said, a wife, a child or grandchild. The president happily provided the autographs.

After it was over, the President went somewhat out of his way to seek out the newspaperman who had supplied the most jagged questions directed at him and thanked him for his candor.

The President then went about his business, which is the preservation of the Republic and reelection next year. The newspapermen returned to their desks and typewriters in Alabama and took up where they left off, we trust, in their varying lines of applause and hostility largely shaped like a congressman by sentiment in their districts.

This is not to say that the conference was without value. There undoubtedly was enlightenment provided both for the President and the Alabamians. It would have been impossible for a man to sit at that table through lunch and until 3:30 p.m. and not learn much.

We venture to suggest that both President Kennedy and Governor Wallace would learn something in such a face-to-face meeting, though it might not alter at all their collision courses inasmuch as they are two politicians working different sides of the street.

Hardly anywhere was it asked why the President had troop drops in Alabama when sufficient local constabulary was on hand, indeed, with officials sometimes spurning reinforcements from Governor Wallace.

Columnist Walter Lippmann, for 40 years a tired old man sagging under the burden of an incomparable and unmanageable load of learning, was writing about Birmingham with Little Rock a precise analogy. Whereas there is no analogy at all: no federal injunction defied, no white rioters. Instead there was a state injunction defied by colored rioters. The rioters were restrained, not rent, by the highly trained dogs. It was white policemen trying to uphold law who were hospitalized.

The newspapermen reached the White House in an appropriate drizzle. They were served a luncheon cocktail or highball to their comfort and after a time were joined by the President.

Herve Charest, president of the Alabama Press Association and editor of the *Tallassee Tribune*, had the position of honor on the President's right; Publisher Walls found his place card on the presidential left. Publisher Clarence Hanson of the *Birmingham News* sat directly opposite Kennedy.

Kennedy looked well. Being abstemious and taking care to exercise, as well as to be under 45. But his face showed his fatigue and a tremor in his hands confirmed it.

Dessert was as long as Kennedy cared to wait and he bored right into it—Birmingham. He did not bark like Bobby; he wanted to converse. He became visibly irritated but once—at the observation that the Revered Doctor King was a White House "pet"—and there could not have been a conference more correct and courteous on the part of all. The windbags were endured with no more chastisement than sly winks on the part of the victims.

Among other things it was brought to the attention of Kennedy by one newspaperman or another that: The law under which the colored marchers were denied a parade permit was originally set upon the books to restrain Klansmen; A grotesque national stir was being made over the use of fire hoses and police dogs when in fact these were standard police inhibitors in every city and the dogs had just been set on college boys at Brown University for no more heinous offense than a springtime urge to ascend the stairs of the girls dorm.

Burke Marshall, Bobby's civil rights gauleiter, would confirm that Birmingham police had acted with admirable restraint (the President agreed); That those the President sponsored such as the Reverend Shuttlesworth had records of bootlegging and that the Reverend Abernathy was fugitive from a husband with hatchet; That reason and justice required that Dr. King be made to obey court injunctions no less than Governor Wallace.

Kennedy, as you read in the wire stories, held to the line that his business was trying to get reasonable whites and blacks together lest the Black Muslims displace such moderates as Roy Wilkins of the NAACP and be enthroned, causing an internal cold war.

3.

The author's article about the March on Washington on August 28, 1963, appeared the next day in the Anniston Star.

WASHINGTON — They came as if to a picnic, with their songs, their hard-boiled eggs and fried chicken—and their demands for freedom and jobs. Then, almost magically, they were gone. The vast body of the 210,000 marchers—hot, dirty, bone tired—was gone by 9 p.m.

They left this: Discarded leaflets blowing in an autumnal wind Thursday morning, papers missed by the sanitation crews plastered to concrete in the flat, straight, drenching rain that dropped when the wind stopped.

And, they also left this: Vast respect for District of Columbia authorities and the Negro leaders who moved this unbelievable, living mass in and out of the nation's capital without incident.

Finally, they left: The unshakable conviction that the revolution started in Birmingham this spring did not end Wednesday. Negroes will march in the streets of other cities. Their protest will continue because when people sing, and sing as the marchers did, their grievances are too deep; they cannot be crushed.

If you saw the march on television and think you know its sounds and smells, and its meaning, you are wrong. The television lens is orderly but cold. Its view is no more accurate than an Admiral in the Pentagon moving ships of a fleet on a board. The sailor has no sense of the movement of the fleet but he is the only one who knows the meaning of the battle. I was there. From 5:30 a.m. until late in the afternoon I was on the grounds of the Washington Monument, at Union Station and finally at the Lincoln Memorial.

This is the way it was:

At 5:30 a.m., Washington was empty, there was the strangeness of early Sunday morning and it was to stay that way for most of the city. One large department store did $22 worth of business. In the early morning dark on the mall, a Parade Marshal's tent spilled a warm, yellow carpet of light on colorless grass. There was coffee there. A burly man with a shiny yellow marshal's armband brusquely turned down my request for a cup. I left and headed for the monument.

About 25 people were there; five had driven all night from Boston to be in the march. There was a girl and four boys. The girl and three boys were talkative. The fifth—a bearded blond with dark sunglasses sat frozen and uncommunicative. Beatnik.

It was 6 a.m., and still no sunrise when Deputy Police Chief George R. Wallrodt arrived on a police three-wheeler. He was looking for Rockwell and his group. A few minutes later, perhaps 150 police had drifted together at a spot on the southeast corner of the grounds. Wallrodt suspended his search to give them instructions. "We are policemen. We have no political or sociological interest in this thing today . . . You may meet some people who have had bad experiences in other cities and are anti-police. Don't let them get under your skin . . . Try not to make any arrests for minor offenses," the big-bellied, weathered and impressive deputy chief told them.

It was 6:30, a dirty, pink stain began spreading behind the Capitol. The grass was turning from gray to green as the sky lightened and a group of about 40 men straggled onto the grounds about 30 yards from where Wallrodt was giving the word to the cops. I talked to two teenagers who described themselves as spectators. Later I found they were there to meet George Lincoln Rockwell, Fuhrer of the American Nazi Party.

The police and the group of men, led by a fortyish man in a fawn-colored coat, were back to back for a few minutes. Then the deputy chief turned, noticing them. "There he is, its Rockwell," Wallrodt said to an aide. Rockwell and the deputy chief talked briefly. It wasn't necessary to talk longer. There had been blunt talk the day before and the Nazi leader knew what he could do.

"This is the counter-demonstration area," said Wallrodt. "My men will seal it off. Nobody can come in here but members of your group and the press."

Rockwell is tall and dark haired, with a strong, cold, angular face. He was decorated some eight times as a Navy commander in World War II. He is not a likeable man. He puffs on a corncob pipe. His eyes move but they do not meet yours, they are always looking beyond.

"No," he said, answering my question. "We are not in uniform (brown with red, white and black swastika armbands) today. This is not a Nazi demonstration. We are here to speak for the decent white people. The vile white people are over there." He pointed vaguely out over the monument grounds where a few marchers were beginning to arrive, several whites among them.

"Look at them!" His finger picked out the bearded beatnik from the monument. "Look at that one," sneered Rockwell, "Look at him! I'll bet he has mushrooms growing between his toes—his toenails must be six inches long."

Rockwell made wild assertions, among them: "Bobby Kennedy had personally signed a warrant for my arrest." A few minutes before, chief U.S. Marshal Jim McShane had walked no more than 10 feet away from Rockwell. I had chatted with him briefly. He mentioned no warrant for Rockwell.

Later, however, Rockwell's deputy commander, a Karl Allen, was arrested by a plain clothes detective for making a speech without a permit after two warnings. It seemed a strange reason to arrest him since no one was paying any attention to the Nazis anyway.

Another reporter and I left the Rockwell group at 7:30. Three buses pulled up and unloaded their marchers. Others were walking to the monument grounds in small groups. We drove through the deserted streets to Union Station. It was there, at 8:30, that the spirit and meaning of the march began to show.

Some 50-shuttle buses jammed the street outside the station when we arrived but the real body of the marchers had not yet started arriving on the 20-chartered trains. Within 30 minutes, however, they were arriving, on two and three separate tracks sometimes. They arrived, some of them, almost simultaneously from Springfield, Massachusetts, and Charleston, South Carolina.

They poured through the gates in dark streams, dotted frequently with white faces. There were all types: the wealthy, self-conscious and over-dressed youths, beatniks, numbers of clergymen; they wore uniforms, bright blue "NAACP" hats, neatly pressed suits of unmistakable quality, overalls and bandanas.

The Union States delegates from the South entered swinging their arms, shoulders swaying with songs that crashed and rolled across the station platform. From the North, they came almost timorously through the gates, looking with interest, but silently, at the streams of singing marchers from the South. A young Negro from New Haven, Conn., explained, "We don't know the words."

These from Charleston and Savannah did. "I got a hammer and I got a bell," the chorus of hundreds sang and then crashed into the refrain, "It's the hammer of justice and the bell of free-e-dom . . . ."

And, there was the hymn, sung joyfully, that I was to hear many times that day, on the monument grounds, during the march and at the Lincoln Memorial: "We are not alone . . . We are not afraid . . . Deep in my heart, I do believe, We will overcome some day."

Then, back through the still empty sections of the city to the monument grounds where by 11:30, there were already 100,000 massed, and yet only half were there. Walking through the crowd, there was no talk of freedom. Just the idle chatter of picnickers. Many sat on the ground. They ate sandwiches, deviled eggs and fried chicken. Some sang along with the entertainers.

The loud speaker announced, "We have a lost child. Larry Johnson, about 12, will his father Roosevelt Johnson report to the first aid tent." It was not hot and there was no sense of pressure from the crowd—then.

There was no jamming or disorder as they marched down Constitution Avenue on one side, and Independence on the other, to the reflecting pool which mirrors the Lincoln Memorial at one end and the Washington Monument from the other.

Police lines kept the mass flowing in two streams. When the Independence Avenue stream merged with the other at the memorial they began to form a pool, then a sea—a hot, thick, sea of people. As I inched through the mass, jammed shoulder to shoulder, a chilling thought occurred. 'How many would be trampled if some lunatic started firing into the crowd from the monument.'

With some relief, I squeezed out of the crowd, mounted the memorial steps and walked to the press tables at Lincoln's left. There is no way to describe that sea of faces flowing away far below. How can 200,000 people crushed together be described? In the crowd moments before, I knew the heat the smell of dust, and felt the awful pressure of the crowd. But, far above them in the cool breeze, they were not real.

For four hours they stood pressed together, the lucky ones at the back sitting with their feet in the pool. The speeches—moderate and militant—were mostly dull. Counting the number overcome by the heat (30 directly in front of the press section) and wondering about how strongly they must feel about their lot to go through such a day, helped pass the time.

On the steps of the Lincoln Memorial, no more than a dozen feet from Dr. King, I wondered about the predictions of violence as the speeches droned on. I hadn't even seen any shoving. I wondered about drunks. I had looked hard but couldn't find any.

My interest and the crowd's mostly responded to the singing. Peter, Paul and Mary were the best. The crowd also cheered the biblical oratory of Martin Luther King "I have a dream . . ." He is a good speaker but I had had enough of speeches.

Then it was over. By 4:30, the sea was draining away. As they left, their discards were exposed. There were no whisky bottles, but there was 400 tons of rubbish to clean up.

There is much more to tell about their going, but this is the cental point: They went away from their Capital feeling the strength and unity of their numbers. For one unreal day they heard the demand, "Freedom," from every throat.

Now they are home in the real world. Their demands are not heard so clearly there. They will try to make them heard and there will be trouble for a long time.

4.

The author's op-ed article, "The Cultural Yeasting of the South," appeared in the Washington Post *on September 7, 1976.*

ANNISTON, Ala.—Last Saturday night, while the tempest flashed and howled around and inside that broken, foolish, old man King Lear, there was a disapproving presence in the Alabama Shakespeare Festival Theater.

The ghost of H. L. Mencken stirred with resentment; hating the fact that one of those rare moments of professional drama was occurring in this improbable place, the county seat of Calhoun County, in the deepest Deep South.

It was not supposed to be. Mencken had said so himself, 55 years ago when he put a curse upon the South in his essay, "The Sahara of the Bozart."

"One would find it difficult," he wrote, "to unearth a single second-rate city between Ohio and the Pacific that isn't struggling to establish an orchestra, or setting up a little theater, or going in for an art gallery, or making some effort to get in touch with civilization . . . You will find no such effort in the South."

What made his curse so irritating to the minority of Southerners who had the income, education and leisure to care was the depressing fact that he was right.

It would remain largely true while the South struggled with more down-to-earth and important priorities: defeating poverty, pellagra and prejudice.

The scrabbling existence of the south Alabama tenant farmers about whom James Agee wrote doused the spark of inquiring humanity and, of course, didn't provide the spacious means with which to organize a ballet or symphony.

Defenders of Southern culture were either defensively shrill or reduced to limply asserting that the first opera was established in New Orleans and that Charleston had built the nation's first theater.

When Mencken rasped back the question, "Yes. But what have you done for civilization since the Civil War?" there was no answer but sullen silence, about the performing arts at least.

In artistic ventures, which were less capital-intensive, however, the South was not silent. No $250,000 sound and lighting console was required for William Faulkner to do his magic. He needed only a battered typewriter. Not only was poverty a barrier but also the narrow, reverse side of the Protestant ethic worked against us. There was something sinful about men and women dancing around in tights (practically naked!) and, of course, performing on the stage is not considered the same thing as working for a living.

But through the 1960s and 1970s, as the South imported cities and capital from the North, change began to be seen.

The first wave of activity was the development of amateur theater and opera on a broad scale, and now there is more activity at the professional level.

State governments, like Alabama's, will have to realize that the quality of life is advanced more by appropriations to the arts than to state sovereignty commissions.

And, most importantly, Southern businessmen must develop a new habit of giving to go along with the region's rising economy. A new ethic and attitude must be nourished which will reach into the locker room of the country club and embarrass the corporate executive who gave $200 to the local theater when the other executives in the foursome gave $2,000.

We're organizing a cultural posse down South. One of these days that posse is going to rise in the dead of the night, seek out the place in Baltimore where Mencken is buried and, at sunrise, drive a silver stake through his coffin.

5.

The author's article about his trip with his wife, Josephine, to China in 1982 appeared in the Anniston Star *on January 13, 1985:*

HUANXIAN, China — Only the well remains.

The house where the operation was performed on a wooden kitchen table was demolished years ago. The surgeon was my grandfather Dr. Thomas Wilburn Ayers, who went out from his home church, Parker Memorial of Anniston, to serve as the first Southern Baptist medical missionary to China.

The patient was a Chinese woman with a jaw infection whose husband threatened to throw her out unless the disfiguring injury was healed.

When this patient stopped breathing under the chloroform, Grandfather feared that his mission work was over before it had begun or that he might even be hanged for the murder of a Chinese woman. He revived her and saved his mission work.

That was in 1901, an anxious time for any foreigner in China. Simmering animosities against years of exploitation burst into a short-lived period of terrorist attacks on foreigners, the Boxer Rebellion. Allied troops were required to relieve a siege of the foreign compound in Peking.

On November 29, 83 years later, my wife, Josephine and I returned to the small town where grandfather had spent 25 years. I had known from a little book he wrote and from dinner-table conversation about his work in China: About the hospital and medical school he built, about the church and clinic for which he raised money, about his preaching, about his work to prevent communicable diseases, about helping organize the Red Cross in a northern part of China, about the highest civil decoration awarded him by the first president of China, Yuan Shikai, and about the monument erected in his honor by citizens of the county after he left in 1926.

But I had never known grandfather as a man. Although he lived to be 96 and died my freshman year in college, I never really knew him. He was not a Norman Rockwell grandfather who played on the floor with the children. In the Atlanta house where he retired, he was an imperial figure—a slender man with a while Vandyke beard, stiff white shirt, black tie and black suit. Unspoken authority silenced noisy boys.

The journey into my family's past was not in search of nebulous roots. I was looking for something concrete. I wanted to meet grandfather before he became an imperial figure, when he was a man who was afraid to operate on that Chinese woman but later joked about the incident.

For westerners, the 20-hour train trip from Beijing to Yantai (the old port of Chefoo where grandfather's ship docked) was an experience. Our two Chinese roommates and we slept in our clothes because there were no curtains to shield the bunks where we also sat. Josephine surely was the only woman who spent the night dressed in clothes from Yves St. Laurent. She became an object of arresting originality to Chinese women when she went out for air during stops. From Yantai, the trip to Huanxian is less than three hours by van. It took grandfather and the family, including Dad, three days by mule-drawn litter.

The main street, Western Street, we found a charming avenue lined with drooping willow trees. Arriving at the small, cinder-block hotel we were surprised to be greeted as celebrities by the county supervisor, the mayor, a television crew and what seemed to be the entire staff of the hotel.

We were indeed objects of friendly curiosity as we walked among the thousands of Chinese buying and selling at the regular county fair. Grandfather, who carried in his head pictures of oppressive poverty, would have been stunned by the sight of that cornucopia of goods in a rainbow of colors.

Seven citizens of the town, old men and women, helped bridge the distance in time and space between grandfather and grandson. What manner of a man was this Thomas Wilburn Ayers. "Willie," as my grandmother and a very few others called him?

What amazed his grandson, a political addict like most editors, was that he seemed entirely untouched by the momentous events he witnessed. He arrived during the 1901 Boxer Rebellion. In 1912, he was there when 2,132 years of dynastic rule ended. From the first president of the Republic, he received the emerald-studded decoration, "The Order of the Splendid Harvest." He left in 1926 just months before Chaing Kai-shek consolidated his regime.

Yet, he never mentioned politics, not in his book, "Healing and Missions," and not in the memory of those who knew him. Instead, he taught, he healed, he made house calls, he raised money, he built and he preached. He invited Chinese to dinner who came curious to see what westerners ate. He was indefatigable during the cholera epidemic and led the fight against communicable diseases for the entire Shandong Province.

"He was a merry man, joshing colleagues and patients alike," said a lovely, 85-year-old schoolmistress, Wang Li Mei, whom grandfather treated for tuberculosis when she was 14. She was describing his bedside manner. "When he met a person, he would smile in order to relieve her worries," she said. "He would say concerning words and joking words in order to persuade me to take some medicine."

Too enmeshed in the intricate webbing of daily life in a small county of 500,000. He did not have time for politics, only for people. Perhaps that spirit was celebrated in the inscription on the miniature Washington Monument erected in his honor. "Regardless of heat or cold he treated the sick both rich and poor." The monument is gone now, too, a victim of terrible and mundane decisions. The church and the monument were damaged by a dive-bomber attack, which preceded the Japanese invasion in 1939. In 1957, both were leveled to make way for a new road.

Not much is left which would have personal meaning for grandfather. He would be pleased to know that grandmother's piano from the old church is now accompanying vigorous Baptist hymns in the new church, finished in 1983. He would be delighted to know that an old student, Fan Shu Zhi, is a deacon of the 600-member congregation.

Only the well he dug and the memories remain. Perhaps that is enough, particularly in arid northern China where water is precious. As the mayor said, "In China we have this old proverb: You who drink the water, do not forget the person who dug the well."

Index

Thank you, Mr. Ayers

10-2013